SEX, DRUGS & GEFILTE FISH

SEX, DRUGS & GEFILTE FISH

Edited by Shana Liebman

GRAND CENTRAL
PUBLISHING

New York Boston

Grand Central Publishing
Hachette Book Group
237 Park Avenue
New York, NY 10017
Visit our website at www.HachetteBookGroup.com.

Printed in the United States of America

First Edition: October 2009

10 9 8 7 6 5 4 3 2 1

Grateful acknowledgment is made to the following for use of their artwork: page 1, Adam
Mutterperl and Matthew Shultz (Why I Only Date Shiksas comic); page 23, Sarah Maxwell
(photograph); page 35, D. C. Benny (cartoon); page 47, Johnathan Ryan Storm (illustration);
pages 64–65, Julie Klausner (Mulatto Incident comic); page 71, Alicia Fairclough
(illustration); page 84, Margot Liebman (illustration of Big Foot); page 101, Nick Kroll and
Julie Klausner (Pool Party Joke comic); page 151, Jon Feinstein (photograph); page 163,
Sophie Crumb (comic).

Grand Central Publishing is a division of Hachette Book Group, Inc.
The Grand Central Publishing name and logo is a trademark of Hachette Book Group, Inc.

Library of Congress Cataloging-in-Publication Data

    Sex, drugs & gefilte fish : the Heeb storytelling collection / edited by Shana Liebman.—
1st ed.
      p. cm.
    ISBN 978-0-446-50462-1
    1. Jews—Identity—Humor. 2. Jewish wit and humor. I. Heeb magazine.

PN6231.J5S44 2009
814'.60803529924—dc22

Design by Joel Avirom and Jason Snyder

For Michael

Acknowledgments

FIRST AND FOREMOST thank you to all the wonderfully talented, good-humored *Heeb* storytellers who gave us their best seven minutes for zero financial compensation—*Heeb*-style. To our incredibly cool editor, Ben Greenberg, and whatever he smoked or drank the night before he dreamed several fantastic covers for this book. To Mike Garten and Yasha Wallin for making that cover come to life, and to Rebecca Weiner for helping me edit the stories. Also many thanks to some of the longtime organizers of *Heeb* Storytelling: Ean Seeb and Eric Elkins in Denver, Amanda Marks in Atlanta, Alessandra Rizzotti in L.A., Amy Tobin and Angela Petrella in San Francisco, Julia Young in Ann Arbor, Byron Kerman and Ran Mano in St. Louis and Kevin Coval in Chicago. We're also grateful to our favorite accordionists Adam Shenkman in L.A., Adam Baruchowitz in New York, Josh Dolgin in San Francisco, and of course, all of our hosts, notably Andy Borowitz in Chicago, the Sklar Brothers in L.A., and Todd Barry—who launched it all on the Lower East Side. A thousand thanks, hugs and apologies to the brilliant Josh Neuman. And last but not least, to my amazing family, for laughing even when it wasn't funny.

Contents

Foreword

By A. J. Jacobs

A FEW WEEKS AGO, I went on vacation with my family to the Dominican Republic. I expected some snorkeling, some beach reading, perhaps a mojito or two. Instead, I spent three days in the hospital with severe pneumonia.

Have you ever been to a third-world hospital? If not, let me tell you: There is much to keep you occupied. I spent a lot of time trying to figure out what liquids the doctors were pumping into my body—my IV drip had no less than four bags of mystery fluids in a range of colors (yellow, clear, red, blue). I also had to puzzle out the best way to swallow the bizarre backgammon-piece-sized pills they kept handing me. That took some time. I got to learn the Spanish words for *mucus* and *searing pain*. I spent hours staring out the window searching for the rooster that had woken me up at 5:30 a.m. every morning. Oh, and I passed several minutes writing my own obituary in my head.

Meanwhile, back at the hotel, my wife was busy freaking out. She was trying to take care of our three sons without my help, and worrying about whether I'd get out of el hospital with a pulse. My father, I later learned, assured her that I'd make it. Plus, he pointed out, perhaps the most important fact of all: I'd get to write about the experience later in an article or book.

My dad knows me well—because that's exactly what I was thinking. Even as I was wheezing and groaning in pain, I was noting the details of the hospital for future use (the cheesy needlepoint flower on the wall, the sound of retching in the next room). It helped get through the ordeal. As horrible as the experience was, a part of me felt almost gleeful. I got me some material!

I think there should be a word for this phenomenon. It's not quite masochism or self-pity, though it might have a trace of each. It's more akin to schadenfreude, but schadenfreude directed at oneself. It's the pleasure you derive from your own humiliation, pain and foibles, fueled mostly by the knowledge that you'll get mileage out of it later. Let's call it auto-schadenfreude.

Auto-schadenfreude isn't restricted to one race or ethnicity. But I will say, we Jews seem to have a knack for it. Almost every good Jewish story I've ever heard is about the pain and humiliation of the narrator, and I bet that a small part of the narrator felt paradoxically proud of the level of his humiliation.

This collection of *Heeb* stories is one of the best examples of auto-schadenfreude I've ever read. These stories overflow with humiliation and pain. And the results are hilarious and tragic and profound. Just a sample:

- Ophira Eisenberg's fantastically horrible sex with a guy who collects stuffed Garfield cats.

- Todd Rosenberg's hilariously disastrous experience with the Hair Club for Men that led to him to weep in front of his parents.

- Wendy Shanker's fear and resolve (never to diet again) after being held up at a Weight Watchers meeting.

A few years ago, I told my own self-lacerating story at a *Heeb* Storytelling event. I was on the bill with former *Gawker* editor Jessica Coen and Schmelvis, the Jewish Elvis impersonator. I told one of the most humiliating events of my life—the time I got a review in *The New York Times* in which the reviewer called me a "jackass."

That was a horrible time in my life. But telling the story to a bunch of appreciative people in a downtown bar—that was freeing and empowering. There's something to owning your pain. It's like you're saying, "Listen, I'm strong enough that I can expose my own flaws." I don't hang around with extreme athletes, but I imagine it's the same pleasant feeling they get when they show each other scars from their motocross accidents and such.

It's especially helpful if you can somehow wring a lesson out of the pain. That's another thing about Jewish stories in general, and the tales in *Heeb*'s great collection in particular. There's often a moral. Jonathan Kesselman tells a heartbreakingly funny story about how he takes meds for his crippling OCD, but that means he can't ejaculate (*retarded ejaculation* is the medical term). His lesson: Freedom comes with costs.

My lesson was that publishing a book was like having a kid. You can do everything right—feed him, clothe him, show him Baby Kierkegaard videos— but a bully in kindergarten can still make him eat clumps of dirt. You have to come to terms with that. And you have to appreciate that your child is able to run around the playground at all, and is even having fun on the jungle gym most of the time.

While writing this foreword, I happened to be reading a book by Harvard psychology professor Daniel Gilbert called *Stumbling on Happiness.* Gilbert talks about how reframing stories is a key to our sanity. Our brains need to create a lesson. Often these lessons are manufactured rationalizations. They are delusions, but they're necessary delusions. "Getting dumped by my wife, run over by a golf cart and addicted to Vicodin was the best thing that ever happened to me. And here's why."

In a sense, the Jewish people have done a brilliant job at reframing their history. Thank God we were slaves in Egypt. Now we know from suffering and can have empathy. Thank God we were attacked by the Romans/Philistines/ Egyptians, so that we can have holidays and eat and revel in God's love. I thank the writers of this *Heeb* collection for turning their suffering into wonderful stories—with real or imagined lessons. Their pain, our gain.

Preface

By Shana Liebman

I WAS NOT A HAPPY CAMPER. Every summer from 1983 to 1988, I pleaded with my parents to spare me from what many girls my age considered paradise: arts and crafts, horseback riding, sing-alongs, dances with prepubescent boys. It wasn't that I didn't enjoy staying up late eating Ding Dongs, but I felt different from my fellow campers—most of whom changed designer outfits between activities, spoke wistfully of acquiring bulimia and taped photos of their Hebrew-school boyfriends to their trunks. (I had filled mine with novels and double-sided stationery.)

My parents, however, thought of summer camp as a luxury that they could never experience, and therefore wanted to give to their kids. So even after four miserable summers at four different camps, they wouldn't give up. Instead they devised a plan: They would send me away with my best friend Michelle. Surely if we were together at camp I wouldn't be so unhappy, they reasoned. Little did they realize Michelle and I had our own plan—to do everything in our power to get the hell out of camp. It started with this letter.

Dear Mom and Dad,

I hate camp. This is the worst summer of my life. It's a nightmare.
Today was boring and awful. I cried all day and I didn't eat a thing.
Then I felt sick and threw up. I will kill myself if you don't pick me up
soon. I mean it. Michelle is miserable too.

Sincerely, Shana Liebman

As if the message wasn't clear enough, I added a visual:

Several similar letters followed.

In the past 20 years, I probably confessed my summer camp suicide threats
to three people. It's sort of hard to make the transition to . . . but now I'm
totally well adjusted. Recently, however, my parents dug up that humiliating
letter in their basement and I decided to tell the story to a bunch of people at a
party—some who knew me and some who didn't. I was nervous until I heard
everyone laugh, and keep laughing and even moan with empathy.

This was the experience that came to mind in 2003, when the editors of *Heeb* asked me, the Arts Editor, to start a *Heeb* literary series: I didn't want to hear young Jews reading from their novel-in-progress; I wanted to create a forum for people from all walks of life to give voice to a panorama of Jewish experiences—no matter how embarrassing.

In the beginning we borrowed heavily from the Moth, a storytelling series created by George Green in 1997. The Moth asked people to tell (not read) stories, so their shows were more dramatic, spontaneous, personal and fun than a literary reading. We did change the format a bit—most importantly, we asked people to tell "Jewish" stories but encouraged them to take liberties to interpret that as they pleased. Like the magazine that launched in 2002, we wanted the series to defy a traditional definition of "Jewishness," challenge conventions and in its own audacious questioning, bring together an unlikely community—those who didn't identify with many of their parents' customs, but still "felt" Jewish.

We rarely rehearsed the shows and we replaced the Moth's timekeeping classical violin with an old-school accordion—which, by some uncertain criteria, felt more Jewish. But the concept was the same, and at the time, we gave credit where it was due. We called our series the "Shmoth" as a friendly homage. When the series began appearing before sold-out, standing-room-only audiences nationwide, we realized we had found a voice all our own and "*Heeb* Storytelling" was born.

The capacity for self-deprecation, extreme guilt, analysis, comedy as coping, therapy-induced self-awareness and obsessive record-keeping are, for better or worse, typically thought of as Jewish qualities, so it wasn't hard to find Jews who could tell a good story—even those who had never been on a stage or had never considered talking publicly about bleaching their arm hair or their search for a tall handsome Jewish sperm donor.

And one of the things that made *Heeb* Storytelling work was that we weren't asking for vetted and perfected routines. As a result, comedians abandoned their schtick; journalists told what actually happened; musicians made up songs with narrative arcs. And the audience ate it up.

From the beginning our shows sold out, and over the last six years the series has traveled to virtually every city in North America. It was only recently however that we started to transcribe, edit, illustrate, edit again, argue about over drinks, reorganize, re-edit . . . ah, publishing.

So here in all their well-deserved published glory are the stories of nerds, ex-girlfriends, liars, rockers, goody goodies, sex fiends, neurotics and, yes, summer campers. The authors are not all Jewish, but their stories are . . . sort of.

SEX

Losing It

By Josh Swiller

I WAS FIFTEEN, IT WAS 1986, and I really wanted to have sex. I know that seems young, but my parents had HBO. And all my friends had done it. Hunter had done it, with Susan. Pat, the basketball star, had done it, with Mary, Dana and Susan. Even Dan, who grew up to become a rabbi and write books about the secrets to a healthy, loving Jewish marriage and raising your kids without scarring them too terribly, had done it, also with Susan.

I'd never met this Susan, but I really wanted to.

Why couldn't I meet girls like Susan? Maybe, I thought, it was because I couldn't hear. I am deaf and wear hearing aids and read lips, and in social situations—especially back then—I was usually a beat or two behind the action. I had, in other words, no game. No game whatsoever.

So I went on a teen tour to Israel—which people do during that year when you're too old to be a camper at your Jewish summer camp and too young to be a counselor. So they pack you on a bus with 20 or 30 other kids for six weeks and drive you back and forth and up and down the country.

You go to the Dead Sea—ooh, the Dead Sea! You can float on it! And man, do your eyes burn! You go to Masada and walk up the cliffs at dawn and see the sun rise blood-red over the desert and think about sacrifice and feel unworthy of your spoiled selfish life. And then kibbutz! You can pick plums for eight hours in a row with one fifteen-minute break to crap behind a bush!

All wonderful experiences, but what I really wanted was to get laid.

Once I got to Israel, I took a weekend away from the tour and through a family connection went to pay homage to a famous rabbi. He was the leader of a big community of scholars and I really wanted to ask him, "Rabbi, when will I meet someone who will love me completely?" (meaning: "Rabbi, when will I get laid?") He was in a room with a big crowd of disciples around him. His beard went to his waist and looked like cotton candy. At the last minute I chickened out and didn't ask him about when I would get to do it. "Rabbi, why am I deaf?" I asked instead.

"I don't know," he said. "I'm not a doctor. Maybe you had a fever?"

Luckily, I had a girlfriend, which is kind of important. You can't have sex with someone you're not dating. Unless you're Richard Gere. (I have no idea what that means, but did you just think of a gerbil?)

Anna was from Connecticut and she was a couple years older than me and she'd been around the proverbial block. That block, like everything else, has gentrified quite a bit since then, but back in those days, there was still hope for a poor, upper-middle-class teenaged Jew-boy. After a month of my pestering, Anna finally said, "OK, Josh, tonight's the night."

I could barely believe my . . . well, my hearing aids. I couldn't control my excitement. We were staying in a tent camp at some kibbutz in the Galilee. There were about forty tents, and we, our tour, took up five of them and the rest were empty. Anna and I took my sleeping bag and walked out through the campground to find an empty tent as far away from the others as possible. My heart was pounding.

We picked a tent, went inside, took off our clothes, lay down on a cot and pulled the sleeping bag over us. And then we started doing it. Now, I could lie and tell you I put in your standard four-song-and-an-intermission porn performance, but the truth is, having no idea really what it would feel like, having no frame of reference, I would say that 0.2 seconds after entering my lovely girlfriend, I started coming. And that I came for about two minutes straight.

"AHHHHHHHHHH—BARUCH-ATAH-ADONAHHHHHHHH," I yelled.

It felt great, let me tell you. I screamed nonstop, I prayed, I gave thanks to God, and Patrick Ewing and Bo Derek and all the other important figures in my life. Anna tried to shush me, but I kept on yelling. And then I started seeing lights, shapes. Anna's face glowed. I thought, wow, I'm pretty good—I'm seeing stars! This is what it's about! This!

"YESSS YESSS YESS AHHHHH—"

The room grew lighter. And then I looked over my shoulder. The tent flap was wide open and three Israeli soldiers with machine guns, alerted by the cries I couldn't hear myself making, crouched there in the ready position, their machine guns pointed on us.

"AHHHHHHHHH—"

I froze, still orgasming. I looked at them. They looked at me. I looked at Anna. She looked at them, looked at me. They looked at Anna. I had a vision, then, a fearful one. Of bullets, of death, of a life unlived. What if they thought I was a terrorist? A Palestinian Orgasm Terrorist? The kibbutz was in a dangerous area. The orgasm terrorists—they get onto crowded buses and whip open their jackets and then: Aha! Try and turn the pages of your holy book now, old man!

No! I wanted to live!

I did the logical thing. I fell off the cot, pulling the sleeping bag with me so that Anna was naked. The soldiers apologized, smirked, closed the flap and stepped out.

I lay on the floor breathing rapidly. Oh my God, oh my God, I thought, what a close shave. And then: Oh my God I had sex! Me—sex! A grin started to grow on my face, one that ended up staying there for a full day. But Anna, I thought, what about Anna?

"Are you OK?" I asked her.

No answer came from the cot.

"Did you come?" I asked.

No answer.

"Want to do it again?"

"No." Loud and clear.

We were silent for a bit.

"You sure?" I asked.

Two days later she dumped me—for an Israeli soldier, actually one of the ones who had walked in on us. His name was Dahveed, which always pissed me off—everyone knows you pronounce it David. I'm deaf and I know that.

A couple weeks later, I went home. Hunter, Pat and Dan picked me up from the airport. "How was your trip?" they asked. "Awesome," I said, and then I told them the big news.

"You did it?" they said. "Wow. Really? None of us have done it! We were all joking. Susan doesn't exist. Wow. How was it?"

They gathered round. I took my time.

"My friends," I said. "It was so good I saw my life flash before my eyes."

The Anti-Mensch

By Ophira Eisenberg

I SCORED A STAND-UP GIG opening for a local headliner at a comedy club in Orange, New Jersey. I hadn't met the headliner yet—some guy named Kevin. He made a big impression when he walked into the prep kitchen, a.k.a. our green room, locked eyes with me and said, "Can you get me a Coke, please?" Instantly I was offended and intrigued. Offended because he assumed that I was a waitress, but intrigued because he was in the 30 to 38 age range and pretty cute. Plus, he did say "please."

I told him that I didn't work there. I was a comic on the show. He scanned me up and down. "Oh," he said.

The lights went down and the emcee hit the stage, wooing the crowd with Ronald Reagan impressions and a handful of Michael-Jackson-is-a-pervert bits. I began to get nervous that the audience would hate me and my autobiographical act. It didn't include a single outdated impression, not even Sean Connery. Noticing that I was wringing my hands while watching the emcee moonwalk, Kevin taunted me. "Scared?"

"No!" I snapped like a kid sister. I quickly matured my outburst with a get-over-yourself glare. I wanted to continue with the insulting flirty banter, but right then the emcee introduced me.

My set went over badly. The crowd wanted me to talk more about blow jobs and less about my 75-year-old Jewish mother's first e-mail, which she wrote entirely in the subject line. The polite applause sounded almost mocking, and I headed straight to the bar in the back.

I gulped my cocktail and watched Kevin bring the crowd back up with jokes that centered on being angst-ridden, bitter and depressed. I felt depressed. I didn't even have a boyfriend or a booty-call boy waiting to hear how the gig went, to reassure me that it was just one night in New Jersey, or just sleep with me to shut me up. With only two years in New York under my belt, the dating scene had taught me that if I continued to hold back on the first date, I was never going to have sex again. Sure, I wanted to find a nice Jewish boy like every other girl in the city, or at least a guy who appreciated the fact that I could make gefilte fish from scratch. Since that was working out about as well as my comedy set in New Jersey, maybe it was time to deviate from the plan.

Maybe I should sleep with Kevin. He was miserable, disheveled and even disrespectful. In other words, attainable. Extra bonus: He had a car.

Kevin's big closing joke was a wince-inducing dog-farting joke, but the crowd howled and he left the stage to wild applause. I could tell he was feeling pretty good about himself, which was going to make my mission easy.

I strolled into the prep kitchen and supplied the perfunctory post-show adoration. "That was great, man! Love that closer! Hey—can I catch a ride with you back to the city?"

"Yeah, sure, I guess."

His blue Datsun was well lived in to say the least. It took him a solid 10 minutes to clear off the passenger's seat, cluttered with paper, balled up T-shirts delivered fresh from a T-shirt gun, and empty food containers. As we drove he mumbled about how he'd been despondent since some girl left him and the business had been wearing him down. He was considering meditation. I wanted him to stop talking. He was ruining the thrill of the chase. I asked him if he wanted to meditate over a drink or four once we got into the city.

We found ourselves in Tribeca and passed by an old bar on the corner of a cobblestone street with warm orange light pouring out of its windows. It was getting late, almost last call, so we took our chances.

Once inside, I realized that we had stumbled upon "magic bar." That's not the name of the bar. It's a time when you catch a bar at its best moment. The lighting was perfect, dancing off of the mahogany bar and making everyone sitting near it glow. The music was at the ideal level to both listen to and talk above, and the other patrons were hip but not trendy, good-looking but still smart. It was *Cheers*, the Regal Beagle and the Village Vanguard rolled into one.

I ordered a Grey Goose martini with three olives. I like to eat one at the beginning, one halfway through and one at the end, as if they were rationed snacks on my hike to intoxication. Kevin ordered an Amstel Light, the beer of champion lightweights. The spell of magic bar started to take hold. I found him irresistible as we bantered in a way you can only do with a one-night stand.

"Really? The last four women you dated were underage? Good for you!"

"You once escaped a mental institution? Wow! Exciting!"

"Your grandfather was in the SS? Did he know Schindler?"

He was different from other guys I'd dated—he wasn't apologetic, he wasn't a mama's boy, he wasn't even nice. And I had to admit, I kind of liked it. It made me feel like a delicate ray of sunshine in comparison.

But my brain started to do this trick: Suddenly I'm picturing us together, 20 years in the future, at our summer house in Madrid. We're sitting on our blue tiled patio, drinking espresso, waiting for our maid to bring out our paella. We're staring out at the sea and laughing about the fact that he used to do a dog-fart joke.

The bar started to close down. Finally, he asked me the question I had been avoiding since I moved to Manhattan.

"Would you like to come home with me to Queens?"

His apartment was a typical Queens apartment in the basement of an Italian family's house. We crept down the brown shag stairs. The place wasn't terrible, it was clean, but it definitely had that bachelor pad feel with its beige walls and lack of decor, except for a vase of silk flowers sitting on a rattan end table near the bathroom. They were so out of place that I couldn't help but think there was a webcam stashed in a rose.

"I have something to show you," he said flirtatiously and swung open the unfinished wooden door to his bedroom.

In that one moment before light revealed the inner contents of his boudoir, I envisioned many things. A harness. A bunk bed. Another man.

To say I was stunned by the actual contents would be putting it lightly. It was like nothing I had ever seen before, and certainly nothing I ever expected from *him*. Kevin's room was full of—I mean covered with—Garfields. Stuffed ones, ceramic ones, bronze ones, little ones in poses on a special shelf. Garfield playing golf, pool, Garfield wearing a beret, Garfield looking angry. Plus a huge Garfield, twice the size of me, adorned with Mardi Gras beads, propped up on his bed. There were so many of them, frozen in orange-and-black-striped action, it was chilling. A dead body would have been easier to deal with.

The sight of this altar to Jim Davis' dynasty killed any sexy, warm or even *safe* feeling. I stared at him. It just didn't make any sense.

"Um . . . How did . . . What's up with all the Garfields?" I asked.

"Oh, I've had them since college," he explained nonchalantly, tossing it off as if hoarding Garfields was a perfectly normal collegiate activity. I was hoping for something more like "They were left to me by my sweet crazy aunt and I have to display them to keep my inheritance," or even "They're a childhood collection that is now worth millions!"

My mind flashed to our earlier conversation at the bar. He went to Boston University, then moved to Providence for a while, then back to Boston, then to Manhattan, then Brooklyn, now Queens. All I could picture was him wrapping each precious Garfield in newspaper and gently placing them in a cardboard liquor box one after the other. He wasn't a sexy man; he was a messed-up man-child. To top it off, I couldn't leave. I was in Queens.

I tried to work with the situation. "Can you take a few of them out of your room? They're a little creepy!" He did, without question, like he had done it before for other trapped, desperate girls trying to make their love den less infantile. He removed the big cat from the bed and carefully selected two other ones from the top of his dresser, setting them neatly on the sofa in the next room. When he returned, he flung me onto the bed and pounced. At least the Garfields were working their magic on one of us.

Turns out the only thing bigger than his Garfield obsession was his penis. It made perfect sense. Only a 37-year-old guy with a dick that big could get away with a bedroom full of stuffies. Without warning, he threw on a Magnum condom and just . . . stuck it in.

The next thing I knew we were having the world's worst, most unskilled sex I had ever had. He lowered his head beside my right ear and pumped furiously like a jackhammer. Like Odie in heat. It felt like he was punching me inside. Like he was fucking a stuffed Garfield, and not even his favorite one in the collection.

I was so detached from the experience that I started making life resolutions in my head. "OK. Tomorrow I'm going to get it together. I'll go to the gym, lose ten pounds, really stick to a disciplined writing schedule and work on my self-esteem. No, first I'll work on the self-esteem. I still have a whole life ahead of me. It's not too late!"

I turned to look at him, but his eyes were shut. He had a tight smile on his face as he continued to thrust at a sprinter's pace. He was lost in some fantasy world: a world of no Mondays and endless lasagna. And then it was over. He rolled off of me and wiped perspiration from his forehead.

The following night, safely back in Manhattan, I rewrote my JDate profile. "Looking for a stand-up guy," I decided on. "Must not love cats."

SJF Seeks Donor

By Lori Gottlieb

AFTER MY LAST RELATIONSHIP ENDED, I decided that instead of signing up with an online dating service, I'd cut out the middleman and sign up with an online sperm bank.

There was no JDate equivalent for sperm—no JSpunk, for instance—but as soon as I typed in my search criteria (tall, Jewish, graduate degree), I had dozens of matches. This was great, but also a problem. You see, for me, ordering the father of my child on a website was especially difficult because I'm not a good online shopper. I can barely choose a blouse from *BananaRepublic .com* without calling customer service and asking, "When it says 'blue,' does that mean 'aqua' or 'robin's egg'?" Likewise, I kept calling customer service at the sperm bank with questions like, "When it says his hair is 'curly,' does that mean 'wavy' or 'ringlets'?"

I called so often that I became tight with this customer service rep named Maureen, who would describe donors to me like this: "He's not *unattractive*, but I wouldn't look twice at him in the subway." Or "He reminds me of that guy on *The Young and the Restless*, the one who plays Victor's daughter Vicky's husband Cole? He's also been on *Days of Our Lives*. Oh, and he was one of the Martin brothers on *All My Children*. He's a hottie!" She was trying to be helpful, but our frames of reference never meshed. I had no idea who her beefcake soap star was; she had no idea who Jon Stewart was.

It took months to find a donor, so you can imagine my disappointment when I hit "click to purchase" and learned he was "out of stock." At 37, I was out of time. So I went through my Outlook and searched for any cute, smart guy friends with musical ability and a low likelihood of having any sexually transmitted diseases. I also didn't want it to be someone I knew well, so I found the perfect guy: a hot 29-year-old cinematographer I'd spoken to for about five minutes at an Ivy League mixer.

The thing is, I'd never even asked a guy to go on a date with me before, so I *really* had no idea how to ask a guy to be my sperm donor.

The solution seemed obvious: a low-key e-mail. A "Hey, remember me, that girl from the Harvard-Yale mixer?" type of thing. I explained that I had "an unusual question," and asked if he'd meet me for coffee.

Which is how I ended up at the trendy Urth Café, making awkward small talk with a guy named Mike. But after dragging out a 20-minute discussion on the weather—in L.A., no small feat—he leaned across the table and said, "So, I'm really curious, what's your 'unusual question'?"

Keep in mind that, as if this weren't mortifying enough, we were on the patio at Urth on a crowded Sunday, where you're about three inches from all the people at the surrounding tables. I tried to think of how an advertiser might spin this, like, "Hey, want to have steamy, mind-blowing, one-night-stand sex—*without a condom?*"

Instead I beat around the bush, mixing lame metaphors like "not having all the ingredients for the recipe" with "It's like donating a kidney, but without removing the organ." I could see from Mike's expression which organ he was picturing.

"Actually, it's more like giving blood," I said, trying not to gross him out, "except there's sex instead of needles, and, well, you know, there's a baby in the end."

Mike stared back blankly, his chai mocha latte literally suspended midair.

The silence lasted so unbelievably long that I became hopeful that maybe he'd just . . . forgotten the question. I hoped I could leave and he'd have no memory of the event.

"Wow," Mike finally said when he came back to life. "I'm really flattered that you thought of me." But then instead of turning me down nicely, he said he'd be open to talking about it.

Now it was my turn to say, "Wow." Over the next few hours, we became oddly intimate, discussing everything from our dating lives to our dysfunctional families. It seemed that simply talking about having unprotected sex had the same effect as having actual first-time sex—the walls immediately came down.

We even talked about whether he'd be OK getting a semen analysis (surprisingly, yes) and sleeping with me (*not* surprisingly, yes). By the time Mike walked me to my car, we were both giddy and infatuated—not with each other, but with the idea of making this happen.

That night, he sent me an e-mail that said: "So far I am a yes, but with more questions." I couldn't believe it. I e-mailed back that I'd be happy to answer each and every one of them.

So, we decided to meet again at Urth. In fact, over the next two weeks, we met at Urth so often that I started calling Urth my "sperm office" and my friend Linda started calling it, simply, "Spurth."

One day at Spurth, though, I learned something disturbing about Mike. He was a member of the Landmark Forum. What kind of Jew joins a cult like the Forum? To me, the Forum isn't that different from Scientology, or heck, being a registered Republican. And I really wanted to avoid both religious and Republican sperm—in case these traits were stealthily genetic. I started having second thoughts, but my WASPy friend Catherine said, "Lori, you're being *neurotic.* You *overthink* things. Besides, what a person does in his *private* life is his *private* business."

A very Gentile attitude, if you ask me.

My Jewish friend Andrea screamed through the phone: "The cult will come and take your baby!"

But I needed a donor, and Mike was cute, smart, talented, healthy . . . and most important, maybe willing to go through with it. So a few days later, Mike and I took a walk in the rain. It would have been romantic, had I not thrown in words like *cervical mucus.*

At the end of the walk, Mike said he wanted to be my donor, and he even asked whether, like a script submission in Hollywood, I was out to others or this was an exclusive offer. Suddenly I thought I should have created a bidding war and played hard to get, sort of like *The Rules* for snaring a donor. "Look, Ben has expressed interest, so if you're interested, you better get back to me by Friday. I'm also out to Steve and Mike. There's a lot of heat around this."

But it didn't matter, because Mike was in. Or at least, he would be.

Then, right before I was about to ovulate, Mike inexplicably disappeared for five days. I got worried that he might, well, pull out. My WASPy friend Catherine said, "Lori, you can't worry about a bad thing happening before it happens. It's not like you can avoid the bad event by *worrying* about it." Again, a very Gentile attitude. My Jewish friend Linda said, "Oy, vey. You're about to be dumped by your donor!"

And she was right: Like a breakup about to happen, the signs were clear. When Mike resurfaced, he left a message on my voice mail saying we needed to talk—leaving his full name and number, including area code—as if we were strangers again.

For our final meeting at Spurth, I wore sexy pink hip-hugger corduroys and straightened my hair. I wanted to look good, the way a woman does when she wants to leave her dumper with a sense of regret. Mike also treated it like a romantic breakup, using a string of breakup clichés: "It's not you, it's me." "It wouldn't be fair to use you just for the sex." "I just can't commit yet, so *for your sake,* I don't want to string you along." And the kicker: "I hope we can still be friends."

"Of course we can be friends," I lied, then added with a wink, "Besides, there are other fish in the sea." But he didn't appreciate my pun. He never did get my sense of humor. Hugging good-bye, I felt reassured by the fact that maybe we weren't right for each other anyway.

Besides, there *is* a romantic ending. Two weeks later, Maureen called from the sperm bank. My first-choice donor—who, Maureen said, looked like "a Jewish George Clooney"—had stopped by the bank to make a deposit. Soon the goods were FedExed to me in a nitrogen tank and—finally—I got knocked up.

Yesterday I learned that I'm having a healthy baby boy—who, being Jewish, will undoubtedly complain one day to his therapist that Mommy embarrassed him by telling the story of his conception to a roomful of Jews at a seedy club in Hollywood, all for the sake of "material."

And no, the bris will not be at Spurth.

Me Make Fire for Lynn

By Lynn Harris

DURING WHAT TURNED OUT to be my last summer as a single person, I flew to Idaho for a weeklong camping and horseback riding trip through the 2.4-million acre Frank Church Wilderness, miles from the middle of nowhere. Through a freak scheduling accident, it turned out I was the only person on the trip. Just me, two horses, four pack mules and—oh, my!—my guide: Justin, a 20-year-old with a baby face and Wrangler jeans. Just the two of us in the largest wilderness in the lower 48, accessible only on foot, horseback or teeny plane. It was like *Blind Date* meets *Survivor* meets *Who Wants to Marry a Horse Whisperer?*

When we arrived at our first night's camp, Justin set about gathering wood. "Me make fire for Lynn," he joked. Yes, we were going to get along fine. We stayed up late, talking and looking at the stars. I kept thinking, "Holy shit, I am alone in the wilderness with a not unattractive member of the opposite sex."

When the fire went out, I went to my tent. Justin slept outside. I didn't dare join him—at least not yet. Sure, Justin could fashion a condom out of a squirrel bladder, but neither that nor the fact that I've got 12 years on him was the issue. Bottom line: You don't want to hook up with your lifeline. And in the wilderness, there's no way to avoid him the next day.

I'm not saying I wasn't tempted. The guys I've dated have been more Muppet than Marlboro Man, but I've always had a thing for cowboys, along with country music and shitkicker boots. My burning desire for men in chaps is, at least in part, a result of my frustration with the higher-maintenance New York men—those who are less likely to say, "Well, little lady, I will name you all the stars in the night sky and then fry you up that elk I felled with my pistol," and more likely to say, "Sure, I can totally meet you for a Gardenburger after my facial. Oh no wait, I have Pilates."

For the next few days, Justin and I rode morning to dusk, through forest, over meadows, along creeks, over fire-scarred mountaintops spiked with sooty skeletons of pine. We sang Merle Haggard. We lay in a miniature meadow of tiny red berries, letting them pop in our mouths like caviar. I learned to tell deer tracks from elk, moose poop from bear. I learned to plot a course three moves ahead, over pick-up sticks of fallen trees, that was wide enough for the mules. I learned that Justin and I had different skill sets. He can hunt, fish, shoot, track, build, farm, break a horse, dissect an elk. I can read French. We talked about our religious differences—so vast there's not much to say.

Justin told me about growing up on a dairy farm, about branding and castrating the calves. "When we cut off their balls, we fry 'em right quick on the branding iron and eat 'em right there," he said, grinning.

"No, you do not," I said. This had become a game of ours, trying to get the other to believe something insane about our foreign-to-each-other lifestyles. I'd made him fall for some tall tale about fighting off Rollerblading muggers, which wasn't that difficult; he'd seen *The Warriors*.

"Yes, we do," he said. "I'm totally serious."

Of course I know people eat cow testicles—excuse me, Rocky Mountain Oysters—which is what made Justin's fib so brilliant, I thought. It was based on fact, naturally, but he had invented the fabulous "fry-'em-up-on-the-iron" detail. Genius.

"Lynn, I'm not kidding. I swear to God."

I thought about our earlier conversation when I rubbed my aching back and made some crack about humans "not being meant to walk upright." And he said something like, "You don't really believe that shit, do you?" Meaning evolution. Meaning that when he swore to God, he was not whistling Dixie.

One afternoon, while we were riding along a ridge, a small (but big enough) bear stepped onto the trail 50 yards ahead of us. Jumping off his horse, Justin handed me her bridle and the mule line. The danger was that these animals would spook, which is one thing in a barn, quite another on a ridge. I held tight, watching Justin run toward the bear, yelling and throwing small rocks at it until it shrugged and lumbered away. It was the coolest, and hottest, thing I have ever seen anyone do.

That night, Justin showed me his .357 Magnum. It looked like a prop.

"You've never even seen one, have you?" he asked.

"I don't know anyone who owns one," I said. Not even my Georgia grand-daddy had a gun, though he'd been outlaw enough to make moonshine on the back stoop of a dry home.

"I don't know anyone who doesn't," Justin said. "I'll let you shoot it if you want." He showed me the safety, the chamber and the feather-light action of the trigger.

"Why am I so scared?" I asked.

"You *should* be scared," he said.

Justin fired first, to prepare me for how loud it would be. The sound bore right into my chest, through my gut, out my toes and back into the trees. Justin made me paper towel earplugs and handed me the pistol. It felt heavy and out of place in my hands. He showed me how to aim at the tobacco tin he'd leaned against a tree. I half-listened, focusing mainly on his instructions not to touch the trigger until I was about to fire. I also imagined the scenario: my finger slipping, the gun flipping, how a bullet would feel in my neck, how Justin would feel having to call my mother.

I eventually chose a moment and pulled the trigger. Boom!

"I'm proud of you!" Justin grinned. The tobacco tin was untouched but we celebrated my initiation with chicken-fried steak. Justin also dug up a bottle of vodka, which, it turns out, mixes perfectly with Country Time lemonade. We tore at the steaks and talked with our mouths full. Then we danced—Justin leading me in a humming two-step around the fire. Suddenly he was flipping me over his shoulder like they do on the country cable channels. I was over the moon, over the bright crescent moon that no one else could see for hundreds of miles.

On our last day, we saw salmon swimming upstream after laying their eggs. Soon after they would become ashy white and fleshless like the skin of molted snakes, only without a new body in which to glide away. How can nature be so cruel as to make them swim upstream on the way to their death?

Justin didn't find this scene as heartbreaking as I did, which made me realize what is so damn attractive about cowboys. Yes, they're macho and save you from bears. But they're both hard as horseshoes *and* soft as flannel. They're not unfeeling, just used to pain. Life cycle, food chain—they see it all closer than we do. They may not "share" so much, but they listen, and they dance.

When we arrived back at base camp, the two other guides, Jared and Shane, were making us margaritas. We drank them in the outdoor hot tub. My first thought: "Dear *Penthouse* Forum . . ." My second: We could totally make a porno called *Laura Ingalls Just Got Wilder*.

Justin told the two guys how the city slicker could handle her horse, her rare steak, her two-step and her liquor, not to mention his gun. And I was glad that firing Justin's gun turned out to be a metaphor for what never happened between us—not even that last night when Jared and Shane turned in, not even after Justin grabbed my hand and coaxed me into jumping with him out of the hot tub, into the freezing brook, and back into the tub, laughing and watching steam rise from our bodies. God knows when I got this mature, but sometimes, I figured, it's better to wish you had than to wish you hadn't. I unrolled my sleeping bag on some horse blankets, under the stars, next to Justin, who was next to his gun. And I slept.

In a Different Light

By Eric Weingrad

I WAS 10 YEARS OLD and only three short years away from my Bar Mitzvah and my first joint. To keep me on the right path to one of those goals, my parents had enrolled me in Hebrew school at the local JCC. Every Sunday, I begrudgingly sat through Mrs. Cohen's four-hour Hebrew class, counting down the minutes until I would be picked up by the carpool parent of the week. Mrs. Cohen wasn't the friendliest of ladies or the most patient. She did, however, fanatically love her culture and religion, and wanted nothing less than for us to share her righteous adoration. Let it be known that we, fourteen little homely Jewish fifth graders, did not. At 5′4″, Mrs. Cohen was an extremely stout woman, but if she'd been a foot taller, she still would have been 30 pounds overweight. Her hairstyle probably hadn't changed since she was a teenager in the '60s, and every week she wore polyester brown math teacher pants and a different silky blouse with one desperate button struggling to keep her chest at bay.

On one regular dreary Sunday, my class was about two and a half hours into studying proper pronunciations of vowel symbols when Mrs. Cohen announced that for the next six weeks she would host two kids from class at her house for Shabbat. "I hope this experience will shed some light onto the beauty of a Shabbat dinner. Now, who wants to be the first two to sign up?" Not one hand rose. It's one thing to waste a perfectly good Sunday in Hebrew school, but to spend a Friday night at your Hebrew-school teacher's house would be insanity. After an eternity, Mrs. Cohen sighed. "Obviously, anyone who partakes in Shabbat services with my family does not have to attend school that weekend." Corey's hand shot up mere milliseconds behind mine.

That Friday night, my mother dropped me off at Mrs. Cohen's home in a grittier section of the city. The roads, the sky, the row homes, even the few Orthodox Jews already walking to early evening services looked gray to me. Mrs. Cohen greeted me at the door wearing a long black dress that made her look like a human inkblot. I dragged my overnight bag, secretly containing my Game Boy and two boxes of Nerds candy, into the house. No sooner had I kissed the mezuzah than I was introduced to Yitzy, Mrs. Cohen's husband. For as big as Mrs. Cohen was, Yitzy dwarfed her. He easily weighed 300 pounds and shook my hand with the force of a Silverback. From the permanent sweat stains on his white button-down shirt, I could tell he wore this very same specimen for every Friday night service. Corey had already been dropped off so he was waiting impatiently for me in the living room, but as I began to walk toward Corey, Yitzy practically yanked me off my feet and tossed me into the kitchen. "You and I will set up the dinner table," he said. There, leaning over the hot stove, was a girl. She turned and introduced herself to me as Sarah, their daughter. I could feel my face warm up and fill with blood. Yitzy and Mrs. Cohen made *her*?

At the Shabbat dinner, Corey stuffed his face with challah and brisket, eyes glued to his plate, unaware of my newfound reverence for the female body. I may have been wearing a yarmulke and reading Hebrew aloud, but what I was thinking was the furthest thing from religious. Sarah sat across from me in a tight red turtleneck sweater. All I knew was her cute, perky breasts looked like two potato knishes packed perfectly into her training bra. And I was still hungry.

After dinner, Mrs. Cohen took me and Corey down into the basement den where we would be spending the rest of our night. Sarah had homework to do, so she was sequestered in her room upstairs for the night. I quietly revealed my fascination with Sarah to Corey, but he just said, "She's gross and her mom's grosser." Corey and I were obviously at two different mental places at this point, so I lent him my Game Boy to play with while I plotted how to sneak up into her room. Around 9:45 p.m., Yitzy came down to get us into our sleeping bags and shut the lights off. "'Night, boys," he said as he creaked back up the wooden stairs.

But I wasn't tired. I sat there in the dark listening to Corey make fart sounds with his mouth and tell nasty jokes that he'd read in one of his older brother's books. They weren't even funny, just an excuse to say "pussy" or "tit." I wanted to do more than just *say* those words. After about an hour, I told Corey that I was hungry and was going to sneak into the kitchen and steal some pretzels—a brilliant cover for my real plan to sneak into Sarah's room and steal a moment basking in her beauty.

Upstairs was pitch black, but I could make out a thin line of light from under the kitchen door. I heard movement from the back of the house and concluded that it was Sarah still awake doing homework in her room. I scrambled into the kitchen, took the lid off of a container of hard pretzels, grabbed a big handful and stuffed them into my pajama pants. Then I quietly and expertly made my way down the hallway toward what I assumed was Sarah's bedroom. Halfway there, I heard a faucet turn on and a stream of water hit tile in the bathroom ahead. As I got closer, I watched the steam build up and push its way out under bathroom door and into the hallway. Was I so lucky that Sarah was standing right there on the other side of the door, naked, preparing to take a shower? I got low to the ground and peered through the sliver of the opening. Someone in a robe was moving around.

The door blew open a little more, then a little more. I was obviously meant to see this. I stood up. My eyes locked onto the display in front of me. There was no escaping. Inside, there, in plain clear view, it wasn't Sarah at all. It was Mrs. Cohen. With her robe gaping open. That's when I saw two of

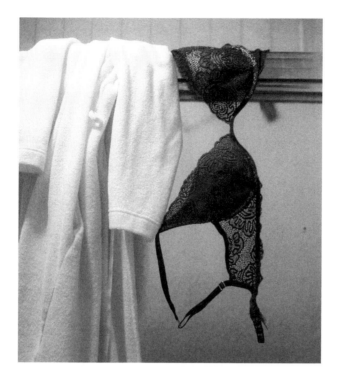

the largest breasts I've ever seen to date. They looked like two round, hairless monsters with single unblinking eyes. I imagined grasping one with both hands, flesh spilling out between my fingers. I was turned on.

I was so turned on that I forgot I was standing right outside the bathroom door, fully erect and slack-jawed. I could hear someone coming toward me from another room, feet slapping on the hard wood floors. After one last greedy look, I bolted back downstairs and hopped into my sleeping bag. Corey asked where the pretzels were so I tossed him some and said to be quiet, we might have been caught.

I squeezed my eyes shut, but my heart and penis both shouted at me, "DO SOMETHING!" I tested to see if Corey was awake by offering him $20 to say "hello." Nothing. I went to work.

I slid my pajama bottoms down to about thigh level and rolled onto my stomach. Something was happening. My schmeckel, as my mother often called it, was begging me to rub it. So I did, against my Transformers sleeping bag. I loved her. I loved this. Unaware that I was popping my masturbation cherry, I kept it up for about a minute when—*flick*—all the lights came on and I heard a very familiar voice say, "Corey, Eric. Come up here, boys."

I was mortified. I was sure she or Yitzy had seen me staring at her in the bathroom. Even worse, I was sure that somehow they knew what I was just doing in their den only moments ago. I was so ashamed. I felt so dirty. My hands were sweaty, my knees were weak, my mouth was dry.

Mrs. Cohen, still wearing her robe, ripped into us. "I know you guys came up here and stole food. And Corey, tomorrow morning your mother and I are going to have to talk to you about your language. The jokes you were spewing out earlier are not appropriate for a boy your age, and Eric, you shouldn't laugh at everything you hear." It turns out Mrs. Cohen could hear everything we said that night because a vent from the den went right into her bedroom. Lucky for me, spanking it against my sleeping bag was as quiet as it gets. My desperate love for Mrs. Cohen faded well before I was due at Hebrew school the following Sunday. But that night, I learned that falling in love can be as simple as seeing someone in a different light . . . or naked.

All Eighteen Inches

By David J. Rosen

IT WAS CHRISTMAS 1996. The city air was thick with CK One. It was a simpler time: Most folks didn't have cell phones yet, the "Macarena" was the #1 song, and I still ate my bagels without scooping them out.

But I was feeling blue. I was in the second longest sexual slump of my life, the worst one being from age zero to eighteen. Plus, life had become routine. My days were transitioning from post-college alcohol-fueled shenanigans to something more mature, long hours at work followed by ethnic food delivery and whatever I could find on basic cable. I was working as a writer in advertising and had spent the last eight months toiling on a campaign for a sneaker company that was killed right before the holidays. When I pressed to find out why, I was told, simply, "The gestalt was wrong."

I was lying on my couch, watching *Where Are They Now: Kirk Cameron*, when my phone rang. It was my friend Darin Strauss, who was not yet bestselling novelist Darin Strauss, but just sloppy, whiny, former camp counselor Darin Strauss. He was all out of breath and giggling; his pitch made him sound like a ticklish castrato.

"Rosen," he squealed, "how'd you like to be on a porn show?"

A porn show? I had so many questions. Gay or straight? Would I have to be naked? Would there be a really hot transsexual on the show who would seduce me and then later I'd find out—whoops—she had a penis? This was a long-standing fear of mine. Plus, I thought Darin might be kidding. He had kidded me many times before. Only recently, when I was really high and hungry, he swore he'd buried a Kit Kat in Tompkins Square Park.

That didn't turn out to be real. But this did. Darin's voice deepened as he told me how this porn possibility had come to pass. On Christmas Eve, he attended one of the myriad Jewish singles events: the Matzo Ball, the Part the Red Sea Hop, the Hide the Afikoman Orgy; parties where Jewish singles met other Jewish singles, then cabbed home together for guilty, kvetchy sex. At whichever one he attended, Darin hooked up with a young woman named Bootsie—Bootsie with an *ie,* the Ashkenazi spelling. In the bright light of the morning after, he found out two things: Bootsie was only 19, and her mom was a woman named Star England. As in, *Sleeping with Star England,* the second most popular porn show on cable access, right behind *The Robin Byrd Show.* (At the time, it was a real Leno/Letterman-esque rivalry.) Bootsie invited Darin, plus a friend, to be on the show.

The next evening we headed over to Time Warner Cable studios on East 23rd Street. We'd already partaken in a few drinks, and the alcohol had us

convinced we were going to be fucking hilarious. We were about to be on a porn show; it was the goddamn American dream. We called all our friends who weren't away for the holidays and told them to prepare themselves for the comedy event of the year. As we approached the building, I had my own internal moment of excitement. This seemed like just the kind of absurd event to get me out of my rut and kick-start 1997 with a bang. Perhaps even literally.

We entered, elevatored up to the fourth floor, and found the studio where the show was broadcast live. It was a tiny, windowless room; picture a walk-in closet with six chairs, two potted ferns and a camera. Bootsie, in an account executive–esque black skirt and blazer, and Star, in a cleavage-revealing satin shirt and pants so tight I almost got a yeast infection, were waiting for us. The first thing that struck me when I saw them was how nice it was that families could be together for the holidays. The second thing was the overwhelming, almost clichéd scent of stripper perfume: equal parts patchouli, hairspray and chlamydia. Darin introduced me to Bootsie, who in turn introduced us to her mom. As she shook my hand, Star glanced down to her chest and asked, "How do my tits look?"

Jewish moms, I thought. They're all the same.

We sat down beside them and made small talk as the single cameraman snaked a few wires around us. Then, without any real explanation of what was going to happen, boom—we were live on the air. I was sporting a striped zip-up sweater and Caterpillar cap for the event, a sort of nerdy Jewish NASCAR ensemble; Darin wore a black leather coat, which, with his long black hair, was an obvious homage to Travolta in *Pulp Fiction*—or Sally Field circa *Hooper*. We weren't exactly ready for our close-ups.

Sleeping with Star England, we discovered, was basically a live call-in show—with strippers. These soon joined us. Guest number one was Angel, a Latina dancer and actress who also had a gig "making private fantasies come true." A porn hyphenate, if you will. The second guest was dancer/actress Honey Mellons. Granted, this wasn't the most original porn name for a woman whose selling point was her enormous breasts, but I felt the two *l*'s gave it a certain je ne sais quoi.

Things started civilly, with Star holding court like a slutty Oprah. She asked us about our latest projects. I mentioned I was working on a new advertising campaign for Fila; Darin said he was working on a novel about Siamese twins; Honey and Angel said they were going to be at Goldfingers all week. Then Star took the first call of the night; it was a dude with a whiskey-and-cigarette rasp.

"I want to see the little guy fuck the big guy."

For all our talk of comic genius, we didn't have any witty comebacks. Darin weakly parried with a quip about the caller being his dad, but it fell short. In truth, we sort of cowered. Star sensed our fear, and like the protective mother she was, she turned to us and threw a softball.

"So, what's it like to be on the show instead of watching it from home?"

I tried to be clever. "Well, it's a lot different without the tissues and moisturizer, Star."

She just sneered and shook her head. "Hilarious, David."

We were not going to be funny on this show.

As the girls' clothes came off, as the vaginal jewelry was displayed, as the whipped cream licking and girl-on-girl kissing began, Darin and I just sat on our stools behind the ladies, dumbly. The whole thing was like the movie *Zelig*. What were we doing there? It wasn't working out remotely like I'd hoped. Darin and I even whispered about splitting at the commercial break. (Yes, commercials ran on these sex shows, mostly for the now-defunct 970 numbers that got so many of us into trouble in high school. Who could resist 970-PEEE?; the extra *E* was for extra pee.) But before we could slink off . . . out came the kielbasa.

Eighteen inches long, two inches thick, smoky-smelling—I'd have been intimidated to barbecue it, let alone deep throat it. But, other than her melons, one of the things Honey was famous for was her lack of gag reflex. And so, she slipped the plastic wrap off the meat stick (price tag still attached: Gristede's, $6.99), opened her mouth and eased the kielbasa in. Inch after unbelievable inch, the whole of it went down her throat. At its deepest, I imagined it must have tickled her spleen. I was awed and I was nauseated.

After the first endeavor, Honey had Darin hold her throat as she repeated the trick to prove she was really swallowing the sausage. There must've been doubters out there, disbelievers who thought she used mirrors or a false throat. And then it was my turn. As I watched her eyes roll back and felt the kielbasa inch down her trachea, I wasn't really freaked out. Well, maybe a little. But more, I was impressed. I thought, "Hey, good for Honey. She was born without a gag reflex and with triple-J boobs, and she's making it work for her the best way she knows how." I started to think about my own life. Here I was, young, single, just starting out in a new city. I had my own apartment, a great job where I didn't have to shower every day—the world was really my oyster. But was I giving it my all, like Honey? Was I swallowing all 18 inches, in my own life?

Then the kielbasa slid back out, Honey coughed a little meat juice onto my arm and I lost the epiphany.

Finally, the show came to an end. In any theatrical production, when the houselights come on, it's bittersweet. All the new friends you've made, all the seemingly deep relationships are suddenly over. As I slipped on my coat,

Honey, still naked, labia pierces clanking like wind chimes, walked over. She handed me her card and shook my hand, like she was a good corporate soldier and we had just finished up at a networking conference.

"It was a pleasure working with you," she said, smiling.

There was a tear in her eye—well, I was guessing, I wasn't really looking at her eyes. But I felt like we'd bonded.

"It was a pleasure working with you too, Honey. Honestly, I feel like I learned something," I told her.

"Thanks, Darin," she said to me.

Then the ladies all went out for post-show drinks—and didn't invite us along.

DRUGS

Let It Breathe

By D.C. Benny

I'M A JEWISH COMEDIAN married to a black psychologist who specializes in sex therapy. We live in Brooklyn and have been described by a neighborhood old-timer as "the Spaniards." A casting director recently referred to me as "swarthy." The West Indians at my wife's job swear she's a closet Guyanese, passing as a black American. One of them actually tried to "out" her by asking for her rice and peas recipe, just to see if it would slip out. We both look like everything but what we really are, which in Brooklyn means we look like everybody else.

Our respective families accepted our decision to be together, but there were some adjustments. Here is an example.

I started hanging out with my wife's recently divorced uncle, Willy, who had grown up in the South and was obsessed with conspiracy theories about racism. Although he wasn't really fond of white people in general, he had a soft spot for Jews, since he was the only black member of a Jewish fraternity at a college in some godforsaken state where blow jobs are still illegal. It was the only fraternity on campus that allowed blacks in and he was the only black person at the school. On display in his home is a sepia photo of him with some guys who look like a gang of tax preparers. He is standing triumphantly in the middle, insulated from a world of whiteness by a sea of curly hair and pronounced noses. The photo could be a target at a Klan shooting range. Willy would be the bull's-eye, but if you hit a Jew, you still win a blueberry pie. A homemade blueberry pie.

When Willy heard that his niece was marrying a white man, he was not too happy and would walk around bemoaning the loss of "good sisters," and how "black men had become an endangered species." When we finally met, however, we took an immediate liking to each other and he even broke out a Jerry Mulligan LP in my honor. "Mulligan was a white too," he said. We closed our eyes and soaked in the sad strains of soulful sax. Well, I listened and Willy talked. "Jazz. You see, the French love jazz. And wine. The key with French wine is you have to let it breathe, which is a metaphor for American's way of life. They just run around in circles, complaining, until they're winded. They need to do like the French and just . . . *let it breathe!*" He then inhaled and exhaled deeply to demonstrate proper breathing.

After that, we started hanging out fairly frequently. When he wasn't talking about France, his other favorite topic was race. He would insist that I was not really white. "You look like you a Mexican, maybe a redbone, or one of them Sepharticus Jewish slaves that wandered in the desert."

It was nonstop. I once mentioned to him that I was going into a Chinese take-out spot to pick up some General Tzo's chicken. He stopped me. "You don't want to eat there," he said conspiratorially. "You see, the chicken ain't chicken. What they do is they get the cats from the Puerto Ricans. See, the Puerto Ricans kidnap the cats, keep 'em in the back of their cars, that's why the salsa music is always so loud, to drown out the meowing. Puerto Ricans kidnap the cats from the Jews, when Jews go on vacation to Florida for those secret meetings at the Center for Controlling the Media."

For my birthday party, Willy showed up with a bottle of French wine, gave me a do-rag as a gift, insisted I try it on, and started to mingle. All night, he trapped my friends in conversations, where he did all the talking about his latest theories. I would walk by and overhear things like: "See, you feel that way because you are white. Whiteness is a state of being without color. Blank. See, white people came from ice, can't feel the cold, that's why they can walk around wearing shorts in October. White people are all descended from albinos. To be white is a genetic mutation like the way a mole rat is blind, white and hairless. See, the word *Caucasian* is linguistically similar to the word *casualty* as in the paleness, or whiteness, of a cadaver. How healthy can it be to have the color of a dead motherfucker if you are alive?"

I also heard: "*Chink* is not an offensive word. It's derived from 'chink in the armor,' a slit designed to let the hot air out when a Chinaman went into battle. Very important cuz they balls got hot as hell under that armor like two water chestnuts cookin' in a wok. And with the little itty-bitty dick, the last thing they need is shrinkage. That's why they eyes all closed up, cuz they angry every time they look down. Got to let it breathe."

Around midnight came a toast. He held up a single malt in one hand and a box of Saltines in the other: "To my nephew-in-law, Benny . . . finally, a cracker with flavor!" He made quite an impression.

The next morning I was awakened by a phone call. It was Willy. "I had a great time with your bohemian friends. A lot of interesting folk; creative types and what-not." Then his voice lowered to a whisper. "I am trying to get some reefer, a dime bag, a nickel . . . if you could arrange . . . discreetly . . . my niece doesn't need to know. . . ."

I hadn't officially bought pot since college so I was a bit out of the loop with the latest hand signals and lingo. Plus, for some reason, people who sell pot always think I'm a cop. Officer Swarthy. Nevertheless, I called around and contacted a stoner buddy and he suggested a bodega on Flatbush Avenue. "Tell 'em you know Flaco," he said, "and don't shave, don't wear blue, don't say 'fuckin' a,' and don't call anyone 'buddy.' "

When I found the bodega, I did a couple loops around it, casing the joint like a pro. Two old men were sitting outside playing dominoes. I nodded to them, walked inside and browsed through the bags of fried plantains. A lady with an ass that looked like a Buick had double-parked in a pair of bike shorts was buying

four "loose-ie" Newports that the cashier carefully wrapped in a piece of paper bag. She left and I approached him with a bag of plantains. As he rang them up, I muttered, "Flaco told me to talk to you about smoke." He looked at me blankly. "Flaco? Flaco who?" My mind was racing. "Flaco. You know . . . Flaco. That's all I know him as. Who uses last names anymore?" He took in what I said then said, "I'm sayin', brother, there's mad Flaco. Flaco from Sunset Park. Flaco from Marcy houses. Then there's Gordo, the nigga formerly known as Flaco. Who you with?" I tried to look hard and distant. "I'm not with anybody, I roll . . . solo." He put my chips in a bag. "You po-lice? 'Cause if you is, you gotta tell me if I axe. That's the law." I thought about how to respond. This guy clearly had the system figured out and I was a novice. "No, if I was I would have busted you for selling loose-ies," I finally replied. He stopped for a second, then yelled to the stockroom. "Yo, Jock, you got a call." I was slightly apprehensive when I learned I was meeting "Jock from the stockroom"—it just had that gay-porn ring.

The door opened and a Korean kid who couldn't have been more than 15 walked in. Joc. Yung Joc. I started to picture him rapping and it was hard not to laugh. "What's up?" he said. "I got fitty bags and hunnit bags." "Fitty," I said, and he gave me a plastic bag with a fat green bud inside. On the bag was a sticker of a guy in a wheelchair, and underneath it was written "The Crippler." I debated for a minute about buying pot that would make one handicapped then handed over the money.

I called Willy when I got home, forgetting how paranoid he could be, to tell him I got the pot. He cut me off and hung up. He then called back from another line and started speaking in code.

"You got the contract?"

"The what?"

"The contract?"

"Oh. Yeah, I got it."

"How many pages?"

"Pages?"

"How many pages was the contract?!"

"Uh, fifty pages . . ."

"Fifty pages?! I told you a five- or ten-page contract!"

"A five- or ten-page contract is gonna have seeds and stems—"

"Got-tammit!" He hung up the phone. An hour later he called back from another number. "It's me. Meet me at the promenade at midnight by the phone booth at the Montague Street entrance."

Midnight came around and I just wanted to get the whole thing over with. As I approached the promenade, I almost didn't recognize Willy. He was in disguise, wearing a trench coat and fedora. He looked like McGruff taking a bite out of crime. He was making a fake phone call at the booth.

I walked over to him, but something was wrong because he looked both ways and started talking to me in code again. As I tried to decipher one code, he hit me with another:

"Blackhawk Down . . . principal's in the office . . . abort mission . . . code red . . . Mutiny on the Bounty . . . flippity-flop on the dip-side . . . hold the onions and definitely NO CHEESE!"

As it dawned on me that all this meant our transaction was to be delayed, he whispered for me to meet him in the all-night diner in ten minutes, and walked off.

I did as instructed and, ten minutes later, walked into the diner, which was pretty empty. I saw Willy in a booth way in the back. As I approached, he put on a show of how he didn't know me: "Uh, waiter, coffee for this gentleman. What did you say your name was?"

When I sat down he slid a napkin across the table. On it was written: "5-0 at cash register. B cool." I turned around and looked behind me. A 70-year-old security guard was buying a cup of tea.

"That guy? That guy's not a cop—" I said.

"Got-tammit!!!" Willy ate the napkin. While he chewed it he yelled at me: "I told you to be cool! That was NOT cool! You gonna get us incarcerated with a bunch of down-low thugs that's secretly sweet, and when the soap drops, I'm not gonna be there."

I had had it. I tucked the bag of weed into his blazer pocket like a green hanky. "That's it. I quit. I don't wanna work for this company anymore. Here's your P.O.T." I left and went straight to bed. The next day, there was a cryptic message on the answering machine:

"It's me. Sorry about yesterday. There has been a new development concerning the last acquisition. I reviewed the contract last night . . . all fifty pages. I can't feel my legs. Call me."

There's an old Colombian proverb that I think sums up this story: "It takes only one donkey to stop traffic, but it takes a real ass to be a drug mule." I'll have to get that translated into French.

Grandma Betty

By Liz Feldman

I, LIKE SO MANY OTHER JEWS before me, had a big fat loud grandma. I also had a tiny sweet gentle grandma but this story isn't about her. This story concerns my grandma Betty, a woman who both fascinated and frightened me. She was a woman who knew what she liked: candy, canasta and cable TV. It was probably the combination of those things that her "big fat" status could be attributed to.

My grandma was above and beyond. She didn't just have that requisite jar of old-lady ribbon candy. She always had a stash of chocolates and gummy fruit slices and what she called "cara*mels*." She also knew what she didn't like. Her most popular expression was "I'm not comfortable." "I'm not comfortable—bring me a pillow," "I'm not comfortable—lemme lay down," "I'm not comfortable—bring me a pillow, get off the couch and lemme lay down."

So it's fitting that my most uncomfortable moments in childhood were at the hand of my grandma Betty. It was my grandma Betty who gave me my first sex talk. I was 11. We were sitting in her Oldsmobile in the parking lot of Jade Winds, her retirement community in Florida. She asked me if I was kissing boys yet and I couldn't even muster up an answer. She then went on a diatribe about what she called "heavy petting" and the "good kinds of rubbing" versus the "bad kinds of rubbing." (By the way—it's a great tactic to have the big fat loud grandma give your kid the sex talk. Guaranteed intimacy issues well into their thirties.)

When I got my period for the first time, I was with my grandma Betty. I was at the Aventura Mall in Florida. I went to the bathroom and saw the bloodstain on my underpants. And I was ecstatic. I had just read *Are You There God? It's Me Margaret*, and I did exactly what Margaret did in the book. I looked at the drop of my blood on my underpants and then looked up to the heavens and I thanked God. I bounded out of the bathroom and realized I had to now tell Grandma Betty what had just happened. I stammered. "I uh, you know, just I got my um . . ." "What is it? What?" she boomed back. "You know, I got my thing, I got . . . you know . . . my period," I whispered. "Oh you got your PERIOD!" she yelled back. And then she promptly smacked me on the face. I learned later that that was a Jewy kineahora thing to ward away evil spirits. But at the time I just thought she was a total bitch. I understood in an instant that I was with the worst possible person to help me shepherd in my ladyhood.

She promised me she had the stuff I needed at home from a prior visit from my menstruating cousin Cami. When we got back to Jade Winds, she handed me a box of what she called "tampoons." She shut me into the bathroom and simply told me to put one in. There were many problems with that plan. The biggest issue being that I had no idea where "in" was. She shouted at me from the other side of the door:

"Put your leg up on the toilet!"

"And then what??"

"Shove it in there!"

"In where??"

"In your vagina hole!!"

"Where I pee out of??"

"No, the big hole!"

I don't know how big her hole was at the age of 78 but mine, at 12, was teeny tiny. I spent an hour poking at my vagina blindly with a tampon. I cried for her to let me out but she wanted to teach me how to use a tampon—which she promised was way more pleasant than bleeding into a maxi. Her heart was in the right place but unfortunately my tampoon was not.

Perhaps the most uncomfortable moments of all were sitting with her on her deathbed. She died slowly of cancer, which allowed for weekly visits to her bedside at a makeshift hospice in my aunt's house. There she would present me with pearls of wisdom that would stay with me forever. Mostly about marriage, something she knew a great deal about, having been married to my grandfather for 62 years—at least two of which were happy. She said I was never going to find the perfect man, which I already knew. I told her I probably wasn't going to marry a man, which I think she already knew. She said and I quote, "Everybody settles." And I swore to her on her bedside that I would not.

We talked about where she thought she was going to go when she died. She had no false hope of heaven or fear of hell. Having never been a spiritual woman, her answer, when asked where she was going to go, was always, "I'm going to Timbuktu."

A week before she died, I had what would be the last uncomfortable moment with my grandma. I showed up for my weekly visit and I found my cousin Seth rolling a joint. I knew he was a big stoner but I thought, "Jesus can't you wait till you're home or she's dead?" But the doctor had told my aunt that she could give my grandmother marijuana to ease the pain and increase her appetite. My grandma Betty, once a voracious eater, was barely eating anymore and this was our last hope. My aunt didn't want to be a part of it; that would be too uncomfortable. So she put my cousin Seth, the stoner, in charge. And I just happened to show up on that day.

"We're gonna teach Grandma how to smoke a joint," Seth said. "You know how to smoke a J?" I was 19. I knew very well how to smoke a J. But I didn't really want my grandma to know how well I knew.

We sat at her bedside and broached the subject. "It's one of those things you have to try once in your life," Seth said. I said, "Hey, Grandma, if you try it I'll try it." Somehow she agreed. She was tethered to an IV so she couldn't really use her arms. I held the joint up to her mouth. I told her to puff, to pull the smoke in, and breathe it in. She puffed a couple of times. She coughed a little. And so did I. About a minute later, she shook her head. "I don't feel anything. This isn't working . . . does anybody have a caramel?" Scott and I laughed. She was herself again. We grabbed her a caramel and unwrapped it for her. She smiled, because she couldn't help it. She laughed. She couldn't help it. We all had the giggles. We couldn't help it. And we sat together for the first and last time, actually comfortable.

I Am Anxious

By Jonathan Kesselman

BEFORE I WAS BORN, back in 1974, doctors didn't use ultrasound; instead they would determine a child's sex by checking the pulse of the baby. A slower pulse meant you were going to deliver a boy. A faster pulse meant you would be having a girl. Needless to say, my mom's friends knitted pink hats for me.

And ever since I was brought into this world, anxiety has been a major part of my life. When I was 13 or so, I came down with a really bad case of Obsessive Compulsive Disorder. And for those of you who say stupid shit like, "Oh my god, I'm so OCD . . ." trust me, you're not. Using Post-its, or cleaning your apartment a lot, or having a "super"-organized closet is not OCD. Flipping light switches in sequences of four or staring at the corner of ceilings while feeling compelled to repeat bizarre phrases in your head for fear that someone will somehow take over your identity . . . that's OCD. To reiterate, a really clean apartment is not.

When I was 18, after years of failed talking therapy and medication, I finally got over the C part of my OCD through a behavioral psychology treatment called Systematic Desensitization. Essentially, during the course of the treatment, you're exposed to the things that trigger your obsessions, but then not allowed to perform any of your compulsive actions. It's sort of like *A Clockwork Orange* when they make Malcolm McDowell into a pussy by clamping his eyes open and forcing him to watch TV . . . or like *Fear Factor*, except you don't have to eat bugs or talk to Joe Rogan . . . that is, unless Joe Rogan is somehow one of your OCD triggers. But how fucked-up of a disease would that be?

About four or five years ago my anxiety got pretty bad. I wasn't working, I was completely broke and I was *enslaved* by my anxiety. The only discernible difference between the Egyptian slaves and me was that I was living in the Valley in Los Angeles, and there was no way in hell I would lift a heavy stone—I have lower back problems.

But I was depressed, drinking a lot and generally not a nice guy to be around. So, when I turned 29, and the hangovers got too bad, I decided to see a psychiatrist and deal with it once and for all. I was prescribed a wonder anti-anxiety and -depression drug called Lexapro. Suddenly I could focus on work. I started making money, and I stopped snapping at people for saying stupid shit like "Oh my god, I'm so OCD."

But with every good thing in life, there is always sacrifice: I stopped wanting to have sex. Even more interesting was that when I did engage in sexual activities I could still easily achieve an erection, but it would take me forever to come. The phenomenon, I quickly learned on Google, is known as *retarded ejaculation*. Sounds like fun, right? Not so much. After a half hour of fucking, both parties desperately want it to end.

At first, I was ashamed to bring up the Lexapro thing with the women I would sleep with. It's kind of hard making words like *antidepressant* or *anxiolytic* or *retarded ejaculation* sound sexy.

"Baby, I want you to come. I want you to come so bad. Come all over my tits!"

"Um, wow. That might be kind of a difficult thing. You see, I have this side effect from my combination antidepressant/anxiolytic medication. It's called retarded ejaculation. Basically, it's a physiological phenomenon that occurs when . . ."

And to make matters worse, because I didn't tell these women what was going on, they assumed that it somehow had something to do with them. That maybe *they* weren't attractive or sexy enough. And so finally, because I felt immense guilt after seeing how panicked and insecure women would become when I couldn't ejaculate, I gave in to the shame and told them the truth.

Oddly enough, upon hearing about my retarded ejaculation, most of these women would instantly relax, and then take the news as some sort of personal challenge. Out would come the lotion and the towel, and after 45 minutes of having my cock stroked, being talked dirty to, all the while having my eyes closed, intensely focused on my most base and perverse sexual fantasies involving a completely shaved, unicorn-loving, blonde shiksa temp receptionist named Krissy who screams out "Fuck me, Captain!" as she's bent over my imaginary high-powered Manhattan mahogany desk . . . or the one in which I use a mind-control agent concocted by a shadowy, classified department of the CIA to assist in my espionage work in South Korea where I'm sent to fuck the beautiful Communist midgets into our way of thinking . . . I might *sometimes* come.

It got to the point where I realized that since I wasn't all that interested in sex anymore, and because it was becoming such a hassle to come up with even more elaborately specific sexual fantasies, that I'd just excise sex from my life completely.

And then something amazing happened. I saved a *shitload* of money. I no longer had to buy chivalrous-man dinners at expensive restaurants, or pay for $125 "Thai" massages. I no longer had to buy flowers, or drinks, or Rohypnol . . . I'm kidding, of course. Buying flowers for a woman is totally lame.

Secondly, my career started taking off. The pursuit of pussy takes up a lot of time that could be better spent writing, taking meetings, networking, watching TV, playing NBA 2K8 on the Xbox 360 Live, napping. And also, I no longer had to deal with all of the emotional baggage that came from . . . what's the word I'm looking for . . . "connecting" . . . with another human being.

So I learned a lot from this experience: Freedom never comes without a price. Moses couldn't come into the Holy Land, and a lot of the time, neither can I.

Benzos and Breast Cancer

By Stephanie Green

I WAS HIGH WHEN I GOT THE CALL. Shit, I'd been smashed for 24 hours, starting with the anesthesia, followed by Percocet and scores of Xanax. After the lumpectomy, I'd gone straight from surgery to Tom's house and smoked a joint. Smoking on top of anesthesia—nice. The lumpectomy was supposed to remove a benign fibroadenoma from my left breast. I'd felt the lump in August. It was small, soft and moved around—not the kind of hard, cystic thing women are supposed to fret over.

An ultrasound told my first surgeon it was benign, but he told me that it might keep growing. "I'm single, take it out. I don't want some guy feeling me up and finding that." It was my first surgery. My BFF Dana and my mom accompanied me to the operation. My body had weathered Ecstasy, acid, 'shrooms, mescaline, coke, crystal, pot and almost every kind of downer. I'd always partied like a rock star. I was a champ under anesthesia.

When the surgeon walked out of the OR, he assured my mom and Dana that the tumor looked clean. It was nothing. He was "sure" of it.

The next morning, I felt so good that I assured my mom she could make the five-hour drive home to Jacksonville. No need for her to stay in South Beach. The doctor said I was fine. I felt fine.

I walked over to Tom's house—he had recently become my pothead partner—and settled into a nice high. A few minutes later, my cell rang. "Mammo" popped up on my caller ID. (Today, eight months later, the number for Mount Sinai Comprehensive Cancer Center is still labeled "Mammo.")

I was sitting at Tom's kitchen counter in one of only four chairs in the apartment. Rene, whom I'd just met, was taking a turntable out of the front door. Tom was helping him. I was in jeans—Rock and Republic—but I can't remember any other part of my wardrobe; odd for someone who remembers what she wore at all of life's pivotal moments.

A woman with a thick Latino accent said, "Ms. Green, when can you get to the doctor's office? He wants to see you soon."

"Uh, I dunno," I said through my pot-thickened haze. Why would they want to schedule a checkup so soon? I thumbed through my Filofax nonchalantly. "I guess I could come tomorrow," I said while thinking that I'd earned myself at least a week of doing nothing but hanging out with Tom and smoking.

"You can come here soon?" The urgency was evident even beneath the layers of incompetence in her voice.

"Uhh, when?"

"Now, miss. Please."

"Now?!"

"Yes, now, the doctor is on his way in just to see you."

I hung up. I was so fucking high. Tom gets the best shit in Miami. Usually when I smoke with Tom, I'm done for the day, but unfortunately this day was only just beginning.

The only other time I'd been in this much shock was watching the Twin Towers burst into flames. My thoughts leapt to Mom. I knew she'd either be on the road or seconds away from hitting the road. Rene had gone. Tom caught my eye, grasped my fear and sat down in a desk chair across the room from me. I dialed my mom.

"Momthedoctorjustcalledhewantstoseemenow.Youneedtocomepickme upnow."

"What? OK, calm down." Her voice got weak and slow. I'd heard that disconcerting tone once before, in 2004, when I'd called in the middle of a hurricane-induced blackout to tell her I was being sued.

Tom was a caricature—ginormous eyes, white skin, chin to the floor— still staring at me. I locked my eyes on his as I panted into the phone.

"Whatever it is, we'll deal with it," Mom said. "No, I'm sure it's not cancer, you'll be fine."

As high as I was, and through the tornado of thoughts swirling in my brain—I was about to be diagnosed with *cancer*—I remembered the most important thing: drugs.

I barked instructions into the phone to my poor mom. "Bring the Xanax! Then pick me up at Tom's behind China Grill. I'll be outside."

I was already calmer knowing that Xanax and Mom were on their way. After I hung up, Tom came to me from across the room panic-stricken, the color still completely drained from his face. He sat down across from me and took my hand. "What happened, Steph?"

"Omigod omigod omigod omigod I have cancer. I have *cancer*, Tom. *Cancer*. I'm 32 and I have cancer."

"You do not have cancer. Don't panic."

He hugged me. I cried just a little into his shirt. He stroked my hair. Tom and I weren't touchy-feely friends. Both straight and single, we'd never crossed that line. But in that moment I grabbed onto him like a boyfriend.

"Think positive," he said, pleading with his brows.

"The doctor doesn't call the day after a biopsy with *good* news."

"Focus on me."

He looked as stricken as a mother would be, a father, a brother, a husband. I would never forget that look. Even though I didn't see much of Tom after that, I knew that whatever happened, he would be an integral part of my life story. I would never forget that room where we'd laughed, argued, smoked, drank and played with his daughter and dog. He was, at that moment, the one thing moving while time remained still.

I walked outside and sat on the curb waiting for my mom. When she drove up, I got in the car and swallowed three Xannies.

"I fucking have cancer, Mom," I yelled. "What the fuck?"

"Whatever it is, we're going to beat it. Everything's going to be just fine."

"Stop jinxing me!" I shouted back at her.

Mount Sinai is on Miami Beach, a mere 10 minutes from my apartment on South Beach. I instructed Mom to drive around the hospital grounds until the pills worked their way into my blood and I was fully sedated.

I knew it was breast cancer, but I wanted to hear it from Doctor El Schmucko who'd told us the day before that the lump was "absolutely nothing."

I forget his exact words, something generic: "The biopsy came back positive for ductal cell carcinoma."

"Yeah, no shit." I was impassive, slightly maniacal and majorly medicated.

Dana, my best friend whom I had called with the news, appeared at the door of the exam room shortly after El Schmucko told me his diagnosis. "What . . . ?" she said entering, looking confused but without alarm.

"Hi-iiiiiiiiii!" I squealed like we were meeting at a bar. "Guess what? I have cancer!"

Dana started laughing and crying at the same time. Her first thought upon hearing my frantic phone messages was that they'd operated on the wrong breast or left a sponge in me. (She watches those medical reality shows.)

I next remember getting into the car. I called Tom, told him the news. He went silent. I may have called some other friends. I remember my mom on the phone with my dad, telling him as we left the hospital: "She's doing remarkably well actually. Xanax is a wonderful drug!"

I was oddly giddy after Schmucko's diagnosis. "I'm registering at Neiman's!" I declared, out of the blue. "I didn't have a Bat Mitzvah, I'm not getting married and I know people will be sending gifts. So I'm going to register, and we're going to have a huge cancer party!"

The next few weeks were a blur of drugs—benzodiazepines mostly—and doctor's visits that entailed a posse of Mom, Dana and Mom's Palm Beach BFF Lynn, a breast cancer survivor diagnosed when she was 31. I dressed for the hospital like I did for a ladies' lunch: head-to-toe designer gear, full makeup and hair, stilettos, jewelry. I looked and felt amazing. That's the scariest part of cancer; you can look fabulous and feel even better while the cells in your body are waging a civil war.

I had nice tits, too. Braless, they were saggy, but in a 34C, they were hot. Men loved them. Women envied them. I liked them in clothes, hated them when naked. In Lynn's car on our way to my first consult with an oncologist, we videotaped me saying (in a slightly nasal, Jappy-sounding voice): "They're not going to chop off my boobs. Fuck that."

After many, many doctor's visits, I finally met Dr. Larry Norton in New York, the head of the Memorial Sloan-Kettering Breast Cancer Program. Norton is the Anna Wintour of breast cancer—if Anna were a nice, humble Jewish man, with a sarcastic, self-deprecating sense of humor. Norton and his team invented the Sloan Protocol, the chemo regimen followed by hospitals throughout the world.

Mom, Dad, my brother and I packed into Norton's office on the Upper East Side. "You know, we could've done this over the phone," he said.

"I wanted to meet you in person . . . and it's the perfect excuse to go to Bergdorf's."

"Ahh, my kind of people."

After he spelled out my treatment options, I asked the question I ask all doctors: If I were your daughter, what would you tell me to do?

"The safest treatment for you would be a double mastectomy and chemo."

This meant a double mastectomy with immediate reconstruction followed by four months of chemotherapy capped off with a year of Herceptin infusions. I had stage II, high-grade, infiltrating breast cancer and was—as the genetic testing later revealed—BRCA1 positive.

Ashkenazi Jewish women have a one in 40 chance of inheriting a BRCA1 or BRCA2 gene, which gives us lucky ones up to an 85 percent chance of developing breast cancer. If I'd chosen not to have a double mastectomy, my chances of recurrence would have been greater than 30 percent. But by chopping 'em off, with added chemo and Herceptin, my recurrence rate dropped to less than 10 percent.

I didn't panic, which is ironic because pre-diagnosis I had panic attacks at the threat of taking mass transit or going somewhere without Purell. I'm usually the neurotic, navel-gazing alarmist, but suddenly I was the strong one. Denial? Probably. But I had no choice. It was what it was.

My friends and family freaked out more than I did. One night, my mom was so out-of-control emotional that I crushed a Klonopin and mixed it into her hummus and salad. It worked. About a month later I told her and Dad about it, after threatening to do the same during one of his tantrums.

When I tell people about this time, they always ask me how I didn't freak out, break down, feel sorry for myself or play the victim card. Meditation? Fuck that shit. Medication is more my speed. "Xanax," I say. Sometimes I'm joking. Often I'm not. The real answer is: Xanax, Ativan, Klonopin, Seroquel, Percocet and Valium. Plus friends, family, excellent doctors and a sense of humor. Pot brownies don't hurt either.

Unprotected: A Confession

By Rachel Kramer Bussel

WHEN I WAS 17 AND 19 and probably around 22, I thought I was pregnant. There was no real reason for the suspicion, other than that I'd had sex with a guy (using birth control) sometime in the previous three months. I was completely paranoid; I'd get my period but still be convinced I was knocked up. Once I even got my period for the second time and still trudged off to Planned Parenthood for a test to make absolutely, totally sure I was fetus-free. I was convinced that I would end up as one of those women who doesn't know she's pregnant until she suddenly gets strange stomach pains. Eventually, I got over myself and trusted that the Pill, and later, condoms, would do the trick. But back then, I thought getting knocked up was the worst possible fate that could befall me. It scared the hell out of me and continued to . . . until I turned 29. I've never been a big believer in the biological clock, but something happened to me at that time, my Saturn's Return (if you believe in that sort of thing). On the cusp of 30, I went from thinking babies were smelly, loud, messy things to yearning for one so much that the feeling physically overpowers me when I catch sight of any infant.

I would liken it to feeling like an alien has taken over my body, making me crave the company of small, helpless children. Even though they are the ones reliant on adults to feed, clothe and nurture them, I feel beholden to the babies, helpless as I look longingly at their tiny forms, requiring the feel of their soft, warm skin for my very survival. I now look at babies I pass on the street the way I once looked at hot guys and girls—OK, not exactly the same way, but with that undeniable urge to reach out and touch them. In this case, to get up in their face and bust out my best baby talk, to offer up my finger for them to curl their minuscule hands around. Holding my 5-month-old cousin Adam to calm him down, feeling his warm, sweet head pressed against my shoulder, kissing his pudgy little cheek, is heaven to me. As impossible and impractical as I know it is at this moment in my life, I want a baby. Which is really the only explanation I can give for why on the night before Valentine's Day I went home with a guy and had unprotected sex, once that night, and once the next morning.

I wish I could tell you it was Valentine's Eve 1996, or 1999, or even 2002, but it wasn't. It was 2006, I was 30, and I knew exactly what I was doing, even if I didn't plan it. I wish I could tell you it was the three dirty martinis I had instead of dinner that made the decision for me. I wish I could tell you it all happened so fast that there was no time to process what was about to happen. I wish I could tell you it was all worth it because it was the best sex of my life, the kind that would make even quadruplets worth it. I wish I could tell you he had a really big cock, and when he rubbed it against me I was so overcome with desire I simply had to have him inside me that very instant. I wish I could tell you it felt so much better than having that latex barrier between us. I wish I could tell you anything that might make me sound like less of an idiot, but I can't.

We had met for our second date at a bar in SoHo. I arranged it so that I could leave afterward and go to a reading, yet part of me knew I was going to sleep with him if it was on the table. I ordered a Diet Coke, but soon after finishing that refreshing carbonation, I sank into the comfort of a dirty martini. And then another one. After the third, I felt the urgent need to show everyone in the bar my bare breast. I remember having that thought you never really want to have when you're drinking: "Wow, now I'm really, really drunk."

I remember giving him a blow job in the cab, then stopping and leaning against his shoulder with my eyes closed. Suddenly we were walking into his just-moved-in apartment. There were boxes scattered around and a bed. I remember seeing my book of erotica, the one I'd given him, sitting on a desk, and then our clothes came off really quickly and we were naked, fumbling around together. That's where things get a little murky, but I do remember lying down, my head spinning slightly. He was on top of me, and there was a moment where I realized he was about to put his penis inside me. There was enough time to think about this, to ponder the surreal fact that in 2006, a guy was about to fuck me without a condom, no questions, no queries, no qualms. And not just any guy, but a nice, Jewish guy, one who had sweetly kissed me on the lips and told me he liked to cook. It was like a *Twilight Zone* episode where I'd become some kind of zombie whose years of sex education had magically vanished from her consciousness.

Part of me wanted to say something—but what? Anything I could've said would've broken the mood, and I started to wonder if I wasn't being a hypochondriac. If he wasn't worried, why should I be? What's the worst that could happen? I'd get knocked up? Well, is it really so bad if your worst nightmare is actually your dream come true? (STDs didn't really enter my mental picture, sadly, because the snobbish, unrealistic part of me figured that if he really had an STD, I wouldn't be in bed with him.) Maybe I'd walk away having broken an eight-month sexless streak and get a baby of my own, one I could cuddle and nuzzle and gaze at adoringly for as long as I wanted. And then I forgot all about that and just went with it. If this was normal for him, well, why couldn't I just go with the flow?

The sex itself was average—that's not to say I didn't enjoy it. I remember the way he looked at me and said, "Beautiful," and made me feel it, his voice soft and reverential. I remember the way he turned over, hands above his head, his perfect bubble butt poised and waiting just for me. I remember falling asleep in his arms and him kissing me all over my face when I woke up, almost like we were a real couple, rather than two near-strangers who might possibly get to know one another better. Or not.

The next morning I remember being grateful for the speared olives and otherwise liquid meal, because my stomach looked flat and felt empty as I slithered off the bed, scampering naked to the bathroom. I wasn't as self-conscious as I normally am, and I was happy to wake up before his alarm clock to curl back up into his grasp. I kissed my way along his bicep, admiring his muscles. I turned over onto my back and again, without speaking, his bare cock entered me. I was so lazy from the previous night's alcohol that I lay there and let it happen. Again. If we didn't use a condom last night, why should we now? The damage, if any, was done, and why should I be such a worrywart?

Maybe that's the heart of it. I worry day and night, even in my dreams. I worry that I'm going to die in a car accident, I worry about my gargantuan student loans, I worry that I'll never write the big book I want to. I worry that some random person will take a sudden dislike to me. I worry that I'll suddenly be fired or evicted. I worry that nobody will ever again want me to be their girlfriend. I usually have extra stamps, pens, sweaters, aspirin—whatever I or someone else might need in case of emergency. But all that gets to be overwhelming after a while—trying to be on top of everything, remember everything, be responsible. On those rare occasions when I simply abandon all the worry, when I almost pretend I'm someone else, someone who glides through life with ease and confidence, I do so with all the passion I have in me.

I was embracing not just a new way of having sex, but a new me, one who expected life to carry her through to the other side safely and securely. I wanted to be the kind of girl who can drink three martinis for dinner and not be near dead the next day, who can flash her chest and laugh about it, not caring what anyone thinks. I wanted to be the kind of girl who can ward off pregnancy by sheer force of will, or the kind who might get knocked up but can turn that into the best thing that ever happened to her.

If I had known exactly what kind of guy he was (the kind who, apparently, could kiss me tenderly on the forehead one day and then confess that he was seeing someone else a week later), would I have wanted him to be my baby daddy? The saddest part, and the real confession here, is that the answer is probably yes. But thanks to two little pills called Plan B, we don't have to worry about any little Rachels running around . . . at least, not just yet.

Out of the Bag

By Noah Tarnow

LIKE MOST JEWISH MALES, I am in perpetual terror of disappointing the females in my family. My sister is Hippolyta among the Amazons of my psyche. She is three years older, and during our childhood—through a combination of her imperiousness and my complete spinelessness—she became a tremendous figure of fear and aspiration. Now that we're adults, we get along well. (I finally figured out that she was almost as screwed-up a kid as I was.) But still, whenever she asks for a favor, I'm more nervous than I should be.

Several years ago, my sister and her husband left New York for San Francisco. They road-tripped across the U.S., so they couldn't take Natasha, their sweet, withdrawn, grossly obese 6-year-old cat. Instead they dumped her at our cousin's house in the New Jersey suburbs, and gave me a vital task: In two months, when I flew out to San Francisco for Thanksgiving, I was to transport the cat with me.

I love cats. Some say that's not wise for a heterosexual single man to admit, but any woman who's shallow enough to let that bother her doesn't interest me. People like dogs because they give unconditional affection— no matter what kind of prick you are, a dog will love you. But cats are more discerning—you have to earn their love, and that's something I appreciate.

Unfortunately at this point, I had yet to earn Natasha's love. Her stance toward me: Don't pet me, don't try to pick me up, don't even fucking look at me. But regardless, I had no intention of letting my sister down.

If you've never taken an animal on a cross-country plane trip, be aware that it's a shitload more complicated than it should be. I had to pay the airline $50 and have the cat's papers with me. She had to fit under the seat in front of me (tricky, considering that Natasha was approximately the size of a newborn rhinoceros), and she had to be removed from her carrier at security so that the carrier could go through the X-ray.

Fortunately, I was prepared. A vet had given me three large white pills. "Just give the cat one of these about an hour before takeoff to calm her down," he said. The second secret weapon: a red leather S&M bustier that I could clip a leash onto while removing her from the bag at preflight screening.

I'm generally a lucky guy, so when that bright pre-Thanksgiving Wednesday morning approached, I was optimistic. I'd done a ton of prep work.

About five minutes before the cab showed up, however, the first sedative was fired from Natasha's mouth with force, skittering across the tile floor of my cousin's suburban kitchen. (This was after several futile attempts to hide it in her food.) I recovered the pill and eventually got it down her throat. But then Natasha put up another violent struggle when I tried to put on the harness. Why does this cat act like a drooling vegetable all of the time except now? And could I blame her? The harness made her look inane—as if she were a feline parody of a dominatrix in an Austro-Hungarian beer hall. I pulled and prodded, dodging and weaving her, finally tightening the last strap as the taxi honked out front.

I jammed Natasha into her carrier. "Good luck!" my cousin wished me. "Have fun, Natasha," she said to the cat. "You look very pretty." Natasha was darting her head around inside the carrier as if she were deciding which way to collapse when the heart attack hit.

As the driver pulled into the maze of airport on ramps, I realized what I was really in for: This was Thanksgiving 2001, barely two months after September 11. One of the busiest travel days of the year, during the most anxiety-ridden time in our lifetimes. I hauled my bag of feline to the end of a very long line. Time wasn't a factor—as a result of my Jew-rosis, I'm always early to anything important, like a flight. But I was growing antsy and I knew Natasha would be too.

I peered into the carrier. She appeared to have settled down, so I started to unzip the bag a little, let her enjoy the view—when this animal made a rocket-powered launch for the sky. Before I could respond, seven-eighths of her body was out of the bag. I acted fast, pushing her skull down, her hind leg caught on the inside of the bag being the only thing preventing her from complete escape. We struggled, her front claws digging into my jacket, me twisting her cranium, forcing her back in the bag, zipping it back up again. People around me laughed.

Few things have ever given me less faith in the competence of American federal bureaucracy than the Thanksgiving 2001 air travel experience. We weren't yet pointlessly removing our shoes or putting shampoo in Ziploc bags, but the whole system was beyond stupid. I had to show my boarding pass to half-interested attendants at four or five checkpoints. Brutish-looking commandos in berets and fatigues sporting machine guns were stationed throughout. And when it came time to deal with Natasha, they didn't know what to make of it and I had to take the reins. "I think I'm supposed to remove the animal and carry her through, while we put the empty bag through the X-ray," I offered.

"Yeah, that's right," said the attendant, not even looking up. But there was too much happening. A dozen other people were trying to put their things through the X-ray, I was removing my cell phone and keys from my pockets, the attendants still had their heads up their asses, the armed men loomed ominously. *Thank God for the leash and harness,* I thought. I held on tight to the leather strap and removed Natasha from her bag, placing her on the ground underneath the X-ray conveyor table. *Just hold on and everything will be fine.*

Seconds later, I felt a slight tug, a call of panic. I looked down and found that I was holding tight onto a leash attached to an empty leather harness. I followed the gaze of several nearby people back toward where I'd been waiting in line, and there was Natasha, bolting her way toward a TCBY. This ridiculously fat and lazy animal was suddenly a turbocharged streak of brown and black, desperate for whatever freedom she thought an airport food court could offer.

I dropped my own bag, left the leash on the floor, and bolted after her. I got several yards, to where the gleaming open expanse of the airport narrowed into the security corridor. There I witnessed one of the more interesting sights of my life: A fatigued military man had Natasha pinned to the ground with his massive soldier-grade boot. He was pointing his gun at her head. Jesus, did he think she was going to spit up anthrax?

"Um, excuse me, that's . . ."

"Oh, here you go." This man could probably have killed me with his mind, but at the moment, he couldn't have been nicer. He handed me Natasha, who at this point was pacified by the shock. He had the kind of smile that said, "I almost split this animal's head into tiny shards with the blast of my government-issued assault weapon, in the process completely obliterating your sibling relationship."

The rest of the trip was anticlimactic. At the gate, Natasha attracted the attention of an extremely beautiful woman who asked me for advice about how to transport her two cats when she moved to Italy in the spring. (I think I told her to commit suicide.) She watched the cat while I visited the men's room; I figured black-market resellers of fat cats don't ply their trade much in Newark Airport.

On the plane, I squeezed her carrier into the space under the seat in front of me. A few hours into the flight, her eyes had completely glazed over, the sedative having finally penetrated her layers of blubber. All was forgiven. I bent over to whisper to her, "We're almost there, sweetie" but those airplane seat belts don't let you bend that far forward, so I ended up whispering it to the 45-year-old tax attorney sitting in front of me. Maybe it made him feel better.

My sister met me at baggage claim and I told her the story. She laughed carelessly. An hour or so later, we were at my sister's new apartment. Natasha did a little exploring, found the litter box, and soon she'd settled into the regular business of being an apartment cat: She was sitting commandingly on her old beloved green easy chair, yawning. My sister made the typical cat joke: "Oh, you must be tired! What a busy day you've had!"

But it was true. Natasha had flown across the country, taken drugs, worn S&M gear, met all sorts of new people, including a man with a gun. Two-thirds of the excitement in this cat's entire life happened today. She better be fucking tired. And my sister better be fucking grateful.

WORK

THE MULATTO INCIDENT

BY JULIE KLAUSNER

RECENTLY, I DID A READING OF MY COMICS. I SHOWED SLIDES OF THE PANELS AND HAD ACTORS ON STAGE TO HELP ME READ THE NARRATION AND DIALOGUE. IT WAS FUN.

Dixon Place presents...
Carousel
Cartoon slide shows and other projected pictures.

Todd Alcott • Leela Corman
Brian Dewan • J. Keen
→ Julie Klausner • Arlen Schumer
Doug Skinner • Jim Torok
Lauren R. Weinstein & Patrick Hambrecht
Plus many surprise guests!
Hosted by R. Sikoryak

I'D WRITTEN A BUNCH OF NEW COMICS FOR THE SHOW, IN ADDITION TO 3 NEW INSTALLMENTS OF MY "RACIST KITTY" COMIC.

Racist Kitty   Rac

I NEVER INTENDED TO MAKE "RACIST KITTY" A SERIES OF MORE THAN 2 COMICS, BUT AFTER I DID MY FIRST COMIC BOOK, "ANIMAL PARTY," THE MOST FREQUENT FEEDBACK I GOT FROM PEOPLE WAS,

I LOVE 'RACIST KITTY'!

I GUESS THE JUXTAPOSITION OF CUTENESS AND BIGOTRY IS A COMEDIC BET ON THE HOUSE.

SO, I WROTE SOME MORE FOR THE SHOW:

I SENSE AN INTRUDER.

I WAS OFFENDED BY THAT HALLE BERRY MOVIE, "CATWOMAN."

THERE WERE DROPPINGS NEAR THE HOLE IN THE WALL, SOME OF MY KIBBLE IS MISSING, AND THE SMELL OF VERMIN IS PALPABLE.

YOU THINK THE SCRIPT WAS PAINFUL?

I BET IT'S A CHINAMAN.

TRY WATCHING A MEMBER OF YOUR SPECIES BE PORTRAYED BY A MULATTO.

DR. MARTIN LUTHER KING, JR. ONCE SAID,

"I REFUSE TO ACCEPT THE VIEW THAT MANKIND IS SO TRAGICALLY BOUND TO THE STARLESS MIDNIGHT OF RACISM AND WAR."

STUPID NIGGER.

I WAS ANXIOUS ABOUT READING THEM ON STAGE, AS I DON'T LIKE TO MAKE A HABIT OF DROPPING N-BOMBS IN FRONT OF CROWDS. BUT I WAS EXCITED ABOUT DEBUTING MY NEW WORK IN PUBLIC. STILL, I DON'T KNOW WHETHER CRUMB WOULD'VE GONE THROUGH WITH "NIGGER HEARTS" IF HE HAD TO DO IT ON STAGE.

JEEZUS! DID I JUST COMPARE MYSELF TO R. CRUMB?

LOOKIT THE *EGO* ON THIS YENTA!

CRUMB-STYLE PANEL DRAWN BY R. SIKORYAK

Prime-Time Playa

By Andy Borowitz

I FIRST MET WILL SMITH IN 1990, in the basement of Quincy Jones' house. (For sheer name-dropping efficiency, that sentence deserves some sort of special recognition.) He wore his hair in the fade style that was popular at the time, a fluorescent red tracksuit and a gold necklace that spelled out the words "The Fresh Prince." It was under that name that he had become a Grammy Award–winning rapper, best known for the novelty hit "Parents Just Don't Understand," the only rap single then or since to make reference to *Brady Bunch* trousers." In addition to rapping, in his brief recording career he had acquired two other skills crucial to recording artists: spending all of his money with lightning speed and not realizing that he had to pay taxes. Which is why he was in the basement of Quincy's house, talking about doing a sitcom, which I was supposed to write.

A couple of days earlier, Brandon Tartikoff, then the president of NBC Entertainment, had asked me if I had ever heard of the Fresh Prince. I told him that I had heard of Prince. My familiarity with rap music pretty much began and ended with the Beastie Boys, unless you counted Run-D.M.C.'s version of Aerosmith's "Walk This Way," or Debbie Harry's song "Rapture." (Counting that last one would truly be an act of desperation.) After Brandon explained to me who Will was, I sensed with some relief that up until a few days before, when Quincy had touted Smith to NBC as a potential sitcom star, Brandon had never heard of him either.

I asked Brandon if he had considered hiring a black writer instead of me. It's not that I thought people should only write about their own ethnic groups— if I'd felt that way, I never would've accepted my first TV job, writing dialogue for *Archie Bunker's Place*. No, I was just being a coward. I doubted that I could pull this assignment off, and I worried about the reaction that rap fans might have to the first hip-hop sitcom being created by a Jewish Harvard grad from Shaker Heights. As it happened, Brandon had already talked to the African-American writers about writing the pilot, but they were either unavailable or uninterested. And so my career in hip-hop began, more or less by default.

It was Quincy who first made me feel as though I might actually be up to this task, or at least wouldn't hideously humiliate myself trying. Quincy, who was in his late 50s at the time, wasn't the likeliest candidate to "get" hip-hop either—particularly Will's brand, which had been pitched mainly to teenyboppers. But Quincy saw a similarity between the bebop artists he came of age with and the rappers his children were listening to. Both beboppers and rappers shared a delight in a secret language that they had created, an out-sider language designed to piss off an establishment that couldn't understand it. Quincy spoke about the duality of the rappers, in whom street bravado coexisted with poetry. As Quincy went on about duality, I noticed that Will had nonchalantly seated himself at Quincy's baby grand and begun playing the opening measures of Beethoven's "Für Elise." This project was starting to seem kind of cool.

I got to work. The concept the network had agreed to involved Will moving in with a bunch of wealthy relatives in Bel-Air (Quincy's neighborhood). My near-total ignorance of hip-hop slang and culture turned out to be an asset, oddly enough, when creating the characters of Will's ultra-preppy cousins, Carlton and Hillary, whose cluelessness helped fuel much of Will's comedy. Having Will define then-current slang terms such as *stupid* and *dope* for his

Bel-Air relatives was a convenient way to explain those terms to an equally clueless white audience—this was 1990, after all, long before the Pillsbury Doughboy started rapping in commercials. When it came time to write the ending of the pilot, I felt as though it had already been written for me. In the final scene, after Will's Princeton-educated uncle excoriates him for being a good-for-nothing street kid, Will sits down at his uncle's baby grand and plays the first few bars of "Für Elise." Fade out.

One year after *The Fresh Prince of Bel-Air* debuted and became a fluky hit, I won the NAACP Image Award for creating it. As I accepted the award onstage at the Wilshire Theater in Los Angeles, I had a sneaking suspicion this moment was going to be the pinnacle of my career in hip-hop. It seemed like a good time to stop.

My Stalker

By Mike Albo

MY NAME IS MIKE ALBO and I'm a D-level celebrity. Well, I'm actually more like a D-minus-level celebrity. A-level celebrities, you know who they are: Madonna, Jessica Alba, George Clooney. B levels are more like Patricia Clarkson, Michael Cunningham or Judge Judy. C levels I would say are Sylvia Myles, a lab technician on *CSI*, and Trista, the original *Bachelor*'s bachelorette. Most D levels are porn stars, local newscasters, separated Siamese twins, famous plastic surgeons. So just bring that down a notch and that's me.

We're the amphibians of the disgusting celebrity world that we live in. We lie there in the mud between the dry herbal land of celebrity stardom and the vast, beautiful ocean of obscurity. A- through C-level celebrities and even some D-level celebrities like Kathy Griffin get a lot of cool stuff, but D-minus-level celebrities get nothing. No free gift bags, no free Reebok sneakers, no tickets to benefits, no money, no love, nothing. The only thing that you get from being a D-minus celebrity is this vague, desperate hope that someday your life is gonna change. And stalkers.

It's late spring in 2001, it's the last gasp of the dot-com boom and I appear on the cover of *Next* magazine. For those of you who don't know, *Next* is the second most important gay weekly. Which makes it like the *Vanity Fair* for gay guys below 14th Street in New York. I start getting these calls on my phone from a guy named Larry Acheball. That's really his name. I was just sitting on the couch one day, deep in my pre-paradigm-shift thoughts ("*Sex in the City* has only two more seasons!" "Will I ever be sick of Prada?" "When will I get the fame and money I deserve as an American?") when the phone rings. I don't pick it up and there's a message: "Hello, I am trying to reach the performer Mike Albo. This is Larry Acheball from my limousine in New Jersey. I am the manager of *Star Search*. Please tell him to call me."

I swear to you, there is barely a DNA molecule in me that isn't dying to return his calls. I'm like, "Oh my God, I could be on *Star Search*!" But something in me, some strange instinct that I usually don't have, tells me not to call back. But he keeps calling, keeps calling, keeps calling.

One night I decide to go out somewhere gay (to this day I still think I am going to find my husband in a bar). I drink two Maker's Marks, get involved in some disappointing sexual menudo, drunkenly take the F train back to Brooklyn, trudge down the street to my building and then I hear someone call my name: "Mike Albo."

It is so clear that I think it's in my head, so I ignore it. But the minute I walk inside my apartment, the phone rings. Another message: "Yeah, Mike Albo, this is Larry Acheball. I just saw you on the street. I happened to be parked in front of your house in my limousine and I wanted to talk to you about *Star Search*."

The next night I go out again somewhere gay to do something gay and drag myself home drunk again and walk up to my building and . . . something is hanging off of the gate to the front door. One of those huge Mylar helium balloons with a picture of Holly Hobbie–esque ragamuffin lovers kissing. And someone had written my name all over it: "MIKEEE ALBO" with hearts and underlines.

I start putting it together—he's not from *Star Search*. That's when he starts sending letters written in that stereotypical stalker scrawl—you know, it's sort of scribbly and turns to the left (someone should copyright that font,

by the way). In the letters he admits that he isn't from *Star Search*, and he says he saw my picture in *Next* magazine. And in the picture, he says, the lips moved and told him that I loved him.

At first I think, "Whatever, there's nothing I can do about it. I'll just sit here in my semi-obscurity and live with it." Of course, neither of those facts stop me from going out again, and every time I do, I come home to more and more gifts at my front gate. A white teddy bear. A glittery plastic butterfly. A stuffed tiger with big, longing eyes. A gallon milk jug cut off at the top with mealy, festering carnations in cellophane stuffed into the opening.

The summer that follows is the worst of my life—I have no money, I'm eating canned food, I'm audited by the IRS and I have a hernia. I spend an entire day at Bellevue registering for hernia surgery and filling out forms to prove I'm "income sensitive." That night, I'm sitting at home watching network TV (no more frittering away my measly paychecks on restaurants and 12-dollar appletinis) and I decide to cook up some pasta with peanut butter (pad thai!) when I hear a buzz at my door. I don't answer, but it buzzes again.

"Hello?"

"It's me."

"Who's me?"

"Larry for Mike Albo."

"He's not here," I said, trying to take the gay accent out of my voice.

I peer outside. There is Larry's "limousine" in front of my house. It's a white Honda Civic. He had driven from Jersey in his Honda to come buzz my door. I can't believe my stalker has more money than me! Why can't he pick on Regis Philbin or someone with a bodyguard and celebrity health insurance and no hernia!? I wait in the dark for him to leave. When I see his taillights drive off, I creep downstairs. He had stuck a big white sticker on my door, with my name written in scratchy red Magic Marker, and there's another gift of festering carnations and a card:

"I have a confession to make. I made up that story about the *Star Search* program. Several months ago, when your picture appeared on the *Next* magazine cover, I said to myself, 'This is my man.' And I know you love me too."

I decide to continue to ignore it and hope he'll forget about me. Then September 11 happens, which is, of course, horrible and awful, and I think that maybe that will change things for Larry, you know? Like he'll have something else to worry about. Then some time in October, I get a letter from him that says that *he* caused the World Trade Center attacks because of his feelings for me, and if I don't talk to him or come and see him he is gonna collapse a building on my head. So I am like, "OK, time to go to the police."

I'm sure you remember what New York was like in October 2001. Everyone was so psychotic and it was the height of the anthrax scare. So I'm walking through Brooklyn, holding my hernia (since my surgery wasn't until November) and all my stalker letters. I go up to the precinct and say, "I have a stalker." They make me open the envelopes before I go inside the building. The world is so fucked-up and freaky and I don't know what's right and wrong.

But then in walks this big Sipowicz Jew cop. I tell him the story and he's like, "Don't worry, we'll put the fear of God in him!" He put his beefy, calming hand on my shoulder and I just wanted to fall into his arms like Whitney Houston in *The Bodyguard*.

The story has a happy ending because Larry actually stopped calling. (He did send me a Christmas card last year. It has a swatch of orange fur in the center with two googly eyes glued onto it.)

So since you guys control the entertainment industry, I have a favor to ask of you. If you could do one of two things, either just elevate me to D-plus status, or just get me a hotter stalker—just one or the other—I would appreciate it.

The Professional

By Jacob Austen

LATE ONE EVENING IN EARLY 1999, I got an intriguing call from a friend who was an editor/sex adviser for *Playboy*. He had scheduled an interview with the rock band KISS for the next day and he was hoping a KISS-loving zine writer like myself could help out. The magazine had planned a photo shoot of the band members, posing with naked women in KISS makeup, that was going to run with just a little explanatory text. But at the last minute, the band had contacted the magazine, strongly suggesting that a full interview run alongside the bountiful spread. Though happy to oblige, *Playboy* was scrambling to get this together at the eleventh hour—which was where I excitedly came in.

My friend explained that the L.A. office would fax over some general naughty questions for the editor to feed the rockers, but I was to come up with more informed topics of discussion. Although as a fan I was overjoyed, the journalist in me was worried. Considering that most of my work prior to this opportunity had appeared in underground publications, I was a little anxious about the prospect of working as a professional. But what made me downright nervous was the challenge of sitting across from one of my favorite bands and actually *being* professional.

Before I tell you what happened, here's a little history for anyone who is not a KISS veteran. During the band's original heyday in the 1970s, the New York quartet most famous for their face paint and fire-breathing was made up of two factions: the Gentiles and the Jews. The two goyim were drummer Peter Criss, a.k.a the Cat Man (inexplicably my childhood favorite), and lead guitarist Ace Frehley, the "Space Ace." Their Gentile-ness was more than the state of their foreskins—they had the basic rock star stuff covered, like abusing substances, crashing cars, going bankrupt. Also, Ace apparently thought Nazis were cool (he reportedly used to party in Nazi uniforms and he designed the KISS logo that is to this day banned in Germany because of the interlocking design of the "SS"). Though these two weren't the creative force behind the band, they are credited with "keeping it real," giving a band that was all about artifice an air of credibility.

The Jewish faction, the two men who still perform as KISS to this day, are ex-vocalist/guitarist Paul "Starchild" Stanley (né Stanley Eisen, whose mother lives next to my aunt Eva on Long Island) and vocalist/bass player Gene "The Demon" Simmons (né Gene Klein, né Chaim Witz, a Haifa-born Israeli immigrant). Their Jewishness comes in part from being menhes (doting fathers without drug or alcohol problems), and in part from their Esau-like hairiness.

But in all honesty, whenever anyone talks about KISS being a Jewish band they are referring to their acuity with finances. From the outset, the band has been a finely tuned money machine, shameless in its endless stream of merchandising (there's a KISS Kondom, a KISS Koffeehouse, a KISS Kasket) and its hard-line business tactics—by the '80s, Stanley and Simmons had taken advantage of their goyish bandmates' woes by buying out their shares of KISS and replacing them with salaried workers.

The face of KISS and de facto leader of the band has always been the lizard-tongued Simmons. Though not a particularly religious man (he attended Yeshiva as a kid, but only because it was free child care for his single working mother), he is a fiercely proud Jew who has summarized Israel's War of Independence as "we kicked their ass, end of story." Not long after arriving in America, the Hebrew-speaking outsider child used two of NYC's great Jewish industries, comic books and songwriting, to craft an ultra-extroverted, attention-hungry persona that is far more interested in the spotlight than in using his riches to pull strings behind the scenes, Elders of Zion–style. Thus, when he saw the opportunity in the mid-'90s to re-form the original KISS lineup and once again become the top-grossing rock band on earth, he put the wheels in motion, and the *Playboy* interview marked the third year of the vastly successful reunion.

I arrived at the downtown luxury hotel in the late morning, and not surprisingly the hard-partying Frehley was not rousable at that hour. So I—along with the mass of *Playboy* editors, photographers and audio engineers—was joined by Stanley, shirtless under leather overalls, Simmons, whose coarse blue-black ponytail looked like it was attached to his cap, and Criss, whose sleeveless shirt revealed an elbow-to-shoulder crucifix tattoo.

The interview went well. Simmons and Stanley had done this so long that they had developed a number of Borscht Belt–esque routines and one-liners ("But that's getting into semantics, not that I'm anti-semantic"). And I quickly earned my shekels, as far better material was yielded by my queries than by the predictable faxed questions about groupies. The musicians reminisced about how important *Playboy* was to them as young men, Simmons recalling how the beautiful nudes represented the true American Dream to his adolescent immigrant eyes, and Stanley remembering how when he actually began dating *Playboy* models he was disappointed in them as people (he later called the magazine and retracted that statement).

Criss, relishing his rare moment in the spotlight, discussed his desire to be recognized by the Rock and Roll Hall of Fame and nostalgically recalled his youthful antics when he and Jerry Nolan (of the New York Dolls) stalked their drum idol Gene Krupa. Unfortunately, the Cat's occasions of oratory were limited. Displaying an almost pathological need to be the center of attention, Simmons consistently cut off his disgruntled drummer. Though the future *Celebrity Apprentice* contestant knew he needed to keep Criss content to keep the lucrative reunion rolling, the following incident was typical of Simmons' antics during the interview: While Criss attempted to wax poetic, Simmons picked up a *Playboy* from the table and started bugging his eyes at the centerfold, grunting "Aooga, aooga!" Criss slammed his fist on the table in frustration, but then Simmons floridly declared, "I will let my bandmate address this question," with a royal wave of the hand. As Criss began speaking again, Simmons gave us a histrionic wink behind his drummer's back.

Unaware that one is not supposed to draw attention away from Simmons when addressing him, I broke this commandment by occasional jesting with Mr. Stanley. So the bassist started working little insults into his answers, at one point referring to a faction of their fans as pathetic obsessives, pointing at me and adding, "like this fellow here." I'm pretty sure he compared me to the fan who got Simmons' face tattooed on his ass, with that infamous tongue emerging from his rectum.

At this point, the *Playboy* editor read the next question on his list: a request for Simmons to pitch his dream porno movie. After some initial hesitation in which he compared skin flicks to the passivity of sports spectatorship (he couldn't comprehend observing rather than participating), he gave in.

"Young girl out of Chicago, dysfunctional family, goes off to boarding school, has her first sexual experience in the back of a Chevy . . . she's a very hot-looking girl and she's only had a kind of a physical effect on people; every time they see her body, they think 'look at them, they're lifted, separated and pointed in my general direction, thank you Jesus . . .' She decides because of that that she is going to disavow her physical attributes and go the other way, and so she becomes spiritual, she becomes a nun in training . . ."

Criss (of the massive crucifix tattoo) was shaking his head with a look of disgust. "I don't like this story. I don't like the Jesus crack, and I don't like this story. . . ."

The *Playboy* editor, somehow mistaking this palpable tension for playful banter, pressed on, "So she's a nun . . ."

"This offends Peter," Simmons apologetically offered.

"But the nun is unobtainable," the editor insisted, pleading for Simmons to continue. "That's part of the appeal, I'm with you on the nuns. . . ."

Thus Mr. Simmons found himself at a crossroads. With his multimillion-dollar empire rebuilt, it was crucial to keep his employees happy, yet here was *Playboy* magazine pleading with him to continue with this story.

"Needless to say, some of the things we've heard about in newspapers occur . . ." and he continued the pitch by segueing into a molesting priest joke. Quickly changing the subject, Stanley stepped in with a Jewish joke. ("Why did the rabbi like watching the porno movie run backwards? He liked the part at the end where she handed him the money.") This led to the *Playboy* editor boasting about a recent article in his magazine on "kosher sex."

"Am I the only Catholic in this room?" a furious Criss injected, pointing an accusatory finger at the soundman to his left. "You're Jewish, aren't you?"

"Yes," the curly haired slacker sheepishly replied.

"You're Jewish! You're Jewish! You're Jewish!" he continued around the table, eventually getting to the Protestant editor to my right, the first to reply in the negative. Pointing his cat claw my way he snarled, "You're Jewish?"

"Yes," I answered.

And here is where the magic happened.

"Hmm . . ." the artist formally known as Chaim Witz said, lifting an eyebrow and looking at me with pleasurable disdain. Then he offered what he perceived as the ultimate put-down. "You could pass for a Gentile. You don't have the Jew thing."

At that instant I knew I was experiencing one of the greatest moments of my life. If it had only been my childhood hero angrily calling me a Jew, it would have been enough. But the glorious absurdity of one of rock 'n' roll's greatest icons, the leader of my favorite band, my Jew-Rock idol, attempting to cut me down like a marauding moyel was so surreal, surprising and bizarre that it made me palpably giddy. Somehow, despite every molecule in my body commanding me to unleash gales of joyful laughter, I managed to stay stone-faced. That was the moment I knew I was a professional.

The Money Was Good

By Robbie Chafitz

I WAS AN ELF ONCE . . . FOR MONEY. Actually I was an elf twice for money. I was also a purple dinosaur, a juggler, a clown, a fire-eater, a human statue, a superhero, Santa Claus, Charlie Chaplin, a ballet dancer, a leprechaun, Dracula, Uncle Sam and a mime. After high school, I freelanced for a special events company in Washington, D.C., and performed at hundreds of birthday parties, Bar Mitzvahs, weddings and strip mall openings. I won't lie, it was fun for a while and the money was good. But by the age of 26, a college graduate with aspirations for bigger and better things, the dressing up was getting old. Not to mention that the run-ins with old girlfriends while dressed as the Easter Bunny were beginning to take a toll on my self-esteem. I had to make a change, so I left the States.

I took a job teaching U.S. film production, English, and American football at the Moscow International Film School in Russia. For the equivalent of three dollars a month, I explained to eager Russian students that one page of script equaled one minute of screen time, that you shouldn't end a sentence with a preposition, and how to count to "ten Mississippi" before rushing the quarterback. To supplement my income I got a job setting up the audio-visual equipment at the Moscow International Press Center. One of my responsibilities was to make sure that the microcassette recorders placed on the podium by the journalists weren't indeed bombs. How did I do this? I had to pick them up and shake them. If they didn't blow my arm off they could remain on the podium. As I explained earlier, I had done worse things for money.

After a very long year in Russia, I returned home broke and had to move in with my folks for a short time. Determined not to go back to my character work, I picked up a temp job at a mail-order supply house processing the returns of a novelty Bill Clinton watch (the arms kept falling off). Knowing I was looking to make some extra money, a friend of the family asked me if I would like to wait tables at her bar on Wednesday nights. I had no waiting experience but how hard could it be? The only requirement was that I show up wearing black pants, a tuxedo shirt and bow tie. This probably would have raised the suspicion of an average person, but I was used to costume requests so I didn't think twice.

Wednesday night at the Rabbit's Foot in Frederick, Maryland, is Ladies' Night. It is the one night of the week that this all-American redneck bar invites the women of the town to take a long-needed break from being objectified. It's the one night of the week that the bar says, "Hey, sweet thing, sit back and relax and allow us to entertain you with half-naked men who will dance upon the stage for you." I was not a stripper, thank God. I was a server. A server dressed in a tuxedo. I was the only server, I might add, whose tuxedo was vintage 1920s, with a real satin finish, made up of hand-stitched trousers and a bib front/back buttoning shirt with a removable starched collar. It was pretty safe to say that mine was the only tuxedo in the bar that wasn't 100 percent polyester, didn't have an adjustable elastic waistband and had never been worn to a junior-high-school dance.

It wasn't long before the male strippers hit the stage and the "ladies" went wild, and I mean wild-animal wild. They ripped at the men's shirts, yelled and screamed lewd sexual comments and touched themselves and each other. The best way to describe the clientele is that they most likely had spent their day in Jerry Springer's greenroom.

I wasn't there for more than a half hour when I learned that I was over-dressed. I was told by the management, Bob, to remove my shirt and to affix my bowtie around my neck. I guess Bob didn't care that my shirt was Savile cut and my trousers were hand-stitched. I spent the next ten minutes finding a safe place to hang my priceless tuxedo jacket and another ten trying to mini-mize my body hair.

Now, I had been in Russia for a year and had not been exposed to the sun for quite some time. So while my fellow servers, mostly off-duty firemen and construction workers with shaved chests and tattooed forearms, titillated the women with their tan sweaty physiques, my pale body glowed in the dark like a ghoulish night-light. I was the server apologizing for my chest hair falling into the ladies' Sex on the Beaches.

One of my tables was a bachelorette party. Their first order was a round of drinks affectionately called a blow job. I placed the order with the bartender, who swiftly filled my tray with a dozen tiny shot glasses. "You know how to serve these?" he asked. "Uh, left to right," I bluffed. Shaking his head like a man who knows another man is about to do something he is not prepared to do, he reluctantly explained the proper serving technique for a blow job shot.

When I returned to the table, the ladies were already lined up to receive their drinks, which is to say, they were on their knees. I proceeded to sit in a chair and place each shot between my legs as each woman, placing her hands behind her back, lowered her head into my crotch, grabbed the shot glass with her mouth and swallowed. My job was to simulate an orgasm for each of the women. Yes, really.

By the third round of shots, I thought I had finally gotten the hang of it until one of the women, kneeling before me, looked up and said, "Hmmm, let me guess, you're either Jewish or gay."

My guess was that up until now, neither Jews nor gays had ever been seen at the Rabbit's Foot. "Just Jewish," I answered, cautiously. I didn't want to start a mass panic. "Yeah, I could tell," she said proudly as she wrapped her lips around the shot glass and gulped. Reacting in false ecstasy, I caught my reflection in one of the many mirrors lining the walls. Now I knew what she was talking about. As the other topless men proudly humped poles and shook their asses in the patrons' faces, I, with my pale hairy chest and unconvincing smile, looked like I had strolled in from the Grossman Bar Mitzvah and accidentally misplaced my shirt.

The night wore on and I was groped, squeezed, licked, rubbed up against and well-tipped. Yes, I was very well-tipped. I was making about 70 dollars an hour, although I had other duties in addition to serving drinks. I had to appear onstage with the other servers and hold a large chocolate phallus for a birthday girl to enthusiastically deep-throat for the amusement of the entire bar. All together, everyone! "Happy birthday to you, happy birthday to you, choke on that big black cock, Lisa, happy birthday to you!" We then surrounded the birthday girl and grinded our pelvises in her face as we poured champagne on her head. They don't call it Ladies' Night for nothing.

I wish I could say that I drove home that night, to my parents' house, swearing I'd never do that again, but there I was for the next few Wednesday nights, shirtless, faking orgasms and presenting big black penises for women to fellate. It was like having an alter ego; mail-order-supply returns processor by day, male topless waiter by night.

All was going well until I was moved from my mail-order temp job to a new temp job at a software company. I was going to fill in for one of the account executive's assistants for a week. On my first day at the new company, I was called into the office of the account executive to get briefed on my assignment when my two worlds finally collided. There I was, sitting across from a very well-dressed professional woman with pictures of her family on her desk, and she was sitting across from the guy whose lap she had slurped shots from the night before.

A week later, I was dressed as a Venetian gondolier at the Italian Embassy.

A Field Guide to the North American Bigfoot

By Ben Greenman

1. Alert.

2. Tired.

3. Thinking of going swimming.

4. Worrying that he is overdrawn.

5. Plotting to avenge himself on his mortal enemy, Alan, who has, over the years, stolen two of Bigfoot's girlfriends, framed Bigfoot for a crime he didn't commit (a minor shoplifting infraction, admittedly, but it's the principle of the thing) and played innumerable pranks that resulted in Bigfoot's humiliation, including one in sophomore year of college in which he dumped an entire pepper shaker into Bigfoot's milk carton and laughed when Bigfoot had to spit out the peppered milk. Bigfoot hadn't had a real enemy since Kenny Labovitz in the eighth grade, and their relationship was as much about formative competition as anything. Bigfoot didn't want to compete with Alan. He didn't want Alan anywhere near him. Alan Tresser. What a jerk.

6. Itchy.

7. Hungry.

8. Enthusiastic.

9. Thinking of Clara—Ah! Clara. What a pity that she had nothing to her name and so was forced to factor in wealth when she felt around in her heart for her real emotions concerning this man, or that one. If only her father had given up his dream of sculpting "the intersection of time and tempo," or "the smallest available unit of rhythm," or whatever it was that he was on about in those masses of knotted metal. "It's a miracle that one of those things hasn't fallen on him and hurt him," Bigfoot said of Clara's father. "Anyway, don't you people love miracles? Water, wine: that kind of thing. Your dad had plenty of water tonight, if you know what I mean." Bigfoot instantly regretted his remark, for her father was a kind man, almost as tall as Bigfoot, though with a stoop when he stood, and he did not put his eyes wide and scream like a child that night that Clara brought Bigfoot home. In fact, he was cordial, gave Bigfoot a firm handshake, let him sit at the table with the rest of them, and the only sign that there was anything amiss came later, when he pulled Clara aside in the hallway and dipped once, quickly, to her ear where he whispered, "Honey, maybe he's not right for you." In the car on the way back, Bigfoot mocked Clara's father. He could do the voice perfectly; it was light and too sweet like a bad dinner wine. "Not right for you, not right for you," Bigfoot said, in singsong. That night Clara wouldn't share his bed, and the next week, she told Bigfoot that she was seeing a man named Paul. "He's a lawyer," she said. "You don't know him. But he makes me happy." Bigfoot stepped backward to protect what was left of his dignity. In his heart he experienced a mild pain.

10. Experiencing mild pain.

11. Experiencing moderate pain.

12. Experiencing severe pain.

13. Wondering how much more he can take. First, there was the kid in the shoe department in the sporting goods store who said he'd go downstairs and check the stockroom when he knew full well that there were no shoes big enough to fit Bigfoot's big feet. Then there was the sleek, impossibly thin woman, probably a model, who asked Bigfoot if he knew where she could get a good wax. Bigfoot didn't know what she was talking about. Some days Bigfoot felt like he didn't understand people at all. Then there was the envelope that he found slipped under his door. It was addressed to him, but it had not ended up in his mailbox. This happened a few times a week; the mailman delivered his letters

and packages to Mrs. Biedermeyer in 3B. This infuriated Bigfoot. The names weren't even slightly similar, except for the fact that they both started with the same letter. And Bigfoot almost never got Mrs. Biedermeyer's mail, although when he did he always made a point of bringing it by, and Mrs. Biedermeyer always made a point of telling him about how her son was doing, out in San Diego, in the videography business. Bigfoot picked up the envelope that had been slipped under his door, opened it, and learned to his horror that Clara was scheduled to marry Alan Tresser on September 8 in a small ceremony in St. Joseph's Church in the center of town. Bigfoot had introduced them, of course, a few years before, when he was still trying to reconcile with Clara, who was dating Paul. Bigfoot and Clara were eating lunch—Clara had said that dinner was too intense—and Alan Tresser was sitting at the very next table. He had come over and pretended that he and Bigfoot were old friends. Bigfoot, trying to save face, had agreed with him. "Very old friends," he had said, not sure who he was insulting. Alan had given Clara the eye, but Bigfoot wasn't surprised. Most men gave her the eye. A few months later, when Bigfoot heard that they were dating, he almost kicked in a door. Now, they were getting married, and he was invited. "This really is the final straw," Bigfoot thought as he went down to the street, got into his car, drove the two hours to the Berkshires, and rampaged in the woods for the better part of the evening. One young hiker scrambled to avoid Bigfoot, slipped on a rock, and got a deep cut on his shin. That should have made Bigfoot feel better, but it didn't. The young hiker wasn't Alan Tresser.

14. Sweaty.

15. Congested

16. Afraid to reply to the wedding invitation one way or another. If he did not accept, could he ever hope to speak to Clara again? But if he accepted, that would be a thousand times worse. He would be standing out on the lawn all by himself, or with a date whose name he could not remember from one minute to the next, and he would be making small talk about the bride and groom. "She looked lovely," one old woman would say. "So pink." Bigfoot would not answer, secretly convinced that he should tear off the old woman's head and push the headless corpse down the rolling hill in front of the church where, just moments before, Clara had turned and lifted her chin and, beaming, given herself to Alan Tresser. A church! This was a concession on Alan's part, as well as a concession that Bigfoot, during his time with Clara, would never have made. Was that the answer all along? Now what would happen? When Bigfoot and Alan Tresser had run into each other at lunch, Alan Tresser was working as the regional sales manager for an automotive magazine. Was that enough to give Clara a good life? And what was a good life, anyway? Certainly not one with too much Alan Tresser in it. Bigfoot was sitting at his breakfast table dragging his claw through the dregs of some oatmeal. "I wish I were dead," Bigfoot said to no one in particular. The lifespan of a Bigfoot was 300 years. Bigfoot had at least 80 to go.

17. Contemplating his death.

18. Dead.

Approaching a Lunatic

By Adam Lowitt

CELEBRITY SIGHTINGS ARE JUST LIKE BREASTS. Entire magazines are devoted to them but when you actually see them in public, staring is not polite. Living in Manhattan, I have had numerous opportunities to gawk at the elite. And with that, let the facetious name-dropping begin.

Once, strolling through Greenwich Village on a beautiful spring day, I passed by formerly televised Superman Dean Cain wearing a pair of sleek sunglasses and judiciously picking through a bowl of pasta. Apparently the rumors are true, Alfredo sauce is impervious to X-ray vision. Years ago, emerging from a subway station in SoHo, completely lost and confused as to my location, I consulted a man smoking a cigarette outside a wine bar for directions. He confidently gave me various routes to travel depending on my scenic desires. That man? MTV news dad, and horrible direction informer, Kurt Loder.

At a bar in Hell's Kitchen, one so financially secure they offer free hot dogs with every drink purchase yet still so financially strapped they cannot eradicate the prominent aroma of urine that occupies their space, I drunkenly spilled my beer on 1992's *My Girl* star Anna Chlumsky. Luckily, I was just sober enough to stop myself from singing my apology, "My fault, my fault, my fault. That was m-y-y-y fault . . . my fault!"

Others have been spotted and admired from afar, but those are the A listers. And although the list continues to grow, one man lives at the top.

It happened a few years ago when my parents came up from Florida for a visit. They were staying at a hotel near my apartment. I walked over to meet them for dinner, mentally preparing myself for the standard five-hour deliberation over which restaurant to eat at. Three passive-aggressive Lowitts, huddled over a *Zagat* guide, conceding suggestion after suggestion until my mom proposed we take this conundrum to the streets and find something as we walked. Passing through the lobby, I noticed a man checking in who looked extremely familiar. Tall, very thin, refined salt-and-pepper haircut, rounded glasses, and most importantly, clad in a suit covered in question marks.

I am aware that most people don't know this man by name; usually he is referred to as "that guy on TV around one-thirty in the morning, screaming from the Capitol steps, 'You can get free money!' " I however knew immediately that this was Matthew Lesko.

My affinity for Mr. Lesko could be traced back to his catchphrase, a saying I had heard, albeit in a much softer tone, on the night before my Bar Mitzvah. My dad, in an attempt to make the religious service a little more interesting, had bet me a hundred dollars to put on a pair of earmuffs before my Torah portion, and in the voice of an old Yiddish Jew, say, "Oy it's freezing in here, turn down the air conditioning."

I had begrudgingly practiced my Torah portion for the previous nine months, as well as doing push-ups every day so I could carry that Torah around the synagogue like a man. And now, on the eve of entering manhood, my biggest concern had become how to securely pre-place earmuffs on the bima without getting caught.

"All you have to do is say it and you can get free money," my father said.

Besides my dad, uncle and one or two cousins, no one was expecting anything other than Talmudic drivel from me on my big day. (Note to self: Talmudic Drivel is a great name for an Israeli prog-rock band.) Still, I put the earmuffs on, nervously uttered the line, and, like most comedy performed by 13-year-olds, it was not funny. My delivery was terrible; timing was poor. I was handed a hundred-dollar bill the next day. I remember staring at that bill deciding what type of frame I would put it in. The day after that, I hung a photocopy of it up in my room and bought seven CDs and some T-shirts.

Obviously the experience resonated. And that day, while my parents were standing outside the hotel, still trying decide on Italian or Spanish, I tried to convey the enormity of a Lesko-spotting to them. They were not interested so I walked back through the large glass doors into an overly carpeted lobby to speak to Lesko. I was nervous. This was not only the first celebrity I'd approached in a long time, but the first I'd ever approached ironically. I took comfort, however, in the realization that there is no delicate way to approach a lunatic.

"Excuse me, Mr. Lesko, I'd just like to say that I'm a huge fan of your work."

To which he responded, in a volume I thought was purely reserved for the airwaves, "Oh yeah!" Then while I was holding back my laughter, he issued a follow-up statement. "You know the government is suing me for libel!"

Amazingly, this high-pitched man in a suit covered in question marks had taken me by surprise.

"Really?"

Lesko immediately delved into his personal life, educated/confused me about his business and even felt comfortable enough to describe his recent divorce. My mind started to wander, enamored by this chance occurrence and yet growing extremely bored with the actual conversation. I kept coaching myself to focus, with the overarching reality that this encounter would never happen again.

By now my parents had come inside and were silently hovering around us. The audacity, I thought, to pretend to care about *my* celebrity *they* were clueless about ten minutes ago.

It was not long before everyone was introduced, fully transforming the conversation into an uncomfortable parent-teacher conference. Now they were chatting and I desperately wanted to go.

Before we left, Matthew Lesko gave me what I now consider my most prized possession: his business card. I proudly carry it around in my wallet like most parents do with photos of their children, showing it off to old friends and strangers at parties. It is a picture of him, riding a child's bicycle with a basket full of cash. I will say that for the brief interaction I had with him, he seemed like a nice enough guy, very polite and gracious to speak with, but it occurred to me that if your on-camera personality screams pedophilia, you might want to pick a different mode of transportation to put on your business card. I think it would be a wise investment to make with your free money.

Hollywood Sucks

By Darin Strauss

BECAUSE THE PUBLISHING INDUSTRY is dependent on luck—combined with a bit of talent and more salesman-unsavoriness than anyone likes to admit— my first novel had done well, and they (publishers, a movie agent) had flown me out to hawk my book to Movietown. It would not be an easy sell, they said. But no one could convince me of that back then.

I had been very lucky so far. My book *Cheng and Eng* was a bestseller right out of the gate. A writer friend of mine calls the period before one's first book comes out "the calm before the calm." So I felt blessed to have gotten any attention at all. And I guess my having had a bit of early success led me to believe that my professional life would just start going according to plan from here on out. Everyone, I was sure, would kill to make a movie about conjoined brothers from Siam who lived in the 1800s and had weird sex.

I had a room at the Beverly Wilshire hotel—my first time being put up in style. I was afraid to order anything, to unscrew the nuts next to the TV, even to open the fridge. The carpet that led from the door to the far window was so soft that I took my shoes off, like a guest in a rich person's house.

Meetings were set up, by whom and how I couldn't say. The first guy I met was a cinematographer who had just been named the "must-have" cameraman in Hollywood by *Entertainment Weekly* magazine. He was being offered a studio deal to direct, and we met at a restaurant where I'd have seven lunch meetings that week. (Apparently, all movie people have a go-to restaurant when they want to take a non-famous possible collaborator out for a bite.) It was an Italian place with what Manhattanites would call an uptown vibe—mirrored walls, expensive but overdone lighting. I sat across from Bob Balaban and near Alan Arkin.

My cinematographer had a smile lit by the first glimmers of real success, and he ended our quick meeting with a handshake and a: "Great—now let's go make a movie!" I was elated. But two days later I heard that he'd just used my meeting to scare the studio into giving him control of another project he'd wanted. It was impressively Machiavellian—a silky bit of quiet knife work. That's how the business works sometimes, I was told. But not to worry, my agent said. There were still more meetings.

The second guy I met with—at the same restaurant—was short and fat and had a blunt way of talking that matched his build. "I want to make this movie," he said.

"Great," I said.

"Chang and Eng, the Siamese twins. What could be a better story?" he said. "One problem, though."

"What's that?"

"They're Asian and they're attached."

"That's two problems," I said.

"We'll have to work around it."

It seemed like maybe he was hoping to make a Jackie Chan/Chris Tucker buddy movie. *I* pulled the plug on that one.

The third guy told me, in that same restaurant, that he wanted to make my book into a movie too—and he wanted to use his mentor as producer. (This time, Peter Riegert, the guy who played Boon in *Animal House*, was three tables away, probably being promised the lead in *Titanic*.)

"Wonderful," I told my meeting partner, and I meant it. This guy not only wanted to make the movie, but seemed like a normal person. I felt we might actually oscillate along the same wavelength. He was smart about the book, funny, warm; he could have been a friend, in another circumstance—a circumstance where he didn't hold my future in his hands.

"So," I said, "who's your mentor?"

"He's the dude who produced all the *Police Academy* movies." His chin rose a few rungs of pride. "*After* Guttenberg left the franchise." I hadn't even known there were post-Guttenberg *Police Academy*s. I ended that meeting.

Finally, after more days of defeat (an allergy attack at Scott Rudin's office, a pointless "get-to-know-you" meeting at *National Geographic*), I met someone at Disney. He and I connected quite well—as best as someone on the fulcrum of such a strange world and a guy on the outside of that world's arc can ever really connect.

He bought the book, hired me to write the script (which I did with a friend's help), and attached Julie Taymor—of Broadway's *The Lion King*—to direct. That was when things fell apart. Taymor was, shall we say, not helpful. I talked to her often—I called a lot about the script I was going to write, and her assistant always put me through to her; after a few weeks, I talked to her assistant more often; and then I got put through to no one. The script moldered on the shelf.

Years later, the book has been optioned five times, and I'm still hopeful. I'm working now with Gary Oldman, who is a genius and who initially found me, though we were both at CAA, by looking me up in the Brooklyn phone book. The script we're writing is great, at least I think it is. But you never know. Hollywood is a tough town to conquer. But then, you probably knew that already.

YOUTH

THE POOL PARTY JOKE

RETIRED BY NICK KROLL*   ILLUSTRATED BY JULIE KLAUSNER

WHEN I WAS IN MIDDLE SCHOOL, I FELT LIKE I WAS GOING TO A POOL PARTY EVERY WEEKEND.

LIZZIE GOLDMAN'S POOL PARTY WAS IN LATE JUNE, AND THE CAPRI SUN'S WERE FLOWING.

AS SOON AS I HIT THE WATER, I HAD TO PEE. I DIDN'T WANT TO GO IN LIZZIE'S HOUSE, WHICH ALWAYS ALWAYS SMELLED LIKE WET DOG & KASHA VARNISHZES.

I SWAM OVER TO THE DEEP END...AS I CASUALLY RELIEVED MYSELF, I WAS HORRIFIED TO SEE THE WATER AROUND ME TURN RED.

I FIGURED THAT LIZZIE'S DAD, IRV GOLDMAN, PROMINENT PODIATRIST & BIG TIME GERMAPHOBE, HAD PUT THAT CHEMICAL THAT TURNS YOUR PEE RED INTO HIS PRIZED "FOOT"-SHAPED SWIMMING POOL.

I WAS SO EMBARRASSED, UNTIL I REALIZED IT WASN'T THE CHEMICAL TURNING THE WATER RED. I HAD FINALLY GOTTEN MY PERIOD, AND WAS TRANSITIONING FROM BOY INTO WOMAN.

*this comic is from a project called Hilarious Graveyard, in which I asked fellow comedians to submit, for me to illustrate, a joke they wanted to retire. Offerings from other comedians can be seen at julieklausner.com.

Baruch Atah Nathaniel

By Simon Rich

AFTER MY PARENTS GOT DIVORCED and my mom went back to work, my brother, Nathaniel, and I spent a lot of time alone in our apartment. Every afternoon, CBS aired four consecutive episodes of *The Price Is Right*. We usually watched all four episodes, but one day, in the middle of episode three, my brother inexplicably turned off the television.

"Follow me," he said, walking over to the window. "I want to show you something."

I shook my head. The only things my brother ever wanted to show me were new varieties of wrestling.

"Come on," he said. "I promise it's not wrestling."

"Is it the thing with the pillows under the shirt?" I asked. "Sumo?"

"No," he said. "It's a secret."

I got off the couch and followed him over to the window.

"If I tell you something important," he said, "will you promise not to tell anyone?"

"OK," I said.

He clasped his hands around the back of my head and pulled my face up close to his. His bottom braces were clogged with Doritos. He had just started getting pimples, and I could see a few oily cavities on his chin, where he had popped some.

"I am God," he said.

I waited for him to make some sort of argument, but he didn't seem to think he needed to.

"No you're not," I said.

He shrugged.

"You don't have to believe me," he said. "That's the whole secret. You can turn *The Price Is Right* back on."

I started to walk back to the couch, but something about his tone stopped me. He was acting overly casual—like there was more to the secret that he wasn't telling me.

"OK," I said. "If you're God, then prove it."

He pointed out the window, at the grid of honking cars and tiny people.

"Do you see that van?" he asked. "The white one that just stopped at the red light?"

I nodded.

"It's going to turn right," he said.

As soon as the words left his mouth, the stoplight turned green and the car turned right. My brother smiled at me and nodded, like nothing crazy had just happened. I tried to come up with a logical explanation for what I had just witnessed. But there *was* none.

"Do another," I said, nervously.

"The blue truck," he said, pointing. "The one at the light. It's going to turn left."

I discreetly made an *L* with my left hand to remind myself which way left was. Then I looked up—and watched the truck begin to turn.

"You're just getting lucky," I stammered. "I could probably guess two in a row."

He pointed down at the traffic going by.

"Right . . . right . . . straight . . . right . . . straight . . . and . . . straight."

I watched in terrified silence as everything my brother had predicted came to pass.

"How . . . are you doing this?"

"I already told you," he said, his voice slightly deeper all of a sudden. "I am the Lord thy God."

I shook my head in amazement.

"Does anyone else know?"

"No," he said. "You are the only one I have revealed myself unto."

"Can I tell Mom?"

"You can tell whoever you want," he said. "But I should warn you: If you spreadeth my secret, it might cause me to become displeased."

"What do you mean?"

He pointed down the avenue at a cluster of flashing ambulances. There had been an accident on 52nd and three men were wheeling a bandaged woman out of the wreckage.

"Did that woman . . . displease you?"

"Yes," he said. "Yes, she did."

"What did she do?" I asked.

My brother hesitated.

"That's between me and her," he said, finally.

"I won't tell anyone," I whispered. "I promise."

Within 40 minutes, my brother was lying in front of the TV on a shrine I had built for him by collecting all of the pillows in the apartment.

"I am displeased," he intoned. "I desire Nutter Butters."

His face and neck were covered in orange crumbs and he was breathing extremely heavily. This was the seventh or eighth time he had desired Nutter Butters that afternoon.

"How many do you desire?" I asked.

He deliberated for a moment and then held up four fingers. I hopped off the couch and sprinted toward the kitchen.

"Aren't you forgetting something?" he called out.

"Baruch atah Nathaniel!"

"Good," he said. "Your faith pleases me. Now, bring me the offering."

That night, when we were watching *Married with Children*, I asked my brother some questions that had been bothering me lately.

"Why do people get sick?"

"Because they have sinned against me," he said.

"But how do you know when someone's sinned? How do you watch everybody at the same time?"

"I have a special TV that shows it all."

"Really? Like the one at the Wiz? With the small screen inside the big screen?"

"Yes."

"Can I see it?"

"No."

"If you're God," I said, "then why are you having a Bar Mitzvah?"

"I don't want anyone to get suspicious."

"What about the rabbis?" I asked. "Can't they tell?"

My brother shook his head. "They know something strange is going on, but they can't quite put their finger on it."

"What happens when people die?" I asked.

My brother hesitated for a moment.

"Do ten Hail Marys," he said.

"Which one's that again?" I asked.

"That's the one where you stand on the couch with your arms behind your back and fall down, onto your face. Then you say, 'Hail Mary.' "

I nodded and got started on the Hail Marys. After about seven or eight, he started to laugh.

"That's enough," he said. "I am pleased."

The truth is: I had always suspected that my brother was God, or at the very least, that he had magical powers. Sometimes when we were watching the Knicks, he'd say: "They're going to put in Mason." And sure enough, within two minutes, Anthony Mason would be tearing off his warm-ups and running onto the court. My brother wouldn't say anything. He would just nod a couple of times, like the TV had confirmed something he already knew.

That's not all: Whenever my brother wanted to, he could magically cause my mother to order in pizza. He usually did it on Tuesdays and Thursdays, when my mother worked overtime. She'd come home at around 6:30, kiss us on the foreheads and toss her small brown bag onto the floor.

"I'll heat up something," she'd say.

As soon as she was out of earshot, my brother would mute the TV.

"We're getting pizza tonight," he'd say.

"But Mom said leftovers," I'd say.

"We'll see about that," he'd say, confidently marching toward the kitchen.

Fifteen minutes later, my mother would materialize in front of the TV with a Domino's menu and ask me what kind of toppings I wanted. She always had an exasperated look on her face, like she had tried to resist my brother's magic, but had lost the fight again.

The other incredible thing about my brother is that he wasn't afraid of anything, not even murderers. By my calculations, it was only a matter of time before a murderer broke into our apartment. *America's Most Wanted* profiled five new murderers every night and there were a finite number of houses in the United States. Sooner or later, our number would come up. I explained this all to my brother, repeatedly, but it didn't seem to impact him in any way.

Sometimes, when we were watching TV late at night, we'd hear a siren out the window, indicating that a murderer had escaped and was on the loose. It never fazed my brother. He just picked up the remote and turned up the volume on the cable box.

When my dad was still living with us, I took most of the sirens in stride. I knew that, sooner or later, a murderer was going to break into our apartment. That was a given. But I always felt that my parents could work together to fend him off somehow. There were *two* of them, after all, and I knew from *Law & Order* that murderers worked alone.

Unfortunately, with my dad out of the picture, our numbers weren't looking so good. My mom was a strong woman. She could carry me all the way to the supermarket and most of the way home before she started to complain about her lower back. But I wasn't sure she could handle a murderer all by herself.

One night, my brother got invited to a sleepover party. My mom had to go out to dinner with friends and my dad wasn't going to be home at his house, so it was just going to be me and a babysitter. She claimed her name was "Tina," but I recognized her as Crazy Hands Wilma, a murderer who had recently been profiled on *Unsolved Mysteries*.

I followed my brother into his room while he packed up his overnight bag.

"Do you have to go?" I asked.

"It's cool," my brother said. "I'll be back tomorrow."

I looked out the window. Lights were flipping on in other buildings. It was almost night.

"You're not really God," I said.

"Sure I am," he said. "Remember the cars?"

I hesitated. I did remember the cars.

"OK," I said, finally. "But if you're God . . . then why can't you *do* anything?"

"What do you mean?" he said. "About what?"

"About *everything*. About diseases and murderers . . ."

"I'm working on it," he said. "Trust me."

"What about Mom and Dad?"

He stopped stuffing clothes into his bag.

"I'm going to have to leave that the way it is for now," he said.

I nodded.

"I'll tell you what," he said. "Here's what I'm going to do about the murderers."

He took off his Knicks sweatshirt and handed it to me.

"This sweatshirt is over four thousand years old," he said. "It's from Israel. As long as you're wearing it, nobody can murder you."

I looked at it for a while, suspiciously. Then I lifted up my arms so he could help me put it on.

"What about the babysitter?" I asked. "She might be a murderer."

"I'm going to put a spell on her," he said. "Watch."

He swung his arms around in a circle for a while, in the direction of the kitchen, where Crazy Hands was studying her French.

"*Baruch atah adonai!*" he shouted. "Now she's powerless."

"Do a spell on me too," I said. "So no one can get me."

He sat down next to me and put his arm around my shoulder.

"Baruch atah adonai," he said firmly. "You are safe, you are safe, you are safe."

"OK," I said, resting my head on his arm. "OK. *Amen.*"

We Want Bo Derek

By Joshua Neuman

I WAS 7 YEARS OLD in the summer of 1979 and I was attending Camp Scuffy, a day camp in upstate New York. Each weekday morning, a yellow school bus picked me up from my home in Paramus, New Jersey, snaking through suburban developments, pausing in front of driveways and circling cul-de-sacs while the boys on the bus snatched each other's baseball hats and the girls giggled and preened.

I didn't harbor any hostility toward girls at the time, but on the Richter scale of libidinous life they didn't register much higher than the New York Yankees' bullpen coach. I recognized the effect that girls had on boys, even boys my own age, but I tended to interpret it as a kind of affectation of manhood—like the way that boys wore gold necklaces or spat in the gutter. The actual desire for the opposite sex was, at best, an unproven hypothesis.

Once the bus had picked up the last kid, it left the residential neighborhoods of northern New Jersey and began its long trek upstate. Along the way, bored boys stiffened their thumbs and unlatched the spring-loaded windows to shout at the pedestrians on the street. But unlike kindergarten, when the boys screamed, "Bite-the-weenie!" and its truncated version, "Bite it!," the boys on the camp bus chanted: *We want Bo Derek . . . We want Bo Derek . . . We want*

Bo Derek. . . . Even some of the male counselors joined in. The only person who I had ever known named Bo was Bo from *The Dukes of Hazzard.* I was pretty sure they didn't mean that Bo, but who was this Bo Derek? And what did all of the boys on the bus want with him?

One summer evening, my mother, father and I were sitting around the dinner table watching *Face the Music,* a spin-off of *Name That Tune,* on our Magnavox 19-inch black-and-white television. The male contestant on the show was trouncing his female opponent so I was particularly in high spirits. During a commercial break, I returned to my plate of food, but was interrupted when I heard ". . . and introducing Bo Derek." I jerked and turned to the film trailer just in time to see a middle-aged man coughing nervously into his fist. He looked like a Jewish leprechaun. So this was Bo Derek?

The film was called *"10."* I asked my mother if we could see it.

Though my mother came of age in the '60s, she was by no means infected with its countercultural spirit. In fact, the closest she came to doing anything rebellious was when she helped a friend of hers get a job teaching with her at P.S. 87 in the Bronx so he could avoid Vietnam. As a psychology student at Hunter College, however, she did not go unaffected by the child-rearing philosophies of Dr. Spock. Throughout my childhood, a tattered copy of his *Baby and Child Care* rested on the tissue box holder in the downstairs bathroom.

My father blamed that book for my mother's tendency to give me whatever I wanted. She let me go to bed whenever I wanted, watch as much television as I wanted and she bought me more G.I. Joes than any kid in the neighborhood. In fact, the only time my mother ever said "no" to me was when I didn't want to wear a jacket over my Superman costume on Halloween. In protest, my future Halloween costumes were: "Gene Simmons with a jacket," "a bum with a jacket" and "the Incredible Hulk with a jacket."

So, when I wanted to see the movie *"10,"* even though she told me that she didn't think it was for children, my mother agreed to take me.

There were three different movie theaters in Paramus: the "tenplex" next to the Toys "R" Us where all of the popular films were shown, the "black theater" in the parking lot of the Garden State Plaza where films geared toward minority audiences were shown and Cinema 35—also known as the "$2.50 theater" (perhaps it was just my parents who called it that). It was the tiniest theater in Paramus and was just a few blocks from my house.

My father didn't come with us to see "*10*." He was busy with something or other in his workshop: a Plexiglas ketchup bottle holder or a contraption that would keep the raccoons from tipping over our garbage cans. We bought popcorn and sodas and sat down in the nearly empty theater. Soon the lights dimmed and the film began.

In the opening scene, "Bo Derek" walks into his surprise birthday party. He's turning 42, but for some reason, he's not happy. He has several drinks before making his way to his telescope, which he aims at a neighbor's house. A couple is playing pool. The lady isn't wearing a shirt. At that moment, I felt a surge of self-consciousness of being seen—with my mother, that is—in an almost empty cinema on a Saturday afternoon, watching a naked lady play pool. My mother, however, didn't flinch.

"Bo Derek's" lady friend catches him looking through the telescope. She calls him a "peeping tom," which leads to a talk that includes references to "leg spreading," "getting [one's] jollies" and an argument over the difference between "a broad" and "a hooker." I tried my best to decipher the conversation, but couldn't. I remembered when the Teen Angel in *Grease* called Frenchie a "hooker" after she had inadvertently dyed her hair pink, so I reasoned that a hooker was probably someone that looked flashy.

Apparently tired of looking through his telescope at the naked party, "Bo Derek" then decides to join the party where naked ladies are on floats in a swimming pool. I had never seen a naked lady before. So *this* is why the boys are screaming about Bo Derek. He had unlocked a universe.

The film's setting soon shifts to a resort somewhere in Mexico, where (the real) Bo Derek is on her honeymoon. Meanwhile, the impish Brit (who I believed to be Bo Derek) telephones his girlfriend back in Malibu. Her son, Josh, picks up the phone. Paramus wasn't a particularly Jewish town so nobody in my class was named Josh. None of the Yankees were named Josh. I could only remember one time when Miss Mary Ann had looked into her magic mirror and seen a Josh on *Romper Room* and that was because my mom had sent her a letter in honor of my birthday.

It is at the Mexican resort where the now iconic beach scene takes place. Wearing beaded/feathered cornrows and a see-through one-piece bathing suit (the real) Bo Derek rubs oil on her body. Meanwhile, the man who I think is Bo Derek is staring at her—at the gold ring on her hand and her golden skin. The ocean's waves are drowned by the sound of the beads in her hair rolling off her shoulder. She lies down. Arches her back. Lowers her legs. Closes her eyes. She never speaks. The only sound she makes is when her beads move, announcing her with the power that John Williams' score announced the killer great white in *Jaws*. She closes her eyes again. And then . . . his fantasy: They're jogging toward each other Bionic Man–style and embrace as the waves cover them with cool ocean froth.

I should've seen it coming. After all, it had felt like a taboo when the boys on the bus chanted Bo Derek's name out the windows. Why else would it feel that way unless this film wasn't for children?

Awakened from his beach fantasy, "Bo Derek" decides to go for a sailboat ride. On it, he spots (the real) Bo Derek's husband, asleep on his surfboard, burning under the Mexican sun. (The man I think is) Bo Derek courageously rescues his would-be adversary from his nap. During the rescue, the dorsal fin of a shark appears. The whole interaction with the shark lasts only about five seconds. "What a rip-off!" I whispered to my mother, who nodded in agreement.

As we walked home from the theater, we didn't speak.

"I thought it was pretty good, but not as good as *Jaws* or anything," I finally said.

I also told her that I didn't see what the big deal was about Bo Derek.

"A lot of men find her sexy," she replied.

Right. *Her.*

My mother and I never discussed the film again and the experience drifted to the same faraway region of my mind that stored the memories of lackluster films like *The Black Hole, Popeye* or *Meatballs 2*. As a matter of fact, nothing really changed after that day. I continued to go to bed whenever I felt like it, watch as much television as I pleased and go to whatever movie I wanted to see.

At camp the next day, I still didn't know what getting your jollies or being good in the sack meant. But I did now know who Bo Derek was, and particularly, that she was a lady. So, when the boys on the bus stuck their heads out the windows and chanted, "We want Bo Derek," I joined in.

Gershon

By Rebecca Addelman

I TURNED 20 ON A NEAR-BANKRUPT KIBBUTZ just south of Tel Aviv. During that summer, I discovered my Jewish roots, I discovered myself and I discovered my sexuality—and I did it all naked with a 55-year-old man named Gershon.

It was the summer of 2000, just before the Second Intifada disrupted the Middle East. It was my first time in Israel, and I was there volunteering on Kibbutz Palmachim, where I knew no one except my cousin Sherry, who'd been shipped off to Israel when she was 17 after getting busted with drugs, and her six fully Hebraic kibbutznik kids whose idea of a good time was to take their action figures and stick them in electrical sockets. We didn't have a lot in common.

But then I met another volunteer, Erin, a nice Jewish girl from the suburbs of Buffalo who'd morphed into a dirty, earthy hippie while studying in New Orleans. Erin had ass-length, fire-red hair, and for her, shoes and bras weren't just optional, they were frowned upon. She was the kind of girl who would happily strip off her clothes to demonstrate yoga moves, "so that you can see the proper alignment." I was the complete opposite. I was still a virgin and pretty prudish when it came to any kind of nudity. I'd been naked with men before, but it had always ended badly, generally in tears or dry hand jobs.

After a week of hanging out with Erin—which included a lot of time averting my eyes as her nipples flopped in and out of her muumuu—she told me about Gershon. "My cousin Gershon lives nearby," she said, "and he knows the country really well. Today we're going to the desert. You wanna come?" It sounded fun and safe—this was Erin's cousin, after all. Plus, I still hadn't been to the desert.

When Gershon arrived, he was older than I'd expected, about 55, and leathery and yellowed from years of caffeine, tobacco and invading Lebanon. He also seemed a little creepy, with his gaping smoker's smile and his raspy voice urging me to "come, come." But I couldn't *not* travel with someone just because they were old and a little worse for the wear, right? So we piled into his car and drove off in pursuit of the Holy Land.

On this particular afternoon, Gershon took us to the Tzin Desert. Equipped with his own ATV, we zoomed into the emptiness as the sun was just starting to dip. It was my first time encountering this kind of landscape, and I was moved by the beauty and ancientness. I felt sad, lonely and content all at the same time as the wind whipped up and off to nowhere, swallowed by the earth and the sky. It was already one of the best moments of my life before Gershon one-upped himself by leading our little party to the edge of a desert lagoon. He'd found a pool of pristine water in the cracked, hardened earth of the Holy Land. It was perfect—until we reached the water's edge where Gershon and Erin stripped off their clothes—*all* of their clothes—and jumped in.

I was shocked—not so much by the nudity but by the fact that these two were related. Related!? Picture one of your oldest relatives of the opposite sex—would you *ever* get naked with that person *willingly?* No, right? Because I'm pretty sure that's a form of incest. A minor form, but still.

"Join us!" they called as they splashed around. "Rifka, you must come in the water. It's part of the experience," said Gershon, implying—by using my Hebrew name—that if I rejected the skinny dip, I rejected Israel.

So I did join them. In my underwear, bra and T-shirt, I lowered myself in the water. I pretended to have a good time, floating and treading water with my naked companions, but the whole thing was a bit distracting. Gershon's pale, flaccid penis kept catching the moonlight, and Erin's bright-red pubic hair would brush against my leg. I kept my eyes on the desert stars and told myself to just be cool.

Over the next few weeks, Erin and I would work at the kibbutz's concrete factory—Spancrete—until 2 p.m. When we were done, Gershon would be waiting with his car stocked with supplies—coffee, nuts, dried fruit, blankets and flashlights—and we'd drive off into the Israeli countryside in search of adventure.

Gershon zigzagged us across the tiny country, showing us wonderful sights and telling us ancient stories, and I started to fall in love with that part of the world—the food, the deserts, the holy buildings. I was spellbound by Gershon's tales of his military days and his parents' trials in Palestine in the '30s and '40s. But inevitably, by the close of every trip, Gershon would steer us to: (a) a body of water that was in (b) a remote location where there were (c) no witnesses. And inevitably, Gershon and Erin would take off their clothes and jump in.

At first I kept on just my bra and underwear, then just my underwear, and finally, nothing. With my clothes went my reserve. I soon found the whole thing beautiful and strangely fitting. It made sense to me to be naked in Israel. This was the homeland. This was the cradle of life. We're in the aqueducts underneath Jerusalem? Of course we should strip! This is the valley where David fought Goliath? Let's fully appreciate it by getting naked in that stream over there. If it really is "more Israeli" to come to the Dead Sea at night when no one else is around, as Gershon says it is, then let's do it nude!

Some might say that Gershon had cult leader qualities, but at the time I didn't see it. "Gershon isn't bad," I'd tell myself. "He's real. He's in touch with the earth. He's Sabra." It helped that things never got sexual. While I wasn't well-versed in the world of erect penises, I'm 85 percent positive that Gershon's was never hard. It never touched me at least.

As the summer came to a close and Erin and I had only a few days left on the kibbutz, Gershon planned something special. He picked us up at the usual time and drove us into empty farmland. We got out of the car and had started bushwhacking through a watermelon patch when Gershon stopped and pushed aside an unmarked boulder. Underneath was the mouth of a tunnel. "Get in," he said. On our bellies, wearing miner's headlamps, we shimmied single file into the earth. He told us this tunnel was part of a network built by the Jews when they hid from the Romans. It sounded plausible, and besides, at this point in the summer, Gershon knew best—whatever he was selling, I was buying. Soon, the tunnel opened up into a huge, perfectly formed underground cave. "This is it," Gershon said. "We're here."

I looked around—no water anywhere. This was very un-Gershon.

"This cave is where Jewish women in hiding gave each other mikvahs," he said. "I thought you two could give each other mikvahs too." I looked around again for a sign of water. How on earth could we give each other baths if there was no water? But Gershon wasn't done. "I want you to do it with this," he said, and pulled a giant bottle of olive oil out of his backpack.

How lucky that on the day we went deep underground, into the dry earth, Gershon had thought to pack a four-gallon jug of oil. In a flash, Erin and I were wearing nothing but our miner's headlamps, and she was drizzling oil over my shoulders and neck. "Don't forget her back," Gershon coached from the corner, also naked even though he wasn't getting a bath. "Get her chest too," he encouraged as he reached into his bag again, this time pulling out a camera. "Good, good. That's great. Just like that. Perfect." And, "just like that," the whole thing turned into a hot, holy photo shoot.

Several hours and two greasy mikvahs later, we felt cleansed, happy and oh-so-very Jewish. We drove back to the kibbutz, proud of ourselves, and a few days later Erin and I got on planes destined for Buffalo and Toronto. We promised to keep in touch but we never spoke again. I've never told anyone about my summer with Gershon. For a long time, I thought I was keeping it a secret because these memories were so treasured and personal. I now realize that I didn't tell anyone out of shame.

But I'm no longer in denial. I know now that what I thought was a beautiful, earthy summer where I discovered my Jewishness and accepted my naked body in the Holy Land was actually nothing but a kinky joyride for a middle-aged man. It wasn't life-altering, it was just plain weird. And I have the pictures to prove it.

The Mossad Bought Me Nachos and a Sprite

By Joey Garfield

AS A YOUNG KID GROWING UP in Chicago, I spent my summers at Habonim Camp Tavor. The camp was affiliated with an Israeli socialist kind of Zionist movement called Habonim or Habonim Dror, and its philosophy was based on the ideals of Israel's early kibbutznik pioneers. Everyone at camp was required to do manual labor, and the summers were joyfully spent working and educating one another about Israeli culture and ideology. I loved this camp so much that I was a chanich (camper) for many years and transitioned over to be a madrich (counselor) for many years after that. I participated in every level of the movement well into my 20s, spending a year in Israel on a kibbutz with an affiliated program. Habonim Camp Tavor was the best camp experience ever.

And then I went to film school in Chicago and wasn't even thinking about Habonim or Israel or anything Jewish when I received a phone call from this Israeli gentleman whose hummus-thick accent was filled with long, drawn-out "eh"s.

"Hello . . . ehhhh may I ehhhhh speak with ehhh Joey Garfield?"

"Speaking," I say.

"Yes, Joey, did you ehhhh participate with ehhhhhhh Habonim Camp Tavor from the years ehhhh 1980 to 1989?"

"Yeah. Who is this?"

"My name is ehhh Shlomo and I received your name from your Sheliach [an Israeli Emissary affiliated with the camp]. I would like to meet with you to speak about a very important matter concerning the safety of Israel. Is there a time on ehhhhhh Friday that I could ehhh meet with you and we can talk?"

And then I start to think that this must be a secret new level to my Jewish youth movement. You start off your mission as a camper, then you become a counselor, then you go on kibbutz and then there is this . . . call to duty. How exciting!

I answer Shlomo with an honorable, "Yes, I will meet you."

"Good. Where should we ehh meet?"

"How about the Sears Tower." He agrees and then asks what I'll be wearing in order for him to identify me in a crowd. I tell him I will be wearing a blue jean jacket and a red Chicago Bulls baseball cap. Then I flip it on him and ask him what he will be wearing so I can pick him out in a crowd.

"That is not important right now, Joey. See you Friday at ehhhhhh noon. Yallah, bye."

I have five days until Friday and I realize that perhaps I made a mistake. "Was this for real?" I ask myself. "Am I the stupidest guy ever? Maybe Shlomo is actually a counterterrorist whose mission it is to take out all the hippie socialist Jews one Birkenstock at a time!"

Friday arrives and in an effort to be all James Bond on Shlomo I arrive at the Sears Tower half an hour early to find him before he can find me. I stand by the food court watching everyone pass by, and you know what? When you are paranoid that this could be your last day on earth, everyone looks like a Mossad agent. The man in the suit reading the paper on my left, the guy cleaning the floor, the lady buying the Sears Tower snow globe, everyone is suspicious. Just as I am beginning to think about quitting this secret socialist Jewish stealth elite squad and returning to civilian life, up walks this burly, short, stocky guy wearing a Russian cap, a long coat and glasses, and carrying a briefcase, which is subtly handcuffed to his wrist.

"Ehhhhhh are you Joey?" he asks

"Are you Shlomo?" I counter.

"Yes," he answers. "I am glad to see you. Is there a place we can sit down and talk?"

I gesture to the very open food court table that I had previously scouted out. We sit down and he looks at the menu.

"Would you like to eat something, Joey?"

I tell him I'm fine, but he insists. I refuse again and he insists again. I refuse again and he leans back and with a hushed kind of fatherly sternness he says, "Joey, when the Israeli secret service asks you to eat something you should eat something!" I order nachos and a Sprite.

"Now Joey, ehhhhhh you may be wondering why I ehhhh asked to meet with you. I am the head of airline security for all flights coming in and out of Israel for El Al. I am ehhhhhh conducting a 'Nis-a-yon' test of all security agents internationally. This is a matter of extreme importance. I need you to help Israel by sneaking a suspicious package through security and onto a flight."

Honestly, all I could think to say at that moment was "Cool."

"Now ehhhhhh the reason you were chosen was because Garfield is not a very Jewish-sounding name, and as we sit here, you don't even look very Jewish. Are you willing to participate?"

I agree to do it and he proceeds to get very excited about this next part.

"OK, this is what you need to do. Go home and make a suspicious package . . . put some Arabic writing on it. I will get you a ticket on a flight from O'Hare to Israel. When you get to the airport, you will need to have a believable story of why you are going to Israel in case security asks you. That way you will have something to say and not 'I am here to try and sneak a suspicious package onto the plane' or something like this. Joey, what do you study in school?"

"Film."

"Ahhh good. OK. You will be a photographer . . . and you are visiting your girlfriend who lives in Israel and her name is . . ." He looks at me for the answer.

"Anna?"

"Anna," he repeats satisfactorily. "She is beautiful and you are in love with her and she lives in . . . Tel Aviv or Jerusalem, pick one it doesn't matter."

"OK," I say

"OK," he says. "Which one?"

"Oh, now? Ummm . . . Tel Aviv."

"You are bringing this suspicious package to your girlfriend, Anna, in Tel Aviv. I will make you a ticket for next Friday evening leaving from O'Hare International Airport to Israel through El Al. Meet me at my hotel across from the airport and we will go over the details. Work on the story, Joey."

I go home. All week I repeat the story in my head: "I am going to Israel to visit my girlfriend, Anna, we are in love. I am a photographer and I am going to take beautiful pictures of my beautiful girlfriend, Anna, in Tel Aviv." For some reason, even though I already got the job, so to speak, I really want to impress Shlomo. So I buy an Arabic newspaper and use that to wrap my suspicious package. Perfect.

Friday comes and I've managed to tell no one about my mission to improve the security of Israel. I pack my duffel bag as if I am really going to fly to Israel, because I am confident that my abilities will be so good, so smooth, that I am going to get on that plane without even a blink from security.

I knock on the door of Shlomo's hotel room and he answers.

"Joey, I am so glad to see you! Let's look at your bag."

I proudly unzip my duffel on the bed. Shlomo looks at the package and then at me. "This is it?" he asks. "Joey, it's too suspicious. It is very obviously a suspicious package. Here take this one. I made one for you." I take a look at the difference between his package and mine and he has a good point. His package was a lot less suspicious-looking than my suspicious-looking package. So I take his.

"OK, Joey do you have your passport?"

Check.

"Your story?"

Check.

"Tov. Here is your ticket. I am leaving for El Al now and you should come in ten, fifteen minutes, OK? Yallah, bye."

Honestly, you would think that sitting in that hotel room having a moment alone to myself I would have come to the conclusion that I may possibly be the dumbest guy in the world doing the stupidest thing ever. But I don't think that. I am so into this idea of sneaking through security and impressing the Israeli secret service that I spend those 15 minutes singing the theme song to *S.W.A.T.* and not once questioning what Shlomo may have put in his suspicious package.

I walk to the airport and hand the woman at the counter my ticket and passport.

"Have you packed your bag yourself?"

"Yep."

"While at the airport, has anyone given you anything to blah blah blah?"

"Nope."

Off I go. I put my bag through the security machine and walk out clean. "Anna, I am coming for you!" As I turn down the hallway I can see way up ahead another security checkpoint. This one is improvised with long folding tables. It's right at my gate with a bunch of tough-looking Israeli soldiers going through everyone's stuff. "Oh, no," I say to myself as a sweat ring forms from my armpit to my ankles. You know that scene in *Midnight Express* where the guy duct-tapes all that hashish to his body and tries to sneak through Turkish customs and all you hear is his heartbeat? That's the sound track to this part of the story.

As I reach the table in slow motion, I am asked for my passport and ticket. "Why are you traveling to Israel?" asks this one superhot Israeli soldier security woman. Instantly, I lose my cool and my story.

"Ah na . . . my girlfriend is a Anna, she is a girl and ummmm I am Anna and Anna . . . and Tel Aviv." While I continue to make words come out of my mouth, I realize that some other Israeli security guy has taken my bag and is opening it. A feeling comes over me that in a matter of seconds someone is going to snap my neck and I'm kind of hoping that if it's this hot Israeli woman it may not be so bad. "Where is Shlomo!?" my mind says to my gut. "You've been set up," my gut says to my mind. The hot Israeli security woman gives me my passport and ticket back, and I take this moment to nonchalantly distance myself from my duffel bag.

"Sir, your bag! Sir, your bag!" the guard kind of panic-shouts in my direction.

"Oh, of course . . . my bag. How silly of me . . . my bag . . ."

And as I reach for my duffel I can see Shlomo walk out from behind a rubber tree plant area. "Stop . . . stop ze test . . . nisayon, nisayon," he says and pats my back. He quickly takes the security guards to the side and has a little conversation huddle with them. I stand there thinking to myself, "Technically I've made it through with a suspicious package and they are probably talking about how to rearrange the tables to make a ceremony for me. Perhaps some champagne in plastic cups. A cookie assortment would be nice. Will I have to make a speech? It will have to be in English. . . ."

The conversation breaks up and the Israelis go back to the line of people not yet checked. Shlomo comes up to me and shakes my hand.

"Joey, I want to thank you for participating in this important security test and want you to know that the State of Israel is a safer place because of you." I am a little teary-eyed at this moment, but I gain enough composure to accept his thanks and ask if it's possible to get an actual ticket to Israel.

"Right now," he says, "I have to get on this flight. We are conducting tests all over the world so I will have to call to talk about this later next week. Yallah, bye."

This happened in 1990. I'm still waiting for that ticket.

Exodus

By Elliott Kalan

SUMMER CAMP AND I HAD ALWAYS had a checkered history. For everything that camp offered that I enjoyed (nature, running around yelling for no discernible reason), it also provided me something I loathed (competition, situations where I might be nude in public). And no matter which summer camp I attended, none of them ever addressed my greatest interest as a boy: sitting quietly and reading. One time, an aspiring bully caught me eyes-deep in *Don Quixote*, one of the few classics of world literature that gets most of its laughs from scenes of uncontrollable vomiting and pooping.

"If you like reading so much," he said to me, "why didn't your parents send you to book camp?"

If only they could have, I thought.

This was typical of most of my interactions with fellow campers, and as a result, I was always looking for a way to get out of camp and back to my home, where I controlled what I did and when I could eat.

I had attempted early exits from numerous summer camps before—so many in fact that my name had become legend in the tristate area. I can't help but think that an alert had been posted to all New Jersey residents living within a 10-mile radius of any summer camp, which is what tripped me up on my final attempt. Of course, like any high-profile alleged criminal, I'd already been convicted in the court of public opinion (i.e., camp directors and my parents) before I could tell my side of the story. The fact is that every incident was a direct reaction to some sort of physical or emotional duress brought on by that great scourge of humanity, bullying.

I was a popular target for bullies from birth roughly until my sophomore year of college. Bullies were attracted to me like hormonally confused metal filings to an extremely bookish magnet. Let's assume, however, that your average bully is merely a misguided Samaritan. I assume what happened in a bully's mind was that, upon noticing me not interacting with another person at the moment but instead reading a book, he assumed I was lonely and decided to ease me from my isolation in the most abusive way possible. Either that, or he thought books were basically poisonous and that he was saving my life.

This is assuming the best about bullies. In the case of the last time I went to summer camp, however, no assumptions should be made. The bully that year, whose name has escaped me the way I always wanted to escape from summer camp—without a trace—decided that for whatever reason he didn't like me. This may have simply been his nature. I don't like to judge a book by its cover, but in this case the cover was a pretty accurate summary of its contents. He was a pale, bald, sharp-nosed, sharp-eared devil of a 16-year-old with a look that screamed "I'm an asshole." He was the spitting image of the vampire Nosferatu, if Nosferatu wore a lot of NBA jerseys and gold chains, and had impaired learning comprehension.

Nosferatu had one main hobby at camp that he indulged often: pushing me off things. Chairs, stairs, benches, tree branches, logs, bunk beds—if it could support the weight of my body, then he enjoyed pushing me off it. This was apparently hilarious to him, especially if he could attack me verbally at the same time, perhaps with some extra back-up from his strange posse of skanky-yet-somehow-mannish teen girls. I have to assume these were his underage vampire brides, because they followed him everywhere but didn't actually seem to like him all that much.

This particular exodus was sparked by an incident during the after-lunch rest period which some 1920s camp jokester had waggishly dubbed *siesta*, completely unaware that decades later the United States would undergo an influx of Spanish-speaking immigrants who wouldn't find calling a rest period *siesta* all that humorous. I had decided to read a book (most likely something *Star Wars*–related) by the side of the camp's picturesque lake, which for some unknown reason didn't meet with Nosferatu's approval.

With the air of confidence that only someone who's already broken more rules than you ever will, he marched up to me and announced that I wasn't allowed to be there, and had to leave. The permission given to me by my cabin counselor was effectively and officially overruled by this self-appointed one-asshole police force. When I explained patiently that I wasn't leaving and he couldn't make me, he replied by pushing me off the bench I was sitting on. Looking back, I should have seen that part coming.

Temporarily retreating before he could somehow discover a way to push me off the earth itself and into deep space, I located the nearest actual camp counselor, a pretty girl whose posture told me she was a mature and hardened veteran of the world. I explained to her what had happened, assuming my assailant would be punished, or at the very least I'd be assured it was OK for me to go back to where I had been sitting. Possibly realizing that approach was absurdly rational, however, she instead told me not to be a tattletale and turned away.

Now, at my wizened age, I realize that the counselor, being an 18-year-old girl, probably had more important things on her mind, like finding a bar with a blind bouncer so that she could use the really badly made fake ID she'd paid her older brother's best friend altogether too much for. But seriously? I was at fault for being a tattletale? I'd expect that kind of childish devotion to playground law from a gym teacher, but from a camp counselor?!

I'm minorly irritated by it now, but at the time my faith in any kind of moral authority in the universe was irreversibly shattered. The Hebrews had prayed to a higher power and been delivered from bondage. My pleas, however, had been rebuffed. Unlike lazy Moses, who had a magic stick and the voice of God to guide him, I was going to have to take matters into my own hands.

Of course there was only one way I knew how to do this: by running away. My skills had, over time, been honed for this kind of last-minute escape. Although none of my attempts were the end result of meticulous planning—more of a spur-of-the-moment response to an instance of bullying or unhappiness—I was always on the lookout for possible means of escape, or weak links in a summer camp's security. The knowledge I had accumulated throughout my abbreviated stay would be used in that instance, but not in a systematic way. I merely felt the need to run and ran with it, without supplies or money.

It helped that this particular camp was almost perfectly engineered for running away, having as its entrance a wide-open road that wound past small plots of farmland before ending directly in the middle of the nearest town. It was like the camp was daring me to escape, begging me even. Frankly, it's a wonder I'd stayed as long as I did.

As you can probably guess, things fell apart almost instantly. I'd barely made it a quarter of a mile before a pickup truck piloted by an incredibly large woman—I assume the spinster daughter of an ornery farmer who named her Bessie after his childhood cow—slowed down next to me. Having seen *Pee-Wee's Big Adventure* many times, I began wondering what kind of strange and ridiculous escapades I was about to embark on, until she asked me whether I belonged at the nearby camp. I told her I wasn't allowed to talk to strangers, which, since I was 14 at the time, was a pretty lame excuse. Giving me a look halfway between "I don't believe you" and "you're retarded," she drove off in the direction I'd started from, returning a few minutes later with the camp director.

Apparently this paragon of rural New Jersey samaritanism felt she'd done her civic duty, and left the two of us to return to camp on foot. The camp director wasn't happy. A more accurate way to put it was that he was furious. For weeks I'd been a thorn in his side: reading books, not going to instructional swim, complaining about being pushed off chairs. Now I'd really crossed the line, and what I did next would decide how extreme my punishment would be.

The trip back was silent and awkward. Except for the walk to the security check at Heathrow Airport on the last day of a trip to England that ended with my girlfriend breaking up with me, it is the most awkward walk I've ever been on. I actually have a very clear memory of the director whipping me in the back with a switch as we walked, though the rational side of my brain tells me that probably didn't happen.

When we got to the camp, I was taken to the reception desk in the administration building, where my parents were called. For the next 15 minutes or so I listened to them tell me how disappointed they were while staring at novelty office signs reading "You want it when?!" and "I can only help solve one person's problems a day. Today is not your day. Tomorrow isn't looking good, either." I assume that's also the sign on God's desk. Finally I couldn't take it anymore and threw the phone at the floor in anger and frustration.

"That is IT, Mister! You are out of here!" shouted the camp director as I stumbled toward the exit. I realized that I was crying, big horrible tears that filled up my whole field of vision, making it hard for me to see where I was going. I put out my hands to push open the front door and somehow managed to push straight through its plate-glass panes. I guess I didn't know my own strength when I was crying and ashamed. My right hand was cut deeply halfway between my thumb and pointer finger, blood dripping down my arm and onto the dirt outside the building. My hand is still scarred from the event, although now, a decade later, it looks more like a poorly placed wrinkle.

I managed to stumble to the conveniently closely located nurse's office, leaving a trail of blood behind me. I don't know what people who came upon it later must have thought, although I assume they imagined something far more exciting had happened. The camp nurse bandaged my hand and showed me to a bed, where I instantly fell asleep. She was the nicest person I dealt with that day.

When I woke up, my parents were there, and my things already packed. They seemed to have run out of anger on the drive up, and the ride back was, understandably, completely silent. It was my last summer in camp. It was also the last time I encountered Nosferatu. A few weeks after the events of this story, he was kicked out of camp for failing a drug test. I have to assume he's working a low-paying janitorial job right now, or running a very successful hedge fund. Let's compromise and say he's a mercenary in the Sudan.

Anyway, I consider this one my most successful escape. Some might argue with this, since it was a complete failure: I got caught, angered my parents, scarred my hand and had to eat at Ruby Tuesday's on the way home (I hate Ruby Tuesday's). Still, they say any landing you can walk away from is a good landing, and exoduses are the same way. Sure, the Hebrews had to wander through the desert for 40 years, but they never had to go back to slavery in Egypt.

Helping Hand

By Todd Levin

ONE ESPECIALLY WARM AFTERNOON on summer break from college, I found myself sitting on the steps of a Conservative Jewish synagogue, eating ice cream. It seemed natural to experience a vague sense of guilt about this. For all my ignorance of Old Testament laws, enjoying a snack in front of a temple could reasonably be considered some kind of decadent affront to God—but since it was very hot and the ice cream was delicious, I just stored this incident in my mental "to atone for" list, and continued licking.

A few peaceful minutes passed, then suddenly the synagogue doors burst open and the rabbi came running outside, heading right toward me, shouting my name. Thinking fast, I tossed my ice cream cone to the ground and screamed, "Unholy temptation, be gone!"

I knew Rabbi Sussman, because this was my girlfriend's synagogue. The rabbi and I never got along, perhaps because I am a Reform Jew and he is Conservative, and Conservative Jews often regard Reform Jews the same way waiters regard diners who wish to pay for their meal with coupons.

Rabbi Sussman was not dressed in what I would describe as traditional Conservative Jewish attire, i.e., flowing robes, sandals, decorative dreidel pouch cinched around his waist and a cumbersome stone tablet cradled in each arm. Instead, he wore green surgical scrubs and latex gloves. "Wonderful," I thought—"he's lost his mind." Alternately, this might have been a Purim costume, although it was August and Purim was back in March. Or October. Really, I had no idea. So as Rabbi Sussman approached I made a fist, just in case I was wrong about Purim and right about crazy.

"Todd. Great to see you."

His warmth was suspicious, and I balled my hand up tighter, remembering not to tuck the thumb inside the fist because that could cause you to fracture your thumb while you're punching the face of a rabbi. Then Rabbi Sussman turned all business: "I wonder if I can borrow you for a minute."

Even if he was insane, it's very difficult to say no to a rabbi. And it's even more difficult to say no to a rabbi dressed as a doctor. So many layers of authority working in harmony.

So I stood up like an adult, dusted the rainbow sprinkles from my shorts and went to him. Rabbi Sussman threw an arm around me and I tensed up, wishing I still had that fist ready to go.

"Listen, Todd. I could use a little help. My son, Akiva, usually gives me a hand but he's at a Little League game today. So, what do you think? Can you give me a hand with a circumcision?"

Absolutely not. "I will surely fail at this," I thought. But then my brain shifted into more Old Testament thinking. "What if I'm being tested by God right now, like when God asked Abraham to sacrifice his only son, What's-his-face? Maybe, if I say yes to this, when I enter the temple there will be no circumcision at all. And instead I'll just be presented with a golden chalice or World's Greatest Jew coffee mug or something. Also, let's not forget how very scared I am of Rabbi Sussman." My decision was made.

"Show me the penis," I demanded.

As we made our way into the synagogue, Rabbi Sussman pitched me the backstory. Apparently, his moyel skills were legendary in the tri-county area and, as such, he was occasionally retained to provide this service to non-Jewish families. Sussman performed these circumcisions after hours, usually in his office with the shades drawn, like some kind of Mafia surgeon.

When we entered his office, the parents were standing off in a corner looking disoriented and sheepish, while their baby wriggled around on a blanket that was spread out across a cleared section of Rabbi Sussman's desk. If seeing their newborn child nestled amongst haphazard stacks of manila folders and Wite-Out jangled these parents' nerves, at least they could find some solace in knowing their moyel would be assisted by the best in the business—a teenaged boy in cutoff fatigue shorts and a white Hanes undershirt hand-lettered with the words, I'M CRUSHING YOUR HEAD. Where's that baby, y'all? The party doctor is in.

My responsibilities during the procedure were refreshingly nonsurgical. Turns out, the rabbi would be handling the more circumcision-y bits. While he prepped, clamped, sliced and discarded things (i.e., skin), I was required only to hold the baby's legs perfectly still. In other words, I was the hired muscle. When asked if I was up to the task, I probably should have just kept quiet and nodded in the affirmative. Instead, I thought I'd loosen up the room with a joke. "This should be no problem at all," I said. "I've held down plenty of babies." High five, everyone.

It's a well-known fact that babies are kind of weaklings. If you're ever surrounded in a gang fight, they say always attack the babies first to quickly even the odds. However, there are no self-defense manuals that prepare you for the superhuman, Hulk-like lower body strength a baby can summon once someone has attached a pair of forceps to his genitals. The instant its penis was clamped, the baby flipped some kind of internal berzerker switch. His thighs pumped so hard and fast I had to dig my heels into the carpet just to keep from being whipped around the room like a rag doll. Fortunately the sticky residue of ice cream on my hands helped me sustain a solid grip and filled the room with the sweet aroma of pralines.

At some point during my life-and-death struggle with this infant, I made eye contact with the father. His expression was understandably troubled, so I started mouthing the words "I'm sorry" to him, over and over again. This was true, I was sorry—though I resisted sharing my other presiding sentiment, which was, "Your baby is acting like a real dick, pal." And, though I didn't know much about the entire surgical procedure—I have only a faint recollection of my own circumcision—I knew that the genital chokehold was by no means going to be the worst of it. And just as this thought occurred to me, the worst of it came.

When Rabbi Sussman made his incision in the dorsal side of the foreskin, the baby produced a sound that had no place in a sanctuary of worship. In the realm of baby-screams this was unprecedented. In efforts to relate this story to friends, I've tried to find a suitable analogy to describe the specific character of that baby's scream—a cat in a wood chipper? A wounded seagull with a megaphone attached to its beak? But nothing has sufficed. I think that's because this scream sounded *exactly* like a baby who just had his penis chopped off. It was in a category all its own.

The screams came in powerful waves. Each new bloodcurdling wail dovetailed with the receding echoes of the previous one, until we were totally enveloped within a seamless wall of shrieks. Now, as the baby windmilled its legs in my shaky grip, I no longer cared about winning any accolades from God; in fact, I was ready to tender my resignation as a Jew altogether. There had to be less savage religions out there. In that moment, Santeria seemed comparatively civilized.

And at the precise moment the foreskin pandemonium had reached its apex—the mother was shielding her face and the father was screaming, "Put it back! Put it back!!"—the rabbi, with expert stoicism, reached for a small wad of gauze, dipped it in some cheap twist-cap kosher wine, then placed the wine-soaked gauze in the baby's gaping, stretched mouth. In an incalculably small instant later, total silence. Those few drops of sugary hobo cabernet were enough to keep the baby pacified. Shit-faced drunk, and pacified. It was, in the parlance of synagogues, a miracle.

I stood over the baby and marveled over his serene expression. It was as if he had no memory of the horror he'd just suffered. I, on the other hand, would not soon forget our brief time together. Minutes earlier, I had been eating an ice cream cone in the afternoon sun. Now, my T-shirt was soaked through with sweat, my hands were shaking, and I was wondering how I could get my hands on an entire roll of gauze, marinated overnight in Wild Turkey. Perhaps the baby somehow registered my duress because for a micromoment his brow wrinkled slightly, and then relaxed again. It was as if he were apologizing for causing me so much grief. And I thought, even though this was not a Jewish baby, maybe the act of circumcision imparted his first uniquely Jewish quality: guilt. It was positively adorable.

Freaking

By Jordan Carlos

MICHAEL ROTH WAS A YOUNG JEWISH PRINCE. His family owned a line of elite department stores in Texas called Roth-Harris, which for a time even trumped its Dallas rival, Neiman Marcus. In other words, Michael had tasted and seen things I as a kid could only dream about—Europe, skiing, tropical beaches.

Michael was a good kid but he was also a total spaz. In peewee league sports, he was always assigned positions where his spaziness could be reined in. In baseball, he played catcher: He never could catch a pitch but he wasn't afraid to charge. In soccer he was a ruthless fullback, taking the scalps of third- and fourth-grade forwards foolhardy enough to advance the ball beyond midfield.

Michael was also one of the most popular kids in school. He had a cool older brother and sister who lorded over the high school and drove expensive foreign cars. His house was nestled in Preston Hollow, an exclusive neighborhood with well-manicured hedges, which was also home to another classmate, Amy Boone—a direct descendant of Daniel Boone, whose parents owned the neurotics' pleasure garden, the Container Store. T.I. titan Ross Perot lived minutes away.

The Roths' postmodern pile sat across from a creek. You had to drive across a small cement bridge to get to it. I had looked through my parents' book of Frank Lloyd Wright architecture and I was sure that the Roths lived in one of Wright's creations. Mrs. Roth was beautiful. She had delicate, sinewy features, and was going gray gracefully. One of her front teeth had a slight crook, which gave her the most wonderful lisp. OK, she was a MILF.

I know all this because one glorious day Michael invited me to spend the night at his house. Now, whenever I spent the night at a friend's house, it always seemed to be the same horrible nightmare. My friend would become unhinged over some small thing his mother asked him to do, like put his Legos away, and he would lash out at her. I would shrink into the corner and hope for an end to the madness. My mom would have never tolerated such craziness in her house. My parents believed that order was far more important than the hide of one child. And Michael's house was no different. He was a brat, used to getting his way.

After that one evening at the Roths', where we dined on gourmet food and I took a bath so hot it burned my brain, I never spent the night again. Michael and I sort of drifted apart. He was very popular after all and I just wasn't. I see now that many of my sleepover invites had a lot to do with me being the only black kid in the class. I think the mothers were trying to broaden their young son's horizons. I can just see the parents saying to one another, "We can't *not* invite the black kid." So I was hardly surprised when I was invited to Michael's Bar Mitzvah, even though we hadn't really hung out since we were kids.

When I got the invitation, my older brother had been diligently studying men's fashion in the pages of *GQ* magazine, and since I wanted to be like my big brother, I also kept myself abreast of all the sartorial dos and don'ts. Hence, I picked out my outfit for the Bar Mitzvah with great care—a tweed jacket I'd gotten for Easter, with a black Polo tie, hunter green Generra shirt, and of course my Bass boat shoes. I was rocking the Kanye West look, sans irony, at the tender age of 13.

I dressed not only to impress the Roths but also Kate Mulvehill, a cute, Scotts-Irish new kid in school who had rich golden hair, freckles, an upturned nose and a lilting laugh that knocked her lovely chin skyward. I was smitten with her. Thoughts of her took up most of the space in my head. (This was before the days of medicating children, so my deluded longing was raw.) I was determined to have Kate, or at least to make all my longing disappear, and I thought Michael's Bar Mitzvah was the night it was going to happen. She'd smiled and exchanged hellos with me when we walked into the synagogue, and she'd made a face at me during the service to express how boring and long the service had been. I was so in there!

After the ceremony, crudités and drinks were served. Michael's parents approached me and thanked me for coming. Then Mrs. Roth complimented me on my outfit and I blasted through the roof into fashion Valhalla. I'd gotten a compliment from the queen of the Roth-Harris Empire. I could die now.

After cocktail hour, the kids all piled into three chartered party buses and I rode with quiet wonder at the depths of the Roth family's riches. We were driven downtown to the West End Marketplace. Once a mess of abandoned warehouses, the West End had been converted into a shopping center complete with fancy restaurants and a Planet Hollywood. Could it get any cooler? Michael's parents rented out an entire floor of the building. The raw loft space afforded great views of all the Dallas skyscrapers. There were amazing gourmet treats and all the soda and candy we could stuff into our grubby little mouths. It was shaping up to be the best night of my life.

As I saw it, I had cultivated my relationship with Kate since the fifth grade, and now the moment had come to step it up and go steady. I'd waited and waited for the right moment. Unfortunately I'd waited too long. Just as I was about to make my move, my friends informed me that some of Michael's New York cousins were dancing with Kate. I took off like a shot for the dance floor, where I was in for the shock of my young life. Kate and another girl, Amy Moye, were surrounded by Michael's four cousins. And they were freaking.

For anyone who doesn't remember, freaking is a ridiculous dance from the '90s: The man leans back, crotch aimed at his dance partner, knees bent and one hand raised toward the sky. With his female partner straddled between his legs, the man makes a bridge with his other arm, so that he has three points of contact with the floor. In short, freaking looks like the MTV *Grind*'s version of the bridge yoga position.

So the boys were freaking Kate and Amy, who were dancing in total ecstasy. I watched in horror. On top of the ridiculous moves, these boys' fashion was atrocious—genie pants with patent leather shoes and steel toe tips, vests and rayon shirts, with Looney Tunes ties. Stuff like this just wasn't done in Texas . . . at least for another couple of years. I wanted to run over and break up the junior high orgy, to grab these gate-crashing Yankees by their scruff and toss them out of the party, but instead I found a dark corner and remained there until it was time to go home.

The next morning my father drove me and my friend David up to the mountains near Norman, Oklahoma, for what was left of a Boy Scout camping trip. David and I had missed the first night of the trip on account of Michael's party. We drove in total silence. I felt like I'd been hit in the back of the head with a frozen sledgehammer. My father, as always, was playing the Four Tops' "Baby I Need Your Lovin'," in his impractical rear-loading CD player.

I actually listened to the words for the first time that day. When my dad tried to eject the disc after the sixth repeat, I begged him not to. Those lyrics were speaking to me.

One Night at Gimbels

By Rena Zager

AT SUMMER CAMP, I BECAME GOOD FRIENDS with Maggie, a violin player, who lived near me in the suburbs of Philly. We'd do fun stuff together like play flute and violin duets. But soon duets just weren't enough for us. We wanted adventure. So we decided to sleep in Gimbels department store. It was to be a suburban homage to the best book ever written, *From the Mixed-Up Files of Mrs. Basil E. Frankweiler*, about a brother and sister who hide out in the Metropolitan Museum of Art.

A big part of our planning was about all the candy we would eat when we were there (We were very adamant that we wouldn't steal it. We planned on leaving money on the counter.) because neither one of us was allowed candy at home. My candy situation was dire. Before AIDS the terrible disease, there was AYDS the diet supplement, which my sister and I would eat just to get a taste of chocolate. At Maggie's house, it was even worse. Her mother made her own bread and she wanted you to conserve water by not flushing the toilet when you peed, so, you know, candy was a very exciting concept for both of us.

To prepare for the stay, we cased Gimbels like two detectives. We found out where the sprinkler system was, where the fire alarms were and what was on each floor. We discovered the greatest hideout . . . two display beds next to each other with plenty of room underneath. We were all set to go except for the fact that we had no way of getting there—we couldn't drive.

Maggie suggested her mom, a psychiatrist who was raising Maggie by herself, might be willing to take us. That might sound weird, but her mom was that kind of woman—bohemian, intellectual, open to new ideas including aiding and abetting her daughter in a little trespassing. She was everything my mother was not, which is why I adored her. I loved going over to their house. I admired how dusty it was and I especially liked that there was a gray metal filing cabinet in their living room. A filing cabinet in the living room? That was mind-blowing. You couldn't sit in my living room—you could get smacked for even looking at it. So a filing cabinet with dust was very impressive.

Maggie's mom agreed to be an accomplice but there were ground rules: We had to keep a journal of our thoughts and feelings, which she wanted to read afterward. We were like, uh, OK, sure, whatever, "I'm scared. Blah blah blah," just drive us there. Also, we had to be out of the store within five minutes of it opening the next day because she had a doctor's appointment and she told us that if we were not out within five minutes she would leave us there. Then this piece of advice: If you get caught, tell them you're reporters from *Kids World. Kids World* was one of those Saturday afternoon TV shows "for kids, by kids." I hated the prissy kids on *Kids World,* but I thought it was a brilliant idea to say we were from *Kids World* because Maggie's mother was brilliant so how could it not be? If you took half a second to think about it though it made no sense. What would two *Kids World* reporters be doing in Northeast Philly . . . in the middle of the night . . . illegally hanging around a department store?

That night, my dad drove me over to Maggie's house. "What are you guys doing tonight?" he asked.

"I don't know. Playing duets?"

Instead, her mother bought us bagels and drove us to Gimbels, wished us good luck and took off. We found the display beds, crawled underneath them and waited for the store to close. Soon after hearing "Gimbels will be closing in five minutes," the Muzak was shut off, but it made the sound—now antiquated—you'd hear when you'd turn off a record player without removing the needle first. It groaned itself down to silence. Then the lights went off. Then the heat went off . . . and then my head started throbbing. Since we had agreed to wait an hour after the store closed to speak to each other, all I could do was lie there listening to my temples pounding, silently screaming in my head: *What was I thinking? This is the dumbest idea ever! Why is my head throbbing? Is this what a migraine feels like?*

The night was terrifying and boring at the same time. (Orson Welles said that about flying once.) The whole place was dark and the mannequins were casting shadows like crazy and it was vast and empty and spooky. The candy raid was definitely off. We were so scared we couldn't even move. We finally got up the nerve to sit on the floor outside our beds, shivering and talking. The big adventure of the night was when we had to go to the bathroom. It might have been the first time I was in a men's bathroom—the women's was locked—and it was filled with graffitti so we thought it would be OK to write our names on the wall. (We were timid scofflaws.) We spent the night gossiping about who was a bitch, who was cute, regular girl talk—except we had to kill hours and hours and hours and we were too scared to sleep and our food had run out and there was no heat on. We made feeble entries in our journals. I think I wrote, "I'm scared" a couple of times.

Around six in the morning, we saw a security guard walking toward us with a guard dog and we dove underneath our beds. Another close call was when I peeked my head out just before the store opened and there was a cashier counting money about two feet from me, but she didn't see me. At 10:05 a.m., we rolled out from underneath the beds and walked down the escalator while people poured into the store. Maggie's mom was waiting for us in the getaway car and we got in and she sped away.

A week later, my mother was reading the local paper and over her shoulder, I saw the headline *Two Girls Found In Gimbels*. I screamed and tore the paper out of my mother's hands. She had no idea why I was yelling and carrying on but I guess she was used to me screaming for no reason. The story wasn't about us. The same night we did it, two other girls were found hiding out in another Gimbels, but they were normal teenagers—they were there to steal clothes—so they got arrested and charged with trespassing.

At school, I bragged about what I had done. And then all these kids started saying that they had done it too. That really pissed me off. First of all, you're losers for copying me, get your own adventure. Second, I didn't believe them. One day, this girl Marianne came up to me all nonchalantly: "Last Friday night, I spent the night in Wanamaker's." She said it way too coolly for it to be true. I knew the hard, worried look of someone who had spent the night in a department store. She definitely didn't have it.

One Night at Gimbels

The True Meaning of Christmas

By Byron Kerman

I WAS A SOPHOMORE IN COLLEGE and I decided that it would be a good idea to explore a new city during Christmas break. Hanging out with 250 other Jews at a T.G.I. Friday's over the holidays, which is some sort of weird St. Louis tradition, had become tiresome.

At the time, I had three not-anywhere-close-to-being girlfriends: Kira, Sarah and Catherine, who, I realized, were all from Atlanta. So I decided to drive the 14 hours from Chicago to Atlanta to hang out with them over the holidays. Each one had a house with a place for me to sleep. It seemed like a good plan. Unfortunately, I didn't really plan. I just sort of said, well, there are three of you who are each willing to put me up, so let's just play it by ear.

I drove down with Catherine, and it was a challenge to keep the bong loaded and lit for the entire 14 hours, but we did our best. Because we were slackers, we didn't actually leave for the drive until 6 p.m., so we drove all night long.

When we arrived in Atlanta, we drove to a house shared by the members of a rock band. Catherine was their groupie—I mean manager. When we got there, a guy came out on the front porch.

"Are you Byron?"

"Yeah. You're Geoff, right?" I was excited to meet some new friends.

"Yeah. Listen, you need to call your mother and the Georgia State Police."

As usual, my mom had gotten worried and been waking up people throughout the South and along the Eastern Seaboard asking if they'd seen me alive.

Catherine and I had a good time for about two days, hanging out with the rock band, watching them practice, farting around in Atlanta, going to the record stores and bookstores, the Little Five Points area, and so on. And then Catherine sprung something on me. She was a bit of a flake, and she said, "Listen, Byron, I didn't tell you this before, but I gotta leave town with my mom. We're going on a little mother-daughter Christmas vacation of our own."

So, I just said OK and figured it was time to call Kira and Sarah to see who I would be staying with next. Sarah's mom answered her phone, and said, "Well, listen, Sarah is in Poland and Germany on one of those concentration camp trips." Oh joy.

So I called Kira who told me, "Sorry, my mom gave up our guest room to one of my cousins."

I had no place to stay. I had 12 days left of a 14-day trip, I had no place to stay in Atlanta and I had no friends here.

So I went to the rock band and said, "Guys, listen, I know we don't know each other very well, but can I sleep on your couch for the next two weeks or so?" And they said OK. They had their own Christmas obligations to attend to.

Over those two weeks, I did this thing that only slackers can do, and it's kind of an achievement. What you do is you wake up at 10 in the morning, and then you wake up the next day at noon, and you wake up the next day at 2 p.m., and you wake up the next day at 4 p.m., and you can do the whole circle if you're really good. It seemed hopeless, but I just kept on going.

Some days I would tell myself that I had to get up before noon, get a bus schedule, find out where the art museums or something like that were in this town, go there, have a good time and stop moping. But somehow, inertia got the better of me, and I did just about nothing except sleep on that leather couch in the band house for pretty much the entire remainder of the trip.

Ten days went by like that, and pretty soon it was Christmas Eve. I didn't even know what day it was when I woke up. For a lot of us, the whole Christmas thing can float by with just a mild sense of awareness—or resentment. I walked down the street from the house where I was staying, and all of a sudden there was a bar that I had somehow overlooked before.

I went inside, got a drink and sat down to read the newspaper. There were about six other people there. That, I figured out from looking at the date on the newspaper, had to be because it was Christmas Eve.

Then from the corner of my vision a hand slapped the table, my table. And where the hand was, there were now four quarters. I looked up and it was the bartender. "Why don't you pick some songs out on the jukebox?"

Now, as far as I know, I am not a pretty girl, but I just said thanks, and picked out some songs on the jukebox. Then this couple, a guy in a cowboy hat and his blonde girlfriend, came over and asked me what I was drinking.

I was sort of buzzed at this point and I kept thinking: This is the best time I have ever had in a bar! People are buying me songs on the jukebox. People are buying me drinks. It's fantastic.

Most importantly, it was a huge relief. I had just suffered for 12 days with no friends but now people were taking pity on me—because I was alone in a bar on Christmas Eve. I decided not to tell anyone I was Jewish. I was having too much fun. I actually had people to talk to!

I talked, I drank, I had a good time and I went home for the first time in more than a week feeling good that my Atlanta vacation had, for a while at least, become something instead of a big nothing.

I told myself that I had just experienced some of that Christmas spirit— the true meaning of Christmas. Reaching out to the widow, the orphan and the stranger, or in this case, the lonely Jew. That's what it's all about. And it felt good.

But you know what? The next morning, I had a much, much bigger epiphany—one that has stayed with me to this day. Why should there be a season or a week or a day dedicated to actually giving a shit about your fellow man? How about every fucking day?

Yes, Christmas worked for me that year, but why should anyone in real pain put stock in a special time of year when people are guilted into being nice to others? I'm sorry, but I think that's some kind of cosmic joke—even funnier than a man in a Santa suit singing Christmas carols while pissing in an alley. And I finally got it on Christmas Day.

Now, the Jews have some pretty funny holidays. We've got one where we make a shack out of fruits and vegetables and we juggle lemons inside of it. We have another holiday where we leave little drops of red wine on a white plate to commemorate the 10 plagues of ancient Egypt. It's very *Macbeth*. But what we don't have is a holiday where we pretend for even a second that this world runs on kindness. Thank God.

Poop Sandwich

By Abby Sher

THERE WAS THE TIME I GAVE a poop sandwich to my rabbi. It was at the confirmation class picnic in my backyard and I was 16 years old—old enough to know it wasn't funny. But I thought he would understand. I thought we had connected on some level, in some corner of our minds that no one else knew about. I thought we had seen each other's soul.

Rabbi Sirkman came to our synagogue the fall I turned 15. He looked like Scooter from the Muppets and he had a thick Boston accent and a beautiful pregnant wife named Susan. I hadn't been to temple much since my Bat Mitzvah two years before, but my mom brought me one Saturday morning to hear the new rabbi give a sermon. After services she made me shake his hand and introduce myself. Rabbi Sirkman's eyes were a warm chocolate brown and he told me he was so glad to see me there. He was starting a confirmation class for high school students to continue their studies after Bar/Bat Mitzvah and he wanted to know if I would be interested. My mom said that, yes, I would be very interested. Great, he'd see me next Tuesday night for a get-to-know-you pizza dinner.

By Monday, word had spread about the new confirmation class. Sara M. announced in gym class that she was going. Jim C. and Andy said they were too. David K. said it sounded boring and Craig said he wouldn't be caught dead there, but the next time I saw him was Tuesday night in the synagogue cafeteria with a piece of pizza and an Orange Crush. David K. was there too. Everyone was allowed to have two slices of pizza and we were each given a folder with a cartoon man on the cover. The man had huge eyes and a big cowlick. His name was Mr. Foof, explained Rabbi Sirkman, and Mr. Foof was going to help us in our exploration. For the next two years, we were going to read Jewish philosophers and theologists and dissect ancient and contemporary texts, hopefully arriving at our own understanding of what it means to be a Jewish adult. He asked us that first night to define God. I squirmed in my seat. David K. said He was an old man in a blue terry cloth robe with a big *G* on it. Tara D. said she didn't think there was a God. Rabbi Sirkman said they were both right.

Each week we started with pizza and soda, standing sullenly in our proscribed circles. But once we entered the library, the world changed. We analyzed Martin Buber and the concepts of I-Thou and I-It relationships. We read aloud from our books about human passions and the true nature of virtue. Rabbi Sirkman challenged us each to identify our place in the world and to think of our religion not as a finite set of rules but as a course of open dialogue. He asked us questions about the state of Israel and who had a right to the land. We debated the feasibility of Jewish-Arab reconciliation and tried to decipher where the conflict began. He told us there was no excuse for us not reading the newspaper, and one night he refused to speak until we told him why we were at war in Iraq. We weren't being graded. There were no tests. But somehow it became important to us to show up in the temple library every Tuesday night and know what we were saying—to know ourselves in the context of history.

I didn't know how to thank Rabbi Sirkman for taking us out from under the high school overpass and bringing us into some place completely unknown. And I didn't know how to tell him that I wanted to spend every Tuesday night for the rest of my life with him. As our confirmation got closer,

I had more and more trouble looking him in the eye. My teeth felt too big for my mouth when I tried to talk in class and I felt like I was going to cry on the carpool ride home. I didn't tell anyone about my feelings. I didn't know how to explain how much I adored him. How much I yearned for his wide smile, or a wink from behind his wire-rimmed glasses. When my mom suggested we throw a graduation party for the confirmation class, I was thrilled with the idea of having Rabbi Sirkman in my house.

The day of the party, Mom laid out bagels, rolls, coffee cake and fancy cream cheeses. I folded slices of deli meat onto a big plate and refilled the ice trays three times each. There were bowls of pickles, herring and chopped liver. My best friend Yael came over an hour before everyone else and we put on blue eyeliner. I was so nervous I poked myself in the eye. Lisa Grossman was the first guest to arrive. She came with her mom and they were wearing matching stirrup pants. Matt Hirschorn was next. He brought a coffee cake and I told him we already had one, but my mom said that I should be more gracious and she put it out on the table anyway. Then Andy and David K. showed up. Alissa and Sue came together. Pretty soon, the backyard was full. Mr. Moss and Mr. Moock stood by the barbecue and Mrs. Turner buzzed between the kitchen and the porch, bringing people sodas.

And then Rabbi Sirkman arrived. When he came into the backyard I grabbed Yael and told her I needed some air and to come with me for a walk. We sat on the rusty swingset down by the woodpile and dug our sneakers into the soft dirt.

"Ew, watch out," said Yael, pointing to a pile of dog poop.

"My stupid sister was supposed to pick it up but she didn't," I said, rolling my eyes.

"It looks like chopped liver."

"But it probably tastes better."

"Yeah, right?"

"Yael . . ." I thought I was going to break into a thousand little pieces.

There was so much I wanted to say about this year, about what was supposed to happen after graduation, about my hidden love. This is what I did say:

"What if we tried to convince Rabbi Sirkman that it was chopped liver?"

"You mean like put it on a plate?"

"Sure, or even on a roll!"

Yael agreed to go along with my hastily conceived plot. I was in charge of grabbing the bread from the basket. She would get the plate and a plastic knife. We would meet back at the swingset in 10 minutes and try not to draw any attention from the crowd. Keeping discreet was actually very easy to do. Everyone there between the ages of 15 and 16 was trying not to look at each other. We wanted desperately for no one to notice our pimples, our fluorescent belts and layered socks, our gleaming braces with slick rubber bands. Yael stood in front of me while I crouched down and smoothed the poop onto the Kaiser roll. The bread was warm from the afternoon sun. Yael handed me a pickle for garnish.

"Perfect," she declared, as I dug a hole and buried the knife in the ground. Then I put the plate behind my back as we climbed up the rocky path and walked toward the porch.

Rabbi Sirkman was busy telling Mrs. Grossman a story. I watched her honey-colored perm shake while she laughed. I wondered if she had feelings for the rabbi too. Finally, she moved back toward the snack table. Yael pulled me forward.

"Yes, ladies?" Rabbi Sirkman asked, turning in our direction.

"Could we maybe talk to you in private?"

"Sure."

Yael led us both behind the bushes where we kept the sprinkler.

"What's going on, you two?"

"Well, we noticed you weren't eating much so we made you a sandwich," she said as we both giggled. I pushed the plate toward him. The smell was intense.

"Thank you, girls," he said slowly. He took the plate and studied the sandwich carefully, his eyebrows pulled together. Yael grabbed my hand and squeezed.

"Are you sure this is for me?" he asked. He tried to lift part of his face into a smile, but the rest of his mouth wouldn't follow. And then our eyes locked. His were wide and watery. They were not amused. I had to turn away. It felt like someone was pressing on my ribs, squeezing out my insides. This was not going as planned. There was nothing funny in this moment at all.

"Go ahead. It's chopped liver," I heard Yael say, but I was already running, running up the porch, past Mr. Moock in between Andy and Peter G. into the house. "Excuse me!" I yelped at Alissa and Tara as I pushed past them and grabbed for the bathroom door, slamming it behind me and bolting it shut. I dropped to my knees and felt my mouth fill up with saliva. I wanted to throw up, but it was all stuck in my chest, this knot of nausea and aching sadness. It was all wrong. I hadn't meant to hurt him. I needed to explain. I wanted to tell him that we thought it would be funny, or at least charming. Couldn't he see that we were honoring him by giving him this hilarious gift? Couldn't he tell from my eyes that I adored him and I wanted only to make him laugh? And then I became terrified that maybe he *could* see my true intent, maybe he *could* tell I was hopelessly in love with him and that wasn't funny at all.

By the time I came out of the bathroom, my mother was waiting for me.

"Young lady, you have some explaining to do," she commanded. "But first you are going to go out there and apologize." She lifted a single finger toward the back door.

Mrs. Turner was collecting empty plates and cups. A lot of people had gone home. Rabbi Sirkman was in the same corner talking with Mr. Moock. And then he was in front of me, just standing there. It felt like there was so much space between the two of us. I stared at my feet and whispered, "I'm sorry." I knew sorry was too small a word for the weight of this moment. I *was* sorry that I had tried to make him eat a dog poop sandwich, but I was also sorry that I didn't realize it could never be fun or funny to watch a grown man whom you loved and admired with a plate of feces. Most of all, I was sorry that I loved and admired him so much. He had given me a sense of time and space and made me believe that I was somehow different, special, but now it was over. I was confirmed as an adult in the eyes of the congregation. It was time for me to act like one. The SATs were three weeks away. Any day now I'd get my period. There were old wars and new religions cropping up in all corners of the globe, beginnings and endings even in this one moment.

"I know you are," he said, kindly.

As Time Went By

By Michael Green

I'll just come right out and say it: No, I have never seen *Casablanca*.

Which is a shame for anyone, but specific blasphemy for a screenwriter. The paradigmatic depiction of love on film, and I have no idea what it's all about. Some guy in a hat. Some girl with an accent. Someone named Sam who plays things again if you ask nicely.

I thought my excuse was a good one—solidly idealistic—at least as romantic as everyone claims the movie is, anyway: I made a promise to the first woman I ever loved. And I kept it.

She was a much older woman. Or at least what seemed much older at the time. She was 34, my age today.

It was the kind of romance that if you scripted, lit and shot it with any elegance, it would be a sumptuous surprise summer hit—Kate Winslet would be heartbreaking as the lead. Horndog preadolescent boys would leave the theater with wonderful unrealistic expectations of what lay ahead once they started shaving. But if I just gave you the basic plot, it could come off a mite creepy.

She was introduced to me as Mrs. Girard, although I quickly came to call her Karin. She was an SAT tutor recommended by my neighbor, who swore that Karin was the reason her dull daughter got into Penn. There are few more saleable statistics in Jewish suburbia.

We worked in her house full of books—all with well-broken spines—where she lived alone. Karin was midway through a divorce. My first thought on meeting her was that she couldn't possibly live alone for long. Long dark hair, almond-shaped eyes a shocking Kryptonite green. She had a voice like warm maple syrup. When she told you not to worry, you stopped worrying. I stared at her a lot.

Unlike my high school teachers, she made you want to work hard for her—which I did. Which in turn earned me the right to crack a distracting amount of jokes while we were supposed to be working. She shared with me a cat's sense of humor: The torment of others was funny.

Because of all this—and because she was often just inches to my left, huddled with me over vocabulary lists—I fell for her, utterly besotted. And at some point I slipped and said so.

And then she told me, irresponsibly, truthfully—impossibly—that she had feelings for me right back. She was wearing a pale blue sweater, loose at the neck. Her dark hair fell forward. We kissed.

I told no one. I had that much sense.

In the weeks that followed I had few thoughts that didn't include her. She wrote me beautiful letters on the thin blue paper used for overseas mail. We talked on the phone for hours.

And then there were the movies.

Before Karin, my taste in film was pitiful, even for a kid raised in the '80s. I had an Atari-inspired aversion to anything black-and-white, preferring *RoboCop* to *The African Queen*, John Hughes to Howard Hawks.

Karin would not abide. She was, after all, my tutor.

So we developed a routine: I'd tell my parents I was going to Ari Weinberger's house and go to hers instead, stopping on the way to buy candy. She would pick the movies.

We watched, in reverse order, every Best Picture winner from 1950 to

1970, more often than not making it to the end of the movie before we'd attack each other, break a few commandments, then eat the candy.

I was surprised at how watchable the classics were.

"Just wait till we get to Billy Wilder," she teased.

"Who?"

"So funny. So romantic. And—oh—there may never come a better way to tell someone how you feel than Bergman did in *Casablanca*. 'I was lonely, I had nothing, not even hope. And then I met you.' God."

I admitted I'd never seen *Casablanca*.

Karin's eyes went wide as MoonPies. "You simply must. Right away."

"Then I will. I'll rent it tonight and watch it at home."

A rare flash of disapproval from the Kryptonite eyes. "You can't watch *Casablanca* for the first time by yourself. Let me show it to you. Promise you won't ever watch it without me."

It was an easy promise to make. We arranged to watch it together the coming Sunday.

But events, as they do, overtook the first round of plans. And the second.

The SATs came soon after (I did well, thanks to her) followed by summer. I assured her I'd keep my promise until we found the time. I'd wait as long as it took.

At the start of my senior year, Karin moved away—just far enough so that the effort highlighted the inappropriateness of any plans we might make. Convenience accounts for much of sin.

We called less and less often. I began hooking up with a girl my age, something Karin encouraged. I think she was coming to regret the indulgence of caprice.

When I went off to college a year later, it was without a call. I wondered if she'd forgotten I was leaving at all until a package arrived for me at my dorm.

It contained a number of well-chosen books, a dozen windup bath toys, a VHS copy of *Casablanca* and a note: "Winter break then."

When my sophomore year roommate, Josh, an encyclopedia of film trivia, asked to borrow my *Casablanca* tape to watch with the girl he currently needed to be with, he was surprised to find it was still in the plastic.

"You haven't seen it?" Josh looked angry. "Come watch it with me and Ginny. See how it makes her love me."

"Sorry. I can't."

"Why not?"

"I promised someone I'd wait for her."

"People break promises. If you'd seen *Casablanca,* you'd already know that."

They watched it in the common lounge while I stayed in our room and wrote a paper on Romantic poetry. By the time the movie was over, Ginny was nuzzled tight under Josh's arm. They dated the rest of the year.

It's been over a decade now. Karin and I have long since lost touch. Much to my surprise, I am now an actual adult with a mortgage, a career and strange hairs growing out of the tops of my ears I pick at absently while reading.

There is another development. Her name is Amber.

Amber: She's funny and smart and filthy and pretty and her goddamn hair sheds everywhere. Sometimes in the kitchen she'll pirouette badly, and some mornings she'll wake me up so I can help pick out her underwear for the day. I love her the way I always wanted to love somebody.

In fact the only time I ever felt anything other than comfort with her was the day she told me her favorite movie is *Casablanca.*

She asked me what I thought of it. I didn't lie. I told her about Karin.

Surprisingly, she completely understood. All she asked was: "Do you want to see it?"

Would I wait forever? I'd never thought of it that way. The truth is, I'd become sort of proud of not having seen *Casablanca*. The blank spot in my edification was a mark of pride, an original sacrifice on the altar of idealized love. As long as I avoided it I could prove my reverence.

On the other hand, I'd been accused of being emotionally withholding by more than one girlfriend, and here was an experience that I was quite literally withholding, reserving for someone all but imaginary by now. I'd squint at a girl asleep in my bed and think, "Sure, she likes to read, and hates shuls that use bongos . . . but is she someone I'd watch *Casablanca* with?"

The idea of finally seeing the damn thing had gotten so built up—sort of the way sex was built up back when I was 17 and lusting after my tutor. It was something I'd romanticized so long it could only come as a disappointment. Then again, isn't a promise made with such a racing heart all the more sacred?

It was the miserable sort of irony Karin would have insisted didn't meet the strict definition: In order to watch the most romantic movie of all time I would have to negate the most romantic moment of my life.

I actually considered finding Karin so I could watch it with her. I could tell Amber I was up all night working a deadline—or better, I went to Ari Weinberger's house.

But I didn't. There's a reason I hadn't called Karin in 12 years. I was over her. It was time to allow for new most-romantic moments in my life.

I went to the store, picked out the two-disc collector's set, declined to renew my Barnes and Noble membership (it seemed wrong to save 10 percent on a rite of passage), made a heap of popcorn, cut up the cheddar cheese I know Amber likes with it . . . and asked her if she would watch *Casablanca* with me.

She slid onto the couch without a word.

She was wearing a blue zippy, stolen from my closet, over a pink T-shirt with a picture of a churro on it.

The movie came on.

For a moment I worried: "What if it sucks?"

"It doesn't."

"That's what everyone said about *Star Wars Episode I* and it sucked like crazy and I waited years for that."

My concern lifted with the opening mockumentary, which explained the circumstances of those struggling to flee the Third Reich, by way of Lisbon, by way of Casablanca.

And it didn't suck. The movie is an impeccable piece of filmmaking, living up to any expectation. The story unfolds like silk. The scenes slide along like stockings over a hardwood floor. Bergman steps into Rick's Café Américain and is as breathtaking as everyone would have you believe. Sam knew it the moment she walked in; trouble follows a face that perfect.

"She's gorgeous," I whispered.

"She broke more hearts than butter," Amber said.

We got to the scene where Rick sits in the dark drinking angrily and making Sam play "As Time Goes By," the song he couldn't bear to hear because it reminded him of his lost Ilsa, and it occurred to me, with some shame, that I'd been avoiding *Casablanca* the same way.

Suddenly uncomfortable, I shifted, and Amber eased under my arm in what I realized had become a familiar routine, an act so much more intimate and nourishing than the sex Renault tried to extort out of that desperate Bulgarian hottie. I am in a relationship with an unspoken choreography.

I saw why the film has been allowed to define love for so long. Love in *Casablanca* is the kind of thing that destroys a man before it awakens his conscience. To be open to it is to be open to mistakes and bullets, and nobody ends up happy. It left Rick a shell of a club owner, well-dressed and popular, but unable to taste the fine brandies in his cellar. And then it made him a hero again, willing to suffer a concentration camp to let the woman he loves live on—with another man.

Yes, Rick makes that ultimate cinematic sacrifice. He lets the girl go. He walks off into the misty night with Renault, fugitives, finally righteous. We don't worry he'll die fighting with the French resistance; we know God protects nobility, even in such a heavy smoker.

I wondered what love would make of me.

The movie ends. A beautiful friendship begins. And my promise was broken.

Amber leaned over, kissed me. "Thanks for letting her go."

She might have been talking to Rick.

FAMILY

And Baby Makes . . . Four

By Caryn Aviv

I WAS 32 AND THINKING ABOUT HAVING A BABY when Michael gingerly popped the question. "Would you be interested in having a kid with me and Adam?" I thought the earth was moving underneath my car (an emotional earthquake of sorts) as we drove down Divisadero Street in San Francisco.

Michael and I had met a few years earlier at the gay and lesbian synagogue. I had recently arrived in town to start a new chapter in life after finishing research for a Ph.D. Newly out of the closet and eager to connect with the gay Jewish community, I signed up as a part-time Hebrew-school teacher. Michael had returned from his graduate school research in Moscow, with his husband, Adam, to resume his post as head of the synagogue's school. We hit it off immediately.

But co-parenting was a life-altering decision. So like any nice Jewish girl from Chicago, I made a PowerPoint presentation analyzing all the pros and cons of our various family options under discussion. Then before I could even decide, Michael and Adam moved to Denver—making the whole issue more complicated. Did I want to be a single lesbian mom in San Francisco? Did I want to act as a surrogate for Michael and Adam to have and raise a baby in Denver? The idea of being a womb factory seemed even more unappealing. If

I moved, would I ever find a suitable girlfriend in Denver (and would it finally close that revolving door of recovering alcoholics and emotionally needy cat lovers I had been dating in San Francisco?). Could I live in a state without a Trader Joe's?

I spent a year exploring a move to Denver. It was a gamble to leave behind a well-paying job, my beloved city and a seemingly endless supply of inappropriate lesbian dating choices. I reasoned that we would either figure it out or not, and if the whole plan didn't work, I could always move back to California and learn to love cats.

As research, I interviewed lesbian moms and gay dads who were doing this already. "Just make sure you have all your agreements in writing in case people split up!" advised one solemn lesbian mom who was battling her ex-wife in court. "Try to find a duplex to make daily logistics easier," said a happy gay dad who lived with his partner next to his lesbian co-parent and kid in the Castro.

A year later, I moved to Denver and rented an attic owned by two notorious gay leather daddies who applauded my moxie and family plans. Michael, Adam and I began to spend a lot of time together, essentially weaving ourselves into a family even without the presence of a kid. After six months of intense conversation, we decided to seal the deal.

We had worked through all the usual things that straight couples negotiate (except the sex), like values, money and which families we'd visit for Rosh Hashana and Passover. We also considered our legal options, given that Colorado law wouldn't know how to handle a family with three parents. I think we all felt giddy about the prospect of trying to get pregnant, and our plan was to start inseminating at the beginning of the school year. All our parents began buying baby clothes as soon as they heard the news. Life was ripe with possibility.

Then things got messy. I met and started dating Jared, a formerly Catholic female-to-male transgender person. Jared was a single parent of an 11-year-old son who he had given birth to before his gender transition. My parents and sister wondered out loud whether I was still a lesbian if I was now dating someone who, although born female, now basically passed as a straight guy.

As if life weren't already complicated enough, I decided to buy the town house next to Jared's only four months into our relationship. I began spending lots of time with Jared's son, assuming the role of stepparent. But I was much more hesitant about Jared becoming intimately involved with my own co-parenting plans, because I knew that would require a whole other level of negotiations. Initially Jared said he was fine with a minimal level of involvement if/when Michael and Adam and I had a kid. He didn't want the added financial burden of another child.

But six months into our relationship, Jared changed his mind—he wanted to become a full and equal co-parent with me, Michael and Adam, *and* for me to become more of a co-parent to his son. Michael and Adam were completely opposed to the idea so I proposed a series of Sunday brunches to explore our options. At our first brunch, Jared suggested that Michael and Adam sell their house so that we could all buy a duplex in a suburban development on the edge of town. Awkward and astonished silence ensued. Adam could barely speak for the rest of the meal.

For the next few months, I shuttled back and forth between the town houses and the boys' house, in fruitless negotiations that rivaled Middle East diplomacy. I realized that I was in two separate and mutually exclusive relationships—one with my lover and his son, and the other with my gay boyfriends. I tried valiantly to please everyone, which of course pleased no one, least of all me. My relationship with Jared began to plummet, and not surprisingly, my relationship with the gay dads suffered as well. In fact, they were almost ready to walk away from our whole agreement that we had worked so hard for years to create.

After several months of conflict, I realized I had two options. I could forgo having a kid with my gay dads and remain with Jared. Or I could end my relationship with Jared and get back on track with the primary reason I had moved to Denver: to become the lesbian co-parenting mom I had wanted to be. After much agonizing, many crying sessions and some useful therapy, I chose the latter option. When I really listened to that small voice inside, buried underneath lots of fear, it became obvious that what I wanted most of all was to become a mom with Michael and Adam, not a stepmom in Jared's already formed family. It was a decision that engendered intense sadness, some lingering regrets, but also a quiet clarity. So once again I became single, and now this time with a town house to sell.

Eight weeks after that horrific and messy breakup, I got pregnant. Who knew it would have been so easy and so quick? (If only it had taken that little time to sell the damn town house!) I wouldn't have chosen to experience the insomnia and hormonal lunacy of pregnancy as a single person, but in a sense, I wasn't really single. I had the support of not one but two excited future dads who watched with fascination and awe at the growing blob in my belly that waved and gurgled on the ultrasound machine.

Almost three years later, I now have a delightful daughter named Sasha who happily runs around after Michael and Adam's infinitely patient dogs. Seeing Sasha laugh, and watching how gently her dads hold her in their arms, I know this was the right decision, even if the pain, disappointment and uncertainty seemed insurmountable at times.

When straight folks ask me how we do it, I tell them, "Think of a divorced family in two houses." Their eyes light up with clarity, but in many ways, the analogy is completely wrong. Unlike divorced families, we intentionally created a family with lots of love, without much legal recognition and without any of the acrimony or rupture that often accompanies divorce. Clearly, we need to find a better analogy (and perhaps we gay folks should stop relying on straight analogies altogether to describe our families). For me, my gay dads and hopefully for our daughter, Sasha, the family we've chosen to create makes perfect sense.

Lesbians at Temple

By Lisa Kron

I'M TRYING TO DECIDE WHAT TO DO for the High Holidays. For the past few years, I've been a member of B'nai Jeshurun on the Upper West Side and my dad, who lives in Michigan, comes to services with me. But this year, my schedule got screwed up and I forgot to send in my renewal. So I'm now trying to figure out what to do. And my friend Leigh said, "Well you should come with us to the gay synagogue." And I said, "Oh, OK, um . . . I don't really know if I can do that." And she said, "No, you know it's really nice. . . ." And I said, "I know, I've been."

I had kind of a bad experience at the gay synagogue. My father started to come out of me at the gay synagogue. It was kind of a bad thing. To explain what happened, I need to tell you first about the synagogue I grew up with in Lansing, Michigan. It was a very progressive synagogue and it was very important to me, my Jewish identity, very important to me as a child. Growing up in the Midwest you have to assert your identity in a way you don't need to do if you grow up, say, in New York. The thing about being a Jew in the Midwest is that even when people know you're Jewish they just assume that you're also a Christian. In the Midwest, Judaism is considered a sort of accessory that you wear on top of your Christianity. So you really have to work to establish your Jewish identity. Like when the High Holidays come and you go into a store and all the Jewish things are out because they think: "Jew holiday. Let's put out the Jew things." And you think, "Oh, good, it's September. And here are the Hannukah candles." You walk into a drugstore and there's the matzo. You think, "Thank God, the matzo's back! Because we didn't get enough of it at Passover." Oh good, more desiccated Manischewitz brownies. I really want more of those. I haven't had all the moisture sucked out of my mouth since last spring. (They're quite extraordinary, actually. One box serves 72. It's like the *miracle* of Passover.)

Anyway, the point is, when I was a kid in the Midwest it was very important to me to establish my Jewish identity, and what this meant was going to services with my father. Now, my dad had grown up in Germany and his father was a chazzan, a cantor, and what this meant was that nothing about the way services were led in Lansing, Michigan, was correct. So my experience of going to services with my father was that I would sit next to him while he muttered things like, "Why are they chanting *that* melody? That's not the correct melody for this holiday." "Why are they going so slowly? What makes everyone in this country think *slow* equals *holy*?" On and on like that. He had it all figured out and he was always mumbling about how it should be. And I was Jewish but I was also a Midwesterner, so my bottom line was that nobody should be raising their voice. And I was always whispering, "Dad!" And he'd answer me in his full voice, "What?" And I'd say, "Dad, *shhhh!*" and he'd say, "Why are you whispering?" And I'd look at him like, "Dad!" And he'd say, "We're Jews! We're allowed to speak out loud!"

So when I was about six or seven there was a major schism in the Lansing Jewish community where one group broke away from the main synagogue to start a new synagogue. (It was like that joke you've probably heard about how if there's one Jew on a desert island there will be two synagogues so there's one he can *refuse* to go to.) This breakaway group thought the main synagogue was spending too much money on the building fund and they wanted to concentrate their efforts on the Hebrew school so they broke away and formed the new, progressive synagogue. We didn't have a rabbi or cantor and all the services were led by the members of the congregation—which was perfect for my father, of course. He got to lead services *his* way. And his favorite service to lead was Ne'ila, the final service for Yom Kippur.

On the High Holidays the setup was that services were led by two members of the congregation—one was the "cantor," who basically led the service, chanting all the Hebrew parts, and other was the "rabbi," who just announced page numbers and told people when to stand up and when to sit down. Needless to say my father had very specific ideas about how Ne'ila was supposed to be done. And there were *no shortcuts* involved. Now, Ne'ila is the very last part of the service before the end of a 24-hour fast. And everyone is really hungry and they're tired and they're ready for it to be over. But this year, my father has transported himself into a state of religious ecstasy and he sees no reason to rush—this is a man also locally famous for the phrase "As long as we're in the car we might as well go to Ohio." So he's chanting, chanting, chanting, chanting. He's got his tallis over his head and it's going longer, longer, longer. And this was making one of the members of the congregation, Murray Edelstein, who was a very tight little man to begin with, very tense. Murray needed the holiday to be over and didn't like the way my father, in his mind, had hijacked this service. Everyone's ready for it to be over but Murray's really hungry and he starts to basically lose his mind. He starts pacing up and down the aisles in a pointed, angry way. My dad's just davening away. And now it feels like it's been dark for about five or six hours. You can smell the food in the other room. The women who are setting it up are like, "You know what? Screw them. The gates are closed. I'm eating." But my dad is still chanting away, oblivious. And Murray Edelstein starts to stalk around the bima, banging his prayer book around, trying in the most passive-aggressive way to signal to my father, "Wrap it up." Everybody's getting tenser and tenser and tenser. Murray is truly losing his shit and it's going to go on forever because my father is forging on, apparently oblivious—until, finally, from under his tallis, the irritated voice of my father comes, yelling, "OH FOR GODSAKES, MURRAY! WOULD YOU JUST SIT DOWN!" I think some people fainted.

So growing up in the Midwest I was all Jew-Jew-Jew and then I came to New York and I was all lesbian-lesbian-lesbian. But after being in New York awhile the Jew part started to resurface. And at some point I thought: "I'm gonna go to services at the gay synagogue." So I decide to go to the High Holiday services at the Javitz Center with my girlfriend, Peg, and our friend Moe, both of whom grew up Catholic. And they're just loving their big Jew adventure. They walk in and everyone's saying, "Good yontif, good yontif," and they keep responding, "Good pontiff, good pontiff." And in the service, you know, there's that unison response to the first few words of a prayer where everyone in the congregation mumbles together, "Baruch Sh'mo." And Peg said, "What does that mean?" And I said, "What do you think it means?" And she said, "Well, *I* think it means, 'Sorry 'bout that.' " And I thought, wow, yes, that's what a Catholic would think that meant.

(One time I asked my friend Moises why people talk about Catholic guilt and Jewish guilt like they're the same thing. I said, "It doesn't feel the same to me but I can't figure it out." And he said, "Okay, here's the difference: Jewish guilt is that you feel like it's your job to save the world and you just haven't done enough. And Catholic guilt is that you just shouldn't be here at all.")

So anyway, we're at this very nice reform, gay, High Holiday service at the Javitz Center, and I start to become crankier and crankier. What's happening, although I don't know it at the time, is that, slowly, I am turning into my father. And I start muttering things like "Good lord, not *another* responsive reading!" Peg keeps shushing me (but in the Catholic way of seeming like she's smiling and nodding at me affectionately but has sprung a small leak while doing it—a habit I call, "shush-laughing"). And I'm ignoring her and my grumbling is getting louder, and she's getting more nervous and digging her fingers into my arm while continuing to smile/shush me. And I say, full voice, "What is it? We're Jews here. We can talk." And Peg shrinks into a tiny, mortified ball. But I'm headed in the other direction. Pretty soon I decide I know when to stand and when to sit and it's *not* when everybody else is doing it. I'm getting more and more irritated. I decide the service is actually over. They've done all the *real* parts and what's going on now is just some bullshit American Jewish filler. So I stand up and say to Peg, "We're leaving." And she's shaking her head and looking at me with large, terrified eyes and she whispers, "We can't leave!" And I say, "We're going." And she says, "No, we can't." But I have now fully morphed into the persona of my father and I announce in my fullest voice, "Of course we can leave. We're Jews. We do not have to sit here like a bunch of PROTESTANTS!"

But you know, as I think about it now, I realize that what came out of me that day at the gay synagogue was not exactly my father. In the Unitarian church, they don't use the phrase, "Please rise." Instead they say, "Stand as you are able." You never have to say, "Stand as you are able" to a group of Jews. If you said, "Please rise" to a group of Jews and there was a little old Jewish man in that group who wasn't able to stand up, you'd hear him announcing, loudly, to the group: "I can't rise! Halachic law *forbids* me to rise! Because I have a *bowel obstruction*!" And what I'm realizing now is that it was him that I turned into at the gay synagogue. That little Jewish man lives in all of us.

Mama Ann

By Joel Stein

AS THE 2008 PRESIDENTIAL CAMPAIGN got close to the end, it became clear that the most important demographic for Barack Obama in November were the old Jews in Florida, and that the most important old Jew in Florida was my grandmother. That's because Mama Ann voted twice in 2000: once normally and once when she sneaked into a booth to help a friend who couldn't see well and she punched the ballot for Al Gore. At least she thinks it was Gore.

But Mama Ann was thinking about voting for John McCain. And she wasn't alone. The situation with old Jews in Florida turning away from Barack Obama was so bad, a political action committee called The Jewish Council for Education and Research organized The Great Schlep, in which hundreds of Jews traveled to the Fort Lauderdale area, visited their grandparents, organized political salons in their condos and ate incredibly bad food. (The grandkids also met up at a bar one night, which—if the psychological impact of spending a few days with frail, elderly, widowed relatives is taken fully into account—may do more to repopulate the world's Jews than the creation of Israel.)

A few weeks before the 2008 election, I made my own pilgrimage to Margate, Florida, to convince Mama Ann to vote for Obama. I was in the Miami area anyway to interview a rapper named Flo Rida.

Before I got there, I had called Tennessee's Jewish U.S. Representative Steve Cohen, an early Obama supporter, for his advice—not so much about etiquette on making it rain at Diamond's Cabaret, but how to talk an old Southern Jew out of a big mistake. Cohen's first suggestion was to appeal to the classic Jewish-grandmother soft spots by telling her what terrific schools Obama went to and that he was a lawyer. Then Cohen started working on the commonalities between Obama and Mama Ann. "Barack grew up in Hawaii," Cohen said. "They have lots of beaches." If Cohen really thinks Mama Ann has left her condo to go to the beach in the past 20 years, he clearly hasn't spent any time with old Jews in Florida. Because Jews had been targeted with anti-Obama e-mails, he thought Mama Ann might believe false rumors that Obama was a Muslim. Again, if Cohen thinks Mama Ann is using a computer, he needs to get to Fort Lauderdale more often.

Armed with these powerful arguments, I asked Mama Ann to explain her concerns about Obama. "First, the man hasn't got the experience," she said. "I also think he's a Muslim." When I tried to convince her that he was a Christian, she said, "There are good Muslims and bad Muslims—just like there are good and bad Jews." When I cautiously reminded her that Obama went to church, she still wasn't convinced. "He went to Muslim schools." I told her that Obama only went to school in Jakarta through the third grade, which meant at worst he wrote cursive in a Muslim style, or used Muslimy fractions, or he knew the Muslim names for dinosaurs, which I assume are close enough, like Abu Brachiosaurus. But Mama Ann told me that those people still "have his ear." The fact that Mama Ann thought friends from third grade were still in close contact with Obama made me deeply suspicious that she somehow knew about Facebook.

It became clear that Mama Ann and all her friends at the condo were still mad at Obama for beating Hillary Clinton, whom they loved because she was feisty and tough, like a fifth Golden Girl. But it was also because he was young, seen as dovish on Israel and black—which is the Jews' second least favorite minority after Nazis. If he were an old Asian guy who knew Krav Maga, he'd take Pompano in a landslide. (I think I've just pitched the plot to *The Karate Kid V*.)

I tried to delicately ask Mama Ann if perhaps her problem was that Obama was African-American, but she told me I was wrong, even when I accused her of being unhappy with the recent influx of blacks into her area. "No. This was their place first. They could take the hot weather. And some of them went far in this world. They're not lazy." Jews and blacks, she explained, have gotten along famously for most of her life. "Now there's some tension on account of the very Orthodox Jews. They're troublemakers. They don't get out enough."

That afternoon, we took a trip to Wal-Mart, because I can drive. Mama Ann told me she needed some elastic, which was not something I knew you could buy. Her first instinct in looking for the elastic was to grab a phone in the store and ask for help. This was not a good plan since all the phones she picked up were actually credit card machines. Eventually she walked up to the first black woman she saw. This woman, unfortunately, was not an employee at Wal-Mart, which I could tell because she was not wearing a Wal-Mart badge. Also because she kept shaking her head and saying, "I don't work here," while Mama Ann explained her elastic-finding problem. Eventually, the woman got her point across and pointed us toward an actual employee. Once we found the elastic, Mama Ann went looking for a battery-operated radio without a clock in it, which, to my horror, required walking through an aisle with the black woman who did not work for Wal-Mart. This was a woman I would have assumed we would have chosen to avoid. Instead, Mama Ann started asking her questions about radios. At this moment, my brain kind of froze in panic and I decided to handle the awkward encounter by smiling broadly and pretending that I was either foreign or mentally challenged and had been hired by an 88-year-old Jewish woman I didn't know to drive her to Wal-Mart. Looking back, it was a lot to expect to convey through a smile.

This was not the only racially charged moment of my visit. After eating chicken breasts, Mama Ann told me that her grandfather used to say, "Eat the marrow, you'll date a black man." I stood there slack-jawed, having no idea that for so many generations, Jews have hated marrow. And while we were in the pool, she walked up to a couple visiting from Spain and said, "If you were any darker, you'd have to move to the other side of town." When everyone in the pool laughed loudly at this, I realized my grandmother wasn't racist. She just says things that are normal for an older person who hates black people.

The next day, we went to Palm Beach to visit her first cousin, Rochelle Bramsen, because I can drive. When Rochelle's daughter and son-in-law argued for Obama, she bristled. I joined in, and asked—as suggested by the talking points—if Rochelle thought Obama was a Muslim. Both Rochelle and Mama Ann said yes. When we were all tired of arguing about that, I asked if it would be such a big deal if Obama *were* a Muslim. "For me, personally, that would be an issue," said Rochelle. Thinking we'd trapped her in a rhetorical corner, her kids and I asked why Muslims in office would be worse than Christians. To which Rochelle deftly responded, "Who says I'm OK with Christians?"

After making some progress with Rochelle and Mama Ann, I decided on my last morning to head down to the condo Hadassah meeting. A few people had Obama buttons in Hebrew. One wanted to tell me how Lyndon Johnson helped the Jews more than people know. Seven wanted to set me up with their granddaughters despite the fact that I was wearing my wedding ring. But many more were sure Obama was Muslim and that extremist Arabs "had his ear."

As I was leaving, I asked Mama Ann if I had somehow persuaded her to vote for Obama. "Yeah," she said. I was elated, until she added, "I'm fine. I have to go for blood work again. They keep me waiting for an hour. I'm all sunburned like a berry. I get in the water, and I forget to get out. I get in conversations." I rephrased my question, this time much more loudly. "Yeah," she said. I cautiously asked why. "You gave me his good qualities. You ought to run for something as a politician."

I left pretty proud of myself, until I started to realize that there was really no great argument I had used, that Mama Ann was changing her mind for no good reason. I started to wonder what my good reasons for supporting Obama were. Did I really think that he'd get us out of Iraq all that much faster, that he could actually deliver health care to everyone or that he'd erase the anger between the parties and races? This is a guy, after all, who is no better than I am at stopping his grandmother from saying racist things. The truth is, I like Obama because he's young and eats arugula and shops at Whole Foods and knows who Ludacris is. Because he's the closest thing to the person I'd really like to vote for: me.

Phone Home

By Avi Gesser

IMPORTANT DISCLAIMER: *This story is almost all true. The voice mails referred to herein are actual messages left by my mom on my answering machine. My mom is most definitely not "in" on this. She is not aware of my Heeb Storytelling activities, and I would greatly appreciate it if it stayed that way. So, by reading this story, you agree that if you happen to be talking to a member of my family, you will take all reasonable steps to avoid any mention of this story and instead select another subject to talk about, such as why there is only one seder in Israel, but two seders everywhere else.*

MY NAME IS ABRAHAM (AVI) GESSER, and this is an actual picture of my family:

We're Jewish. In the center of the photo is my great-grandfather Abraham, whom I am named after. Apparently we look a lot alike, although it is kind of hard to tell. The baby is my mom. This is not a recent picture.

My story is about my mom, and there is one thing you need to know about her by way of background: Although she lives in Winnipeg, which is about 5,000 miles away from me, she needs to know where I am at all times. Her day can be divided into two roughly equal parts: those times when she knows exactly where I am and those times when she is actively looking for me.

I work at a large New York law firm and my days can be pretty hectic. I have almost no time for anything other than work, and all my friends and family know not to try getting ahold of me at the office for nonemergency personal matters . . . except for my mom, who calls me at work every single day and sometimes several times a day. I will often be in my office with some other lawyers gathered around my desk, discussing some case, and the phone will ring. I see from the display that it is my mom calling, so I don't answer it. Then my cell phone rings. It's Mom, so I don't answer. Then my BlackBerry rings. It's her. I ignore it. Then there is a pause while she tries me at home.

My office phone rings about 45 seconds later as she starts through the cycle again, this time leaving long messages on each device with vital and pressing information, such as the following:

Avi, it's Mom dear. We are going to the JCC—Eli Weisel is going to be broadcasting. We're going at about 5:15. We got to be there at 6:30, but they're having some food so we want to have something to eat there too. So . . . call us either before 5:15 or about 9 o'clock in the evening. Talk to you later dear. Bye bye.

Here is a more recent picture of my family:

That's my mom and dad, Esther and Hymie, in the middle. The three kids are Abraham, me, on the left, Isaac and Sarah. As I may have mentioned, we're Jewish. My parents are observant and being Jewish is pretty important to them. My brother is quite into the Jewish stuff, but me . . . less so. This is a source of great concern for my mom. As part of her efforts to bring me back into the fold, she calls me to remind me of upcoming Jewish holidays—as if the only reason I never build a sukkah in my apartment is that I keep forgetting when the holiday is. Knowing that my complete adherence to all the requirements of a particular holiday is highly unlikely, Mom always provides me with partial compliance options. So, for example, she knows I won't fast on Tisha B'av, but maybe I could skip breakfast or have a light dinner? Here is a recent message I received along these lines:

 Avi . . . don't forget, don't eat meat for lunch tomorrow. Happy Shevu'ot. Chag Sameach.

That was the voice mail I received at the office. At home, I got:

 Avi, it's Mom . . . I'm just reminding you to eat dairy tomorrow. OK dear. Bye bye.

The next day I was in a meeting at my office with several board members of a major client. In the middle of my conclusions regarding the conduct of a senior executive, my administrative assistant knocked on the door and walked over to me with a note. In these circumstances, being handed a note is reserved for very bad news that cannot wait—a family member has just been rushed to the hospital, the FBI is in your office going through your e-mails, there is blood pouring out of your left ear, etc. The note read:

Don't eat meat for lunch today.
Love, Mom

Although I was initially furious at the completely unnecessary and inappropriate interruption, which she obviously had insisted upon, I could not help but smile at the addition of the "Love, Mom." As if I may have otherwise been unsure as to who had sent the message.

My brother and I are not that close. There are several reasons for this. He is eight years older than I am. He lives in California while I live in New York. We don't have much in common. We don't share the same interests. When we were kids he tried to kill me on several occasions. And so on. This is also a source of great concern for my mom, mostly because she honesty believes that if we were closer, perhaps some of my brother's love for Jewish ritual would rub off on me. So, in an effort to build that relationship, every year, beginning about three weeks before my brother's birthday, I begin to get this kind of voice mail:

Avi, it's Mom dear. Listen. Thursday, January 27 is Isaac's birthday. So don't forget to send him an e-mail card or whatever you call those things.

[talking to my dad] Umm, Hymie what do you call those e-mail cards . . . Blue Mountain, yah.

OK dear. Bye bye.

This year, I was very busy at work in January and simply forgot to send my brother an e-mail card. So, on the morning of his birthday, I received this message:

Hi Avi, it's Mom. Just wanted to remind you that it's Isaac's birthday today and it would be nice if you gave him a call.

Bye bye.

That day, I was tied up in court all day, so I didn't listen to the message and didn't call my brother. When I finally got around to checking my voice mails at around 11 p.m. that night, I heard that message from my mom, along with the following message from my dad, who absolutely never calls me:

It's your dad. You haven't called Isaac and that's not nice. If you haven't . . . If you haven't got . . . he's home all day because he's got a cold. Bye.

At that point it was too late to call either my parents or Isaac and the next day was equally hectic, so I didn't get around to calling him. When things finally calmed down that next night, I realized that for the first time in as long as I could remember, my mom had not called me. Wow, could my parents really have been that angry about this? Apparently so, because the next day came and went, again without a single call from Mom. I decided that Mom and Dad were overreacting and, as a matter of principle, I was not going to call either them or Isaac to apologize. After a full week of no calls I started to think to myself, "What am I going to do with all this extra time I have? This little family squabble has freed up about five hours a week for me—probably enough time to learn French." But just as the Berlitz language tapes arrived at my apartment, the quiet ended.

Unbeknownst to me, an event was about to occur that was so momentous, my mom could no long maintain her silence. That fateful day, this vital message was left on my machine at work:

 Hi Avi. Tomorrow is the holiday of Tu Be'shvat, the birthday of the trees, the beginning of the spring in Israel. Get some figs or dates or pistachio nuts if you can.

Bye bye.

Happy holiday.

And so I did. I called my mom the next day to tell her how tasty the figs were and to thank her for the important reminder.

Little Isaac's Nozzle of Love

By Steve Almond

I FLEW DOWN TO MIAMI to visit my big brother, Ev, for a week because he and his wife, Carmen, had their first baby a couple of months ago. So I guess, in a sense, I was actually visiting the kid, whose name is—check this out—Isaac Diego Ornstein. Half Jewish, half Cuban. "Our little Jewban," Ev calls him.

They've got this great house in South Miami, very tropical, overgrown and so forth. The first night, Carmen made us a feast: flank steaks, black bean soup, these fried plantain chips with garlic sauce that are basically crack cocaine, and flan. After dinner, Ev and I headed out to the back porch with the kid to watch the sunset. It was the middle of February and we were in shorts.

"This is the life," I said.

Ev grinned. "I told you." He'd been trying to convince me to move down from New York for the past year. We were sitting there digesting, when all of sudden, Isaac Diego started making these weird faces.

"What's going on?" I asked.

"Little dude's hanging a grunt," Ev said. He handed me the baby and went to get the diaper bag. He had this mat, which he laid down on the picnic table, and he set the kid down and took off his diaper. It's not like I was watching the process that closely, but I couldn't help but notice that my nephew had—how do I want to say this?—a weird-looking wiener. I sort of drifted over to the table to take a closer look.

"Is it just me," I said, "or is that kid a little long in the foreskin department?"

Ev was wiping the baby's bum, getting the diaper tabs all lined up. "Yeah," he said. "Carmen didn't want to have him circumcised."

"But we're Jewish," I said. "Did you explain the whole Jew thing to her?"

"She knows about the Jew thing."

"Like, the whole commandment deal."

"It's not a commandment."

"Sure, it's a commandment."

"No, it's not. It's not one of the Ten Commandments." Ev taped up the diaper and kissed Isaac's belly. He was doing this thing where he doesn't look at me. "To tell you the truth, I never considered it that big a deal," he said. "We're just happy the bambino is healthy—ten fingers and toes."

He was referring to the fact that Carmen had this condition, I forget the exact name, but basically her placenta got infected and her blood pressure shot up, and for a while the doctors were worried that Isaac might have gotten infected too.

"Yeah," I said. "I mean, obviously it's not the biggest deal in the world. I'm just wondering what she has against circumcision."

"She doesn't like the idea of him being caused any unnecessary pain," Ev said.

"He's just a little schtunk. He's not going to remember anything. Besides, you've seen how these rabbis do it. They get the kid all boozed up. You could even give him a local anesthetic."

Ev yawned. He was finishing up his residency in internal medicine at UM, sleeping about four hours a week. "If it was up to me, I'd have done it. But Carmen dug her heels in, and I didn't feel like arguing with her. You have no idea, bro, how stubborn she can be."

We heard the screen door behind us slide open.

"Did I hear my name?" Carmen asked. "Are you talking about me, sweetie?"

"Singing your praises," Ev said.

Carmen smiled. "You better be, papi."

She took Isaac from my brother and walked up to me and stood there, striking this Madonna pose. "Isn't he the most beautiful baby you've ever seen?"

"Pretty amazing," I said.

"But isn't he the most beautiful baby you've ever seen?"

I didn't know quite what to say. I mean, the kid was cute.

But his head, to be honest, looked sort of hammered-down.

"I hadn't really thought about it in terms of a hierarchy," I said.

Carmen sighed in a way that made it clear I'd missed the whole point and kissed Isaac on his soft little hammered-down head. "Remember to bring the diaper bag inside," she said to Ev.

Ev patted his belly. "That was some meal, huh? I never would have thought I'd be at risk for heart disease. But Carmen's cooking. Man!"

"Does Mom know?" I asked.

"Know what?"

"About the nozzle."

"If you're referring to my son's penis," Ev said, "I'd prefer if you used the term 'love gun.' "

"Does she?" I repeated.

Ev paused. "Yeah. She talked it over with Carmen. I didn't get the details."

Our mom wasn't all that religious, actually. It was our dad who'd been serious about Judaism, but he'd died when we were little.

"To tell you the truth," Ev said, "it's just not a big deal for me. She gave birth to the kid. If she wants him to keep the extra ten percent, that's cool with me."

We were both quiet for a minute. Off in the distance, the clouds were turning from orange to red.

"Right," I said finally. "I mean, I'm not going all Lubavitcher on you."

I looked over at Ev. He was snoring softly.

The truth is, it pissed me off a little. I mean, I felt for the guy. Carmen was a ballbuster. But it was like, come on: Represent the tribe. This woman knew you were Jewish. She agreed to a Jewish ceremony. The least you could do was get your son properly outfitted on the genital front.

That night, I lay in bed and thought about little Isaac's nozzle. I couldn't get past how ridiculous it looked. Like a tiny cowl-neck sweater. Then I started thinking about—and I know how terrible this sounds—but I started thinking about the word *smegma*. I couldn't get it out of my head. Smegma . . . smegma . . . smegma. That's what little Isaac was looking at, a lifetime supply of the stuff. And not only that, but there was no way his little Jewish friends were ever going to accept him as a Jew once they saw the nozzle. What Carmen had done, in effect, she'd pulled off a palace coup.

When I got up the next morning, Ev had already left. Carmen was in the kitchen fixing eggs, with the kid plopped next to her, asleep in his little portable baby La-Z-Boy.

"Smells great," I said.

Carmen turned and smiled at me. She had this knockout smile.

"Did you sleep okay?"

"Like a horse," I said.

"Like a horse?"

"Or like a stone, maybe. Maybe stone makes more sense."

Carmen brought me a plate of eggs and some sausage and this ultra-buttery Cuban toast and café con leche, which, if you don't know, is basically a cup of hot milk with a shot of espresso and about a pound of sugar. I dipped the toast into the coffee and let it get nice and soggy.

Carmen laughed. "That's what my dad does."

"Great minds," I said.

She sat down across from me. "Man," I said. "These eggs are delicious. What's in here?"

"Just such some cheese and chives."

"Chives," I said. "Wow." As you might have gathered, I'm not much of a cook. The act of spicing tends to amaze me.

She smiled again. "I'm glad to have such an appreciative audience."

It was another gorgeous day there in Miami. The sun was beating down on all the plants in the backyard and a soft breeze was coming through the screen door. I thought to myself: This wouldn't be so bad, to live here. What was so great about New York anyway? It was cold as hell and dirty, and the business I was in was full of people who smiled at you while they knifed you in the back.

"So," Carmen said, "Evan tells me you'd prefer if Isaac was circumcised."

I glanced across the table. She was still smiling, though I couldn't really see her teeth anymore.

"Yeah," I said. "We talked about that a little last night."

"He said you were kind of upset." Carmen raised her eyebrows.

"The thing is, I realize we're not the most Jewish family in the world. But Isaac is half Jewish anyway, that's a part of who he is. And what with modern medicine and everything, it doesn't seem like that big a deal to just get him circumcised."

"It's not that big a deal to you," Carmen said, "because it's not your penis they're going to slice."

"Wow," I said. "I'm not sure I'd put it like that."

"How would you put it?"

Here's the thing: I liked Carmen. I really did. She was a tough cookie. And Ev needed a tough cookie, someone who could call him on his bullshit. But she also had this hunger for drama that made me a little suspicious. "I just think it's something that could make his life a little easier down the line. I mean, most men are circumcised these days. And his dad is circumcised. Don't you think he's going to feel a little funny when he sees his dad and then looks at himself?"

"Actually, I think he'd find the size discrepancy more disturbing," Carmen said. "That's been my experience with men."

"I can't argue with that," I said. "I realize this is your and Ev's call."

"Right."

"All I'm saying is that it's part of our identity, the Jewish identity. Kind of like our trademark."

"But you just got done saying how almost all men are circumcised."

"Right," I said. "Because the idea caught on. But it's still something that's associated with Jews. We were the ones who started it."

"Actually," Carmen said, "there's considerable evidence that many of the ancient cultures practiced circumcision. So actually, it was the Jews who got the idea from someone else. They were just the first ones to link the practice to God." Should I mention that Carmen had studied classics?

"The biblical scholars say circumcision was just a way of preventing disease. Because, back then, obviously, men couldn't wash as much. So you had all kinds of infections down there." Smegma, I thought, idiotically. Smegma.

"But today, with our standards of cleanliness, those risks don't exist anymore. There's really no reason to circumcise a child."

"Of course there is," I said. "Because God said to do it."

"But you don't believe in God," Carmen said. This was true.

"It's not so much a God thing," I said. "It's more like a cultural thing. Like, respecting that part of his identity is Jewish."

"You really think the shape of his penis is going to make him a Jew or not?"

"Well, I mean, it's not a one-to-one ratio."

But before I could say anything else, Isaac started to whimper, and Carmen picked him up and carried him to the couch. She pulled her shirt up and stuck him on her boob. "I'm not trying to be dismissive," she said. "I realize that my husband is Jewish. That's part of the reason I love him. We plan to raise our kids in a way that respects his religion and mine. Look at his name.

He's named after your father. We just felt like there was no reason to subject our baby to a painful, barbaric custom."

"You mean you felt that way," I muttered.

"Excuse me," Carmen said.

"Nothing."

"Are you implying that I forced this decision on Evan?"

"I'm not implying anything. It's none of my business. Listen, I didn't come down here to cause trouble."

"That's what gets me about Judaism," Carmen said. "It's so clannish. It's like all those laws you guys have are really just a way of dividing people."

"I'm not sure the Catholics have any kind of record to brag about," I said.

I could feel Carmen glaring at me as I finished my eggs, so I just got out of there, took my rental car to the beach and lay on the sand and fried.

That night, Ev came into my room. He looked exhausted, his eyes all hollowed out.

"I'm sorry," I said.

"For what?"

"All that stuff with Carmen. It got a little nasty."

He plopped down at the foot of my bed. "So I gathered."

"I should have kept my mouth shut."

There was a silence.

"No," he said quietly. "You were right."

"I was?"

"Yeah, I mean, I feel the same way. Should have had the kid snipped. If you don't insist on some things, the thing just disappears." Ev laid his head back against the wall. "That's what the Orthodox say about us already. We're not even Jews to them, because we don't follow the laws."

"Yeah, but Carmen had some good points," I said. "She's no dope. You can't base a whole religion on laws. It should cut deeper than that." Ev closed his eyes. I thought he might be sacking out on me again. But then he cleared his throat.

"You remember what Dad used to say whenever I'd complain about having to come in to light the candles, or waiting to eat at the Seder? He'd say, 'You're a part of history, Evan. Don't you want to be a part of history?' It's a silly thing to say to a kid, because kids don't care about history. They just want to play, whatever. But I was thinking about that today. I want Isaac to know where he comes from, that he's a part of a history that's greater than all of us." Ev laughed. "Jesus," he said. "I sound just like the bastard."

"Was he really a bastard?"

"Not really," Ev said. "Just kind of severe. Old school. Here's something you probably didn't know—he circumcised both of us."

"You're shitting me."

"No, it's the law. If the father is trained, he's required to perform the bris. Mom told me those ceremonies were two of the happiest moments of his life." Ev shook his head. "The thing about Carmen, she acts all tough on the outside. But inside, she's as soft as they come. She can't stand for Isaac to cry. It's something to do with her family. Not like her dad was some kind of ogre. But he wasn't around much, and the women, Carmen and her mom, they were stuck trying to keep everyone happy."

"Sure," I said.

"She loves him," Ev said. "She loves that guy so much."

He opened his eyes, and I could see that they'd watered up a little. And it will seem strange to say, but I knew right then that he wasn't just talking about Carmen and his son, he was also talking about himself and our dad, sort of remembering those moments when he'd felt the pure, dangerous beam of our father's love.

I didn't know what to say. I mean, we're not the kind of family where this heavy stuff comes up too much. We're more of a duck-and-weave kind of operation. But I could see that Ev was really struggling with this thing and that made me feel bad again, for sort of barging in and making things complicated.

"It's late," I said. "You shouldn't worry about all this now. See if you can catch some sleep."

"Listen," he said. "I don't want you to feel bad. I'm going to work this thing out. The important thing to remember is that Carmen and me, we both, you know . . ." His voice sort of wobbled there a second. I was scared to death that he might start crying, that I'd be expected to say something deep and rescuing.

Ev closed his eyes and took a deep breath. "All I'm saying is that we both care about you. And if anything should ever happen to me."

"Jesus," I said. "Nothing's going to happen."

"Yeah, I know. But I'm saying if it did, whatever, I'd be counting on you to look out for Isaac. And I'd hate to think that anything would stand in the way of that."

"Are you kidding? No way, Ev." And then I saw what he was talking about, the nozzle thing. "Oh God," I said. "Not for a second. You don't even need to say it."

Ev patted my leg. It was something my dad used to do. I felt like hugging the guy, because I could see how hard he was working, to support his family, to keep the peace with his wife, to fulfill the promise he'd made to our dad. He was worn out from making his own history, I guess you could say. And it was clear to me that my devotion to him was the most important thing here, more important than any flap of skin, or God's orders or whatever. We had to stick together. And I don't mean as Jews so much as brothers, as guys who shared the same blood and the same history. It was like Carmen had said: Circumcision was really just a sign of devotion, of loyalty. All those 614 laws—however many there were—they were just a way of trying to maintain the brotherhood.

From the other room, we heard Isaac start to whimper.

And then we heard Carmen get up from the bed and pad over to his crib.

Ev didn't say anything. I didn't say anything either. We both got up and went to the doorway and peeked into the bedroom. The kid was latched onto her boob, one of his hands set right there and the other clutching a curl of her hair. It was quite a thing to see.

Carmen looked up at us, through the dimness of the room. She squinted. For a second I thought she might be pissed that we were spying on her. But then she smiled, a little shyly. "What are you two doing up? I thought it was just the baby and me."

"Nope," Ev said softly.

We were both just standing there, smiling like idiots at her and the kid.

"You guys look like you've been conspiring," Carmen said.

"Always," I said. "Forever."

True Tales from Katzalot

By Mark Katz

I DON'T REMEMBER MUCH about that terrible day in November, as I was just a fetus at the time. But here's what I've been told: By the time the third shot was fired from the book depository behind the grassy knoll, the phone rang in my parents' Brooklyn apartment. My mother, eight months pregnant and prone to hysteria, was watching the horror happen on live TV. On the other end of the phone was my grandma Rose, a can-do matriarch calling from her home on Avenue U, six blocks away. The tone of her voice had the calm, cool resonance of a hostage negotiator.

"Adrienne, listen to me. This has nothing to do with you. Now, turn off the television and go lie down. I'll be over in five minutes. . . ."

Like Camelot itself, my family's history with the Kennedy administration may have been somewhat mythologized. My parents raised four kids (for Jews we were practically Irish!), and four times a year, the birthday child was traditionally regaled with the story of the day he or she arrived, perhaps slightly embellished from year to year. Mine always began with this incident from when I was negative five weeks old. The next beat of this time-honored tale takes place two days later: a nearly identical phone call from Grandma Rose that rang moments before Jack Ruby had been wrestled to the ground. For the second time in those frightful 48 hours, my grandmother managed to successfully reason with my mother's uterus.

These details from the weeks before my birth only hint at the effect that the Kennedy era had on a child born in its aftermath. And like the birth itself, this was mostly due to a determined effort by my mom.

Mom's ex post facto fixation began with the arrival of the Kennedy memorial issues of magazines like *Life* and *Look* that began piling up in the living room of the split-level house we moved to in the summer of 1964. Page after page featured photographs of John and Jackie, John-John and Caroline—impossibly attractive, effortlessly stylish people in godly repose—and flipping through them elicited the palpable lifestyle yearnings of a J. Crew catalog. Before long, my mother had begun to use these magazines as how-to manuals for creating a little Camelot of her own. And in my first five years, those between *Dallas* and the moon landing, I was raised in a suburban enclave of Kennedy culture entirely of my mother's making.

Phase One began innocently enough, when my mom joined the ranks of the millions of women taking fashion cues from America's stylish first lady. In the Jewish fashion week otherwise known as the High Holidays, she started showing up at synagogue in Oleg Cassini knockoff dresses, her bouffanted hair beneath a pillbox hat. Young, slender and pretty, she carried off the look better than most—but would probably have elicited fewer stares had Nixon won in 1960 and had she shown up in a respectable Republican cloth coat instead. As time wore on, my mother's fascination with all things Jackie led her to replace the buttons on her dresses with larger, more pronounced ones, accessorizing each dress with a coordinating wrap. And if there had been a tailor who could have lengthened her neck or widened the distance between her eyes, she might have done that too.

Phase Two focused on my father. She set out to refashion a short-but-sturdy, round-faced dentist with sparse, flaccid hair into a chiseled, toothy Kennedy. Dentists are notoriously bad dressers, and my father was color-blind to boot. Dad proved immune to the Jack Kennedy accents she added to his wardrobes:

thin ties, tie clips, crisp shirts and athletic cut sport jackets with narrow lapels. Clothing that looked effortlessly good on JFK looked belabored on him. One Father's Day, she gave him monogrammed handkerchiefs, but the embroidered JSK protruding from his pocket seemed more than just one letter off. She had to face the fact that the most she could accomplish by dressing up a short D.D.S. was to make him resemble a short M.D.—and then only from a distance.

Phase Three was me—the child she nearly had the day he was shot and that she hugged through her belly the day he was buried. And when I arrived, five weeks into the Johnson administration, my life began as my mother's very own living, breathing, crying, pooping John-John doll.

I make no apologies for the fact that I was a stunningly beautiful child. My eyes were big and blue, my hair was golden and silky, and I'll be damned if my face wasn't cherubic. Later in life, I'd stare at the photographs that only partially captured my beauty and curse the irreparable damage of puberty. But at the time, my mom looked down to see a baby prince and set out to raise a John-John of her own, the templates for which were right there in the pages of those magazines on the coffee table.

Both of my grandfathers were professional clothiers: Her father, my grandpa Joe, was the proprietor of Joseph's, a children's clothing store well-known to those who lived in Sheepshead Bay, Brooklyn. My grandpa Max was a tailor, and the owner of the Parkway Cleaners in St. Albans, Queens. At my mother's behest, they worked in tandem to customize, to her specifications, the finest children's clothing on the market: velvet jackets with embroidered crests; knit jumpers in regal purples, reds and blues; and short pants lined with satin that hung from matching suspenders.

As if the princely wardrobe weren't enough, the first pair of shoes ever strapped to my feet were red, open-toe, faux-leather Stride Rite sandals—near-perfect replicas of the pair John-John wore the day of the poignant salute.

For my very first haircut, she took me to the stripe-poled barbershop in the local shopping plaza and asked the old Italian gentleman for a "John-John," then pulled out a collection of photographs showcasing the front, side and back of

John-John's head. She explained in exact detail the hairstyle she sought: bangs pushed forward for the effortlessly tousled look. The sides should be trimmed above the ear and the back left longer and fuller. The nice old man promised to do his best, but as he lifted the electric buzzer, my mother snatched me from his chair. On the way home, she stopped off at the pharmacy and picked up a new pair of stainless steel scissors, long and slim with a Q-shaped finger rest. This was the day I received my first mom-administered haircut.

After that day, my mother began amassing a sizeable collection of scissors, combs, neck buzzers, thinning sheers, plastic aprons and hair tonics (the kind of equipment the state requires one to have a license to use on the general public but which somehow is available for purchase over the counter). Every six weeks or so she would open the bathroom cabinet where the haircutting arsenal was kept, and one by one, my brothers, sister and I would go in for our turn in the home-style barber chair—a sturdy upholstered chair that started its life as part of a dining room set. Having your hair cut by your mother in the bathroom is not necessarily a bad thing; it was just an uncommon practice this far from Appalachia. But the sad fact was that none of my brothers or my sister or I ever had a professional haircut by a licensed barber until we went off to college. And even then, the positive effects of professional hair care were largely undone over Thanksgiving break. Most people associate the smell of astringent and talc with getting a haircut, but, to this day, a waft of L'Air du Temps makes the hair on the back of my neck stand on edge.

On a drizzly Sunday morning in the fall of 1994, I got a call from my friend Mitch, once a regular in the after-school driveway basketball games of my suburban youth and now a Manhattan Assistant District Attorney.

"Hey, a bunch of guys from work are playing touch football in the park. If you want to play, come by at Sheep's Meadow around noon."

"It's raining out" was my response, but I'd have been just as likely to beg off on a crisp, sunny day. Football has always been my least favorite playground sport, as it is premised on speed and size, both of which I lack. To make matters worse, I can only throw a wobbly spiral, and passes thrown directly at me have a way of bouncing off my chest. But Mitch added the detail that he knew might overcome my disinterest:

"My buddy John is supposed to show."

He knew that I knew whom he meant.

An hour later, I arrived at Central Park in sweatpants and a slicker, along with another good friend from high school, Rich Rosenthal. We hopped the fence that was supposed to keep people from playing football on the recently reseeded lawn and approached some guys tossing a football around. As I got closer, I could see that the one wearing the backward Jets cap was John F. Kennedy Jr. I was about to play touch football with John-John and I could almost smell the chowder.

Quick introductions were made among the 10 or 12 of us, and I took my cue from the group when we all pretended that John was just another one of the guys, no different from all the Daves, Steves and Mikes. We chose up sides and I was assigned to John's team. Mitch and Rich were on the other, not-John team.

On offense, John played quarterback while I quietly assigned myself the task of trying not to be an obvious detriment to our team's effort. As we played in the cold, light rain, I noticed some photographers huddling on the other side of the fence. From that point on, I stayed close to John in the huddle, mindful of the expression on my face that might be seen in the next day's *Daily News*. As good-looking as he was, I would describe my response to him as a heterosexual crush. I wanted to play well so that he would like me, but that was unlikely, as I had never played well in my life. As the game went on, the team on defense quickly learned that I was the weak link on our offensive line and they assigned larger, quicker players to line up against me to get to our quarterback. I was reassigned out of necessity to be one of two or three eligible receivers but never tried terribly hard to break free from my defender. This gave John little choice but not to throw to me and he seemed happy to oblige—except on the one occasion when the guy covering me slipped on the wet grass as I left the line of scrimmage, leaving me wide open as I ran down the field. John spotted me as I broke free, pumped once, twice and then released a tight spiraled ball, thrown with some zip, as I waited near the end zone for it to arrive. The ball hit me like a precordial thump, bounced off my sternum and went two feet up into the air, giving me a chance to drop the same ball twice, which I did. It was the last pass he threw to me for the rest of the game. There was no way I was going to be invited to Hyannisport now.

As the game disbanded and the East Siders headed east and the West Siders headed west, I worked my way into the circle of sweaty rain-soaked guys who surrounded John. We had met once before, I reminded him, at the White House Correspondents' Dinner, and segued sharply from there to tell him a story I thought he might find amusing: that once upon a time my mother cut my hair to look like his and that was the reason for a childhood of home haircuts. He smiled graciously at my anecdote. Then he had a question for me.

"Does your mom still cut your hair?"

"No."

"Good for you."

Bar Mitzvah:
The Musical!

By Matthew Loren Cohen

YOU MIGHT THINK THAT A BAR MITZVAH would be an uninspired topic for *Heeb*. But I'm going to bravely challenge your assumption and tell you about mine anyway. It's worth discussing, not because it was the most momentous or the biggest, but because it was the gayest.

My Bar Mitzvah took place on May 13, 1989. And as you can see from this photograph, I had to stand on a stool to actually be seen over the lectern.

(I haven't grown, by the way.) The place was Temple Beth El in Boca Raton, Florida. I grew up in Boca—we were the poor family. Our house was the one with only four bedrooms (and no, Dorothy, Blanche, Rose and Sophia were not home at the time this photo was taken).

Because almost every Jew in Boca Raton is some kind of ludicrously wealthy doctor or lawyer, Boca Bar Mitzvahs are exercises in excess. No expense is spared. During my seventh-grade year (Bar Mitzvah season), I received several invitations so elaborate that they arrived not in envelopes but in boxes complete with confetti, and occasionally an embedded chip that would play, say, "Hava Nagila" when the card was opened.

One invitation, for example, was printed on a mini tallis. The production of these easily cost more than my entire Bar Mitzvah. However, as you can see in the following photograph, my mom's Scottish terrier can now properly attend shul.

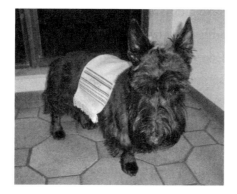

Anyway, the receptions of the Bar or Bat Mitzvahs I attended were held in country clubs and hotel ballrooms to which we were often shuttled in stretch limos. There were cocktail hours with mock game shows for us to play, parties with live bands *and* DJs (for when the band took a break, of course) and decorations that would have made Brooke Astor blush.

My parents were part of Boca's much-less-known breed: the middle class. And at the time of my Bar Mitzvah, they'd been divorced for two years. My mom was raising me and my brother on child support from my dad, a building contractor, and her own teacher's salary. So knowing that my Bar Mitzvah could not even begin to compete with some of the extravagant galas I'd attended, I had to come up with something affordably superlative for mine. I mean, the reception was going to feature only husband-and-wife DJ team Mike and Bobbie Roberts and I was not allowed to invite all my friends. (Once and for all: mea culpa, Erin.) I had to make a splash somehow.

I've loved musical theater ever since I attended my first Broadway show, *Joseph and the Amazing Technicolor Dreamcoat*, at age 5. I even acted in my first professional musical (a local production of *Pippin*) when I was 8. Because there's an unwritten rule that every Boca Bar Mitzvah has to have a theme, when it came time for me to choose one, I forewent such common choices as sports or movies or piano, and opted for . . . Broadway! My mom, because she loves a good show, was delighted with my choice, and my dad, because he still calls pants "dungarees," couldn't have cared less.

At a Bar Mitzvah reception, like at a wedding reception, there are assigned tables, and the tables are often named in relation to the reception's theme. So you can imagine each adult's delight upon entering my reception to learn which Broadway theater they'd be spending the night at. For instance, my mom's friend Stephanie Margolis was seated at the Belasco, and my dad, thanks to my mom's seating plan, was most likely at Broadway's smallest theater, the 593-seat Helen Hayes. My mother, as you may have assumed, was front-and-center at the Majestic. This table-naming, by the way, was entirely my 11-year-old idea.

The centerpieces on each of the theater-named tables were pillars comprised of lots of sparkly stuff. The least gay item was a small wooden piano spray-painted black. The pillars themselves were placed in upturned red, gold and black sequined hats, and they had actual Playbills attached to them (which my cousin in New York City helped procure), as well as long sprigs of gold-and-silver musical-note garlands. Each table was covered in shimmery confetti.

Above the kids' table, at which I sat front-and-center (even though, according to the Talmud, I had just become a man), was a giant sign that read "Matthew's Opening Night" in an Art Deco font. And all my friends (those who were allowed to be invited) received glittery silver hats. You can see the hats in action in this photo of my friends doing a kick line as Mike and Bobbie Roberts energetically spun the *Chorus Line* cast recording. That night, one singular sensation was me.

My special-edition Bar Mitzvah–specific yarmulkes were not made of the usual black fake velvet but instead were shiny silver fake satin. And for souvenirs, instead of the typical "I was a star at Jessica Grossman's Bat Mitzvah!" T-shirts, guests received a lovely chocolate in the shape of . . . a theater ticket.

Finally, the temple's social hall was filled with silver, white and black balloons. (Admittedly, not so gay.) But when combined with giant Art Deco-esque floor-to-ceiling black and white standees, seen in the kick-line photo, the gayness quotient went up measurably.

The tiny woman in the photo with the balloons is my late great-grandmother, Rose Stirberg, and the primary genetic reason I've been 5′4″ since the late '80s. I mention her and the balloons together for a specific reason. In 1989, Rose was 86, and she no longer could see very well. When she was led into the social hall for the reception, she glimpsed the black balloons, turned to my grandmother, her daughter, and whispered, "The band is all *shvartzes*?!" Even though that really has nothing to do with the gayness of my Bar Mitzvah, it's clearly worth passing on.

So you can see that my Bar Mitzvah was not lavish or fancy or extravagant. In fact, if you study the photos closely, you'll notice how . . . um . . . cheap it was. But it was also really gay. And while it certainly wasn't the gayest in the sense of Pride parade gay, with drag queens on floats and a midnight performance by Daphne Rubin-Vega, I'm proud that it was the most intellectually gay Bar Mitzvah, at least by Boca Raton standards. And even though we weren't wealthy, it ended up paying off—literally—to be able to invite a bunch of rich kids obliged to bring presents.

Most importantly, despite the event not being one of Boca Raton's more notable social engagements, I ended up having a gay old time.

Herzog Versus Davis

By Hal Sirowitz

MY MOTHER AND FATHER USED TO ARGUE over which side of the family had the most famous relative. My mother claimed it was her side: Al Davis, owner and president of the Oakland Raiders football team. He was related to her stepmother, but she wouldn't let that disqualify him. He treated her like a first cousin, so that was what she went by. To prove he was a relative she called his mother, Rose, and asked her to get him to send me a football autographed by the team. My sisters were mad that she didn't ask him to send them something. But she was afraid he might send them cheerleader's outfits. The last thing she wanted them to be was cheerleaders.

The problem with the autographed ball was that whenever I used it, the ink would come off on my hands. I tried to throw the ball so it wouldn't land on Daryle Lamonica's signature, but he was the John Hancock of the Raiders, which made that difficult to avoid. The more I threw the ball, the fuzzier the signatures became, until I could only make them out from memory. I had to retire the ball to preserve the names that were left. Playing with the ball decreased its value. I wished Al had sent me a plain one.

Al Davis also arranged for me to see his team play the New York Titans, who later became the Jets. After the game, I was taken into the locker room. I had the football so the players could sign their names again in darker ink. My mother had lent me her laundry pen. But the players were in the shower. It didn't make sense to ask naked men to sign the same ball again. But more importantly, I was transfixed watching the blood from their wounds flow down the drain. This cured me of my fantasies of becoming a professional football player.

Not everyone was impressed by my Al Davis connection, especially Jets and Giants fans. I also felt like an outsider because before and during each game I had to decide whether to be loyal to my family and root for the Raiders, or to my city and root for the local team. I chose the Raiders. But it was a philosophical nightmare.

On the other side, my father was related to the Chief Rabbi of Ireland, Isaac Herzog, a position made more interesting by the fact that Ireland was never known for having many Jews. The most famous Irish Jew was Joyce's Leopold Bloom. He wasn't even a real person. Herzog was eventually appointed Chief Rabbi of Israel. His son Chaim became a general in the Israeli army, a United Nations Ambassador and Israel's President.

While the Herzogs rose in stature, Al Davis was going through tough times, trying to replace losing quarterbacks with winning ones. Al had this theory that a good quarterback should be able to throw the ball almost the length of the entire field. He drafted quarterbacks with great arms but bad aim. The purpose of throwing long was to open up the field for smaller gains. But like Icarus, who thought he could fly, the Oakland quarterbacks thought the ball would land in the arms of the intended receiver. They were both proved wrong, though the quarterbacks didn't die like Icarus. They were just traded.

At some point, I thought having famous Israeli relatives would make Jewish girls like me more. But most weren't impressed, and they were even less impressed when I told them I'd never been to Israel. I said my father paid for a lot of trees to be planted in the Israeli desert. Therefore, I was indirectly responsible for the increase in shade. That didn't work either.

My father would say, "How could you compare a general with a football owner? Even if the team loses, it's not kicked out of the conference. It's rewarded with higher draft picks. But if General Herzog loses a battle, the Jews might be kicked out of their country. And even though Jerusalem is old, the Jewish State is new. It's like a baby having to take care of itself. But don't tell your mother I've said that. Just play along and tell her how great Al is. She knows his team is losing. They both need all the support they can get."

That's the story I was going to tell Chaim Herzog, the son of Isaac, who's also the Minister of Social Affairs and a member of the Knesset, Israel's parliament. I was in Israel attending the Kisufim Jerusalem Conference of Jewish Writers in April 2007. Isaac was gracious enough to take time off from the upcoming elections and to bring his wife along to meet me at a coffee shop. It was the first time I met someone important enough to have bodyguards. I ended up telling him another story about how my mother rewrote my Bar Mitzvah speech because I mentioned God too much. Instead of the speech being about my relationship to God, it was about my two famous relatives. When Isaac heard this, he said he felt bad about his family getting in the way of my search for God.

I never really looked at it that way.

Fake Farm

By Laura Silverman

THE FIRST FAMILY PET WE HAD was a beagle named Ginger. I don't remember much about her, but I'll always be indebted to her for giving me a good porn name: Ginger Chestnut. If it hadn't been for Ginger, I would have been Petey Chestnut. Still sexy. But not as sexy.

Petey was the fox terrier we got when I was 8. Soon after that we got Nicki, same breed, who was brought in to be Petey's wife and bear his children. After Nicki had her litter of puppies she pretty much went bat-shit crazy. We had a swimming pool in our backyard, and she became obsessed with biting our ankles every time we tried to go off the diving board. It would start as soon as you even got near the diving board, with a sort of warning growl, and by the time you got to the end she was going in for the kill. You had to hope she didn't have a good grip on you when you took that first bounce, which either forced her to retreat or tossed her into the water. The whole thing resulted in summers filled with bruised, bloody ankles and some crazy-assed dives, which I think is at least partly responsible for who we are today. Some crazy-assed divers.

Petey, the male dog, had his own obsession. He swam laps, back and forth, all day, every day, a task from which he would not be distracted. If you got in his path he would simply swim around you and rejoin his course. It was as if he were training, compelled by some unearthly force to condition himself for the day that he would receive his calling. Which brings us to the following.

My parents never loved each other. On their wedding night, my dad took a walk on the beach alone and cried. I imagine that my mom was glad to have him out of the room for a while. Having realized at the outset that their marriage had been a terrible mistake, they did what any reasonable two people would do. They had children. By the time I was nine the situation had become unbearable, and there was only one logical action left to take. Pack up the family and move to a farm.

Not a real farm. A real farm produces things. On a real farm, animals are acquired, bred and raised to provide labor, or to yield various consumable products. This was a fake farm. A few acres of land with a big red barn, a pond, a creek and some sheds where animals were brought in to create a farmlike appearance, and were otherwise left to enjoy an idle life without purpose. A few days before we moved to the fake farm, my dad's best friend gave us a baby goat as a gag gift. It's a great idea to give animals as gag gifts, by the way, because it's not like the animal is a living thing that continues to exist even after the joke is over. If left alone, the baby goat cried constantly, and we had to take turns sleeping with it in the garage. On moving day, the goat was staked out in front of the new house and its constant crying went unheeded, until someone happened to notice that Petey had the back end of the baby goat in his mouth and was trying to pull it free from its tether.

The goat was rushed to the vet, and Petey was scolded for his behavior, "No, Petey! No eating live baby goats we got as gag gifts! Bad dog!" But it was no use. The blood of decorative farm animals on his muzzle was intoxicating. He wanted more. And he was about to be shamelessly indulged.

The first thing you do when you move to a fake farm is to get some ducks, which can be purchased at a real farm. We started with three, one for each of us. We kept them in a little shed and we named them.

But it wasn't long before Petey found a way into the shed, got them each by the neck and shook them dead. So we went back to the real farm and bought more ducks, 10 of them, which the farmer bundled in twos and threes into burlap grain sacks and loaded into the back of our station wagon. This time we brought them down to the pond, where we thought they would be safer and have more freedom. They were as pretty as a picture on that pond, swimming around like ducks do, cutting swirly figures into the surface of the water. But Petey was a swimmer, a great swimmer, and one by one those ducks were hunted down and turned into little white feather storms on the water.

We began to find them almost daily, on our front doorstep, with Petey beside them, eyes bright, shoulders high, grinning like the village idiot with a new pair of shoes.

Another perfectly good duck would meet its final resting place—the big plastic trash can in the garage. What else were we supposed to do with them? It wasn't like we were going to eat them. That would mean ripping out their feathers and chopping their heads off, and that's just not the kind of thing that fake farm people do. We're not savages.

My dad tried to teach Petey not to kill the ducks. He would push his nose into the carcasses and say, "No! Bad dog!" He even went so far as to try and shame the dog out of killing, by tying a dead duck to him with a rope and making him walk around with it all day, which is a really disturbing thing for children to witness, but as far as Petey was concerned it was a reward, and he wore that duck like a medal, proud as the day is long, while at the same time enjoying the convenience of having his jaws free for more killing.

I don't remember how many times the ducks were replaced, but I remember the last time. I remember going to the real farm to get them, the whole family together on this particular day, and I remember watching the farmer stuff them into the grain sacks, 15 of them this time, packed in twos and threes, noisy, noisy ducks; piled into the back of the station wagon, flapping and honking and just going nuts back there. And all of us, uneasy about the grain sacks as usual, as we were about all the harsh realities of real farm things, but excited by it too, having ducks in burlap sacks like grain or any other cargo, like real farm people do, with all their calluses in the places where they need them. And those ducks just making the biggest racket you've ever heard, and all of us laughing about it. And then quieter, settling down now; and then quieter still. Then pulling up the driveway, opening the back of the station wagon, and it's too quiet, too still, and then a wave of panic, realizing that things change and become more modern every minute, and how could that farmer not know it when it's so everyday to pack up ducks in sacks, but then there's always going to be that one day when things are suddenly different and everybody has their own reasons for not seeing.

The sacks were made of plastic.

We pulled and ripped at their knotted tops and started dumping ducks onto the driveway, some dead, some stumbling, half-flapping, gasping, long languid necks swaying like drunken snakes reaching for some hallucinated prey. And then my parents on the ground, together on their knees on the ground, massaging duck hearts and blowing into duck beaks, saying, "This one's gone, hand me another," but it was no use, and duck after duck quit struggling toward life and stiffened into the unyielding posture of the dead.

And there we stood, stunned, embarrassed, distraught, silently observing the downy quilt of horror that lay at our feet, already dreading the inevitable heaping of a record 15 ducks into that trash can, when a kind of miracle happened: a tiny chest rising and falling. The extension of a wing. Back from the dead, as if by the hand of God, one little duck got to his feet, gave himself a good shake, and looked right at us, as if to say, "What?"

We named him Lucky, and it was not without ceremony that we carried him down to the pond and released him and watched him swim out, cutting those pretty swirls into the black shining surface of the water, glossy white feathers shimmering like angel's wings in the summer sun. Petey killed him later that afternoon.

BODY & SOUL

My Whole Hair Story

By Todd Rosenberg

I'M BALD. When it first started happening it freaked me out totally. I was 24 years old, living at home with my parents and managing a bookstore. I couldn't believe my hair was falling out. I dug through old family albums and looked at my family history hair-wise. Great Uncle Schlomo? Bald! Cousin Sol? Bald! Grandpa Max? Bald! Bald baldy bald!

Around this time, Hair Club for Men was running their late-night infomercials—practically on a loop. And like any shedding insomniac I watched this program over and over into the wee hours. I knew it backward and forward. The guy getting out of the pool. The guy in the convertible. The guy with the bikini chicks. The before (sad loser) and after (happy winner) photos. No problem they said! Wash and go they said! I finally went . . .

When I walked into this cheesy place, I saw one of the guys from the actual commercial! The guy from the pool! I recognized him immediately. It was like seeing a minor celebrity! I was surprisingly thrilled. But then I started really looking at his hair. It looked terrible.

Like this:

Before I could put two and two together, this hot chick named Stephanie came out and brought me into this "consultation room." Stephanie's cleavage looked like this:

Stephanie told me how important it was that I was doing this *now*. Because after I lost more hair people would "know." Stephanie told me it was still early enough that people would never be able to tell. So I signed up and gave Stephanie my life savings of $3,500. Some lady took a hair sample and explained the process. Here's how it works: They take your side hair ("strong hair") and weave a very tight braid with it all around your head. The horseshoe part. And they cut hair on top of your head extra short.

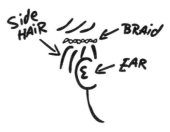

Then they take this mesh hairpiece and basically "anchor" it to your new side hair braid with fishing wire so it holds tight on top of your head. They tighten it down.

After that they style it up and I was quickly realizing that it was more styled up than I ever styled up before. It took, like, an hour. Gelled, brushed, gooped, shaped, hair-sprayed and finally done.

Stephanie told me how much better I looked. She said I looked *amazing*.

Did I mention Stephanie's cleavage looked like this?

I left in a daze and drove home almost crashing my car while checking my new look in the rearview mirror every two seconds. I walked in the door and shamefully showed my parents what I'd done. They were like, "Umm . . . If that's what makes you happy . . . We want you to be happy." I didn't feel happy.

I went to sleep that night and remember feeling strange because I didn't feel naked when I was totally naked. I kept touching my new hair. Gently pulling at it. I couldn't sleep. It itched. I wasn't naked anymore.

I woke up around 4 a.m. to get a jump start on my new hair before work. (I had to open the store at 9 a.m. and it was 10 minutes away. It was a big day at the bookstore that day because we were starting the move to a new location and the big boss was going to be there.)

My first day of wash and go! I took a shower and put all the shampoo and goop in it then tried to style my hair with the gel. The wash worked but the go wasn't going. I started panicking. The hair looked *nothing* like it looked the day before! It wasn't *90210*! It was this big matted tangled mess! Attached to my head! I couldn't get a comb through it! I couldn't make it look normal in any way! It was like a hair sculpture. It was so thick!

I kept adding more gel thinking that would help. It made things worse. It wouldn't dry. And eventually the obvious hit me—if I feel self-conscious about my thinning natural hair, I was going to feel 10 times more self-conscious about this crazy thing on my head!

I woke up my parents crying (I was 24) and told them how I had made a terrible mistake and I needed this thing off of my head immediately!! Problem was it was seriously totally attached to my head! I couldn't get it off and I had to go to work!

My dad and I got out the scissors and we cut the whole braid off. It was the only way. It was humiliating. I cried through it. When it was finally off, I had this weird no-hair hairline around the side of my head where the braid was—and it was cut really short on top but still kind of long on the sides. My "haircut" was bizarre.

But I went to work that day with a smile. The crazy anxiety panic was about completely gone. I actually felt good about my newly horribled hair. I knew I'd done what I could do to fix the problem and now I was free! Coworkers asked what happened and I told them I was drunk and my friends screwed with me.

Anyway, to this day that was the best $3,500 I ever spent because I learned such an amazing lesson from it. I knew there was nothing more I could do about what was happening—so I just let it go. If I had kept that hairpiece on I just wouldn't have been me. And I like this me.

Half and Half

By Raven Snook

WHEN I WAS ABOUT 5 my parents sat me down and explained that I was half
Christian and half Jewish. My father had been raised as a Christian Scientist
and my mother had been brought up a Brooklyn Jew, and even though neither
of them practiced anymore, they wanted me to understand my heritage, that
I was half and half.

Now, I was a very literal child so I decided that my right side was Christian and my left side was Jewish. This imaginary divide was emphasized even
more when I sprouted a tiny pointy growth on the left side of my head. The
doctor said that it was just a benign tumor, but I knew better. Jennifer—the
most popular girl in my kindergarten class because she wore all-purple all the
time—had told me that all Jews had horns. Since I was only half Jewish, it
made sense that I only had one on my left side.

As I grew up, I was obsessed with keeping both of my sides in balance.
I didn't want one side to outweigh the other. My Christian side already seemingly had the advantage in that I was right-handed. So I wanted to make sure
my Jewish side never felt left out.

This was really hard because my parents opted to send me to a grammar
school at the Cathedral Church of St. John the Divine. It wasn't as Christian as

it sounds. This was the '70s so the school was very multi-cultie, hippie-dippy, embracing all creeds, colors and confusions, so I fit right in. The pastor was even cool when I told him that even though I was willing to go to chapel once a week, only the right side of my body would be participating. When I recited the Lord's Prayer I looked like Billy Idol singing "Rebel Yell."

While the pastor was understanding, my fellow classmates weren't, and after a couple of weeks I realized I was going to have to talk through both sides of my mouth if I was going to make it through school without a perpetual wedgie. After a couple years at Cathedral—not to mention a lifetime in our predominantly Christian culture—it became clear that my Christian side was beating the crap out of my Jewish side.

So in fifth grade I asked my mom to send me to Hebrew school. This was a really tough transition for me. Every day I would leave the beautiful gothic arches of St. John the Divine to go to the claustrophobic yellow brick walls of the SAJ Reconstructionist synagogue. The rabbi, Allan Miller, didn't seem to believe in God, and throughout every service, he would try to convince us of that too, just so he could have atheistic company. Every time the cantor finished davening, Rabbi Miller would read a section of the Torah and then deconstruct it as if it were a Thomas Pynchon novel. Then he'd end the service by singing "Adon Olam" to the tune of "Rock Around the Clock."

Despite my best efforts to find religious equilibrium, I remained pretty imbalanced until I got to ninth grade and went to my first secular school, the High School of the Performing Arts (yes, the *Fame* school). It was there that I found God, or specifically, Jesus. I wore all-black clothes. I dyed my hair jet black and I started to collect crucifixes. Big ones. Which I wore right between my tits. Even though my mother had no problem sending me to a school that had the words *cathedral* and *church* in its name, my crosses were more than she could bear. She pleaded, she prodded, she grounded, she threatened, she even bought me a rhinestone-encrusted Jewish star—and trust me, those are hard to find—hoping I'd trade my crosses for a shimmering Star of David. But I was like, "Um, sparkly Jewish star over a dead guy on a cross bleeding profusely? I don't think so!" The best my mom could do was guilt me into not wearing crosses during my Bat Mitzvah—after which I promptly quit synagogue.

Around the same time I more or less quit school. I was too busy hanging out at places like the Peppermint Lounge and the Pyramid Club to be bothered with academics. Suddenly crosses were no longer my mother's main concern. My 20-year-old Aryan-looking boyfriend, who was in the Navy and liked to deal heroin on the side, was. She knew she had to do something drastic to get me to change my ways. So the summer after I failed all my ninth-grade classes, she announced that she had accepted a job transfer and that we were moving . . . to Paris.

As if I didn't have enough issues being a Jew already, she moved me to France, a block from Notre Dame, a structure so stunning it could seduce anyone into converting! After school and on weekends, I would get stoned, go into this gorgeous cathedral and watch the colors in the stained glass windows kind of like . . . go together.

I attended the American High School of Paris, where I did my arty Goth thing. I was in choir, and after a couple of weeks the director, Mrs. Pruitt, came up to me and asked if I wanted to join the choir at the American Cathedral in Paris where she was the conductor. "I know you're half Jewish," she said. Apparently my mother had made sure everyone knew. "You won't have to participate in the religious service if you don't want to. You can just come in on Sunday mornings and sing hymns. You have a lovely voice."

I don't know if I just wanted to piss off my mom even more, or if I truly wanted to sing, or maybe I wanted to go to that dark side, my Christian side, just a little bit more, but I said, "Sure." That next Sunday, when any self-respecting Goth would be asleep, I got up, put on my crosses (hey, it was the right place to wear them!) and went to the American Cathedral in Paris.

Mrs. Pruitt introduced me to the rest of the choir, a combination of congregation members and ringers: professional singers hired to give glory to

God on key. We quickly sang through the morning's hymns, donned billowy black gowns and headed upstairs.

"Now, I know you're not that familiar with church," Mrs. Pruitt said. Little did she know. "Just follow Kathy, the woman on your right. Whatever she does, you do it too."

We sang a hymn as we walked down the aisle and filed into the pews as the priest began the service. He preached. He prodded. He pleaded. He guilted. He sounded like my mother. I tuned him out and soon I had lost track of what was going on.

Suddenly Kathy got up, so I jumped up alongside her. She exited the pew. I exited too. She started heading up the steps toward the altar. I followed. Then she knelt down. That's when I realized I had fucked up.

The priest stopped in front of me and dangled the wafer in front of my face. "Oy vey," I whispered, as the priest gave me the Sacrament, after which I took a really big swig of that awful cheap red wine. But in that moment, as I consumed the body and blood of Christ, it hit me: It didn't matter that I was technically half and half. In my body and in my blood and in my soul, I felt 100 percent Jew.

To this day, I always feel a swell of Semitic pride whenever I pass a Catholic church. Thanks to their Communion I was finally made whole.

Weight Watchers at Gunpoint

By Wendy Shanker

I FINALLY STOPPED DIETING a couple of years ago. Now I feel quite content with my juicy, Jewish, curvy (a.k.a. "voluptuous" on JDate) bod. But back in the day, I tried every diet there is, from South Beach to the hot-dogs-and-vanilla-ice-cream diet (oh yeah, it exists) to Jenny Craig. And I spent a mad amount of money at Weight Watchers.

Although Weight Watchers constantly changes their language—for example, WW is no longer a "diet" but a "flexible food plan"—the gist of the thing doesn't change. Stop eating. Start moving. Lose weight. The clientele is mostly women wearing their 12s and 14s over their Spanx, who've been told their whole lives that they're "big-boned." There's always one Midwestern 300-pound woman at the weekly meetings, there with her equally large mom. They'll both end up on the "Half Their Size!" cover of *People* magazine. And of course, there's always one overweight guy who will lose 60 pounds in about three weeks. Damn you and your male metabolism.

The Weight Watchers leaders are truly inspiring people who've somehow followed the plan and made it a lifestyle. Most have reached their goal weights and maintained them. Except this one guy who used to lead the group I went to in downtown Manhattan, who hadn't seen his goal weight for at least 25 or

30 pounds. He used to tell us, "When we talk about one bread, we mean half a Lender's Bagel. Not a bagel store bagel, like a Pick-A-Bagel. You know the big ones that weigh about half a pound? Hmm, I love me an everything bagel at Pick-A-Bagel. Toasted, with veggie cream cheese . . ." He always left me hankering for a bagel with a schmear.

Someone at a Weight Watchers meeting, like the Midwestern lady, always asks this kind of question: "If I eat three to-may-tohs, instead of two to-may-tohs, how do I account for those points? Should I use some of my optional calories, or . . ." Now, points are confusing. But you and I know that the problem is probably excess Two-Bite Brownies, not excess tomatoes. Very few of us end up at Weight Watchers because we overdid it on veggies.

One night I went to my weekly meeting in a hotel conference center on the Upper West Side of Manhattan. I was in line, waiting to be weighed in, when I heard a crash. I turned around to find a guy standing there, wearing a ski mask and pointing a gun at me. Another masked man lurched out from behind the desk, clutching a poor Weight Watchers clerk by the neck and holding a gun to her head. For a minute I was confused, thinking this had to be some sort of dramatic new scare tactic. Like: "Weight Watchers—Lose Weight or Die!" Then, horrified, I understood that we were being held up.

The masked men forced all of us (including the Midwest Tomato Lady and the Fat Guy Who Loses Weight in No Time) to lie down on the floor in the conference room. Part of me longed to do a quick roll, kick one criminal in the balls, grab his gun and somersault over to crack the other guy across the skull. But because I'm not exactly La Femme Nikita, and because I was terrified, I stayed put. I tried to do whatever I could to shelter myself from the reality of the situation and distract myself from the panicked whispers of the other members around me.

As I was lying facedown on hotel carpeting with my hands clasped behind my head, my heart was beating a mile a minute. Why us? Why threaten a group of nice, moderately fat people who were already humiliated enough by having to show up at Weight Watchers? They probably assumed that we were dumb and slow and weighed down by the Ding Dongs in our pockets. I imagined the cops bursting in, taking the thieves by surprise. The cops would shout, "Put down the fat-free Smart Snacks, you bastards! I will give you to the count of three to put down the Smart Snacks!" The criminals would declare, "We will give up the hostages in exchange for one box of berries 'n' cream muffins, two *Get It Moving* exercise tapes and a year's supply of Smart Ones frozen dinners!" Then the cops would come back with: "Will you accept a case of pineapple beef teriyaki dinners and a complimentary subscription to *Weight Watchers* magazine instead?" The crooks would confer and say, "Yes, we will!" We'd all jump up and cheer, and someone would make some air-popped popcorn with no salt or butter (three points) and we'd all go to a spinning class at Crunch.

But that's not what went down.

I prayed for safety, figuring it was Shema time, as the crooks came around to strip us of our jewelry and the contents of our purses and wallets. When they finished making their rounds, they told us that if we moved they'd kill us. Then they left. After a couple of silent, scary minutes, the Weight Watchers leader courageously got up and called the police. We all checked in with each other as we shook off the fear. The cops arrived moments later.

As a cop took my statement, he noticed that he was standing next to a scale. He asked, "And then what happened? Did you hear anything?" Then, thinking I wouldn't notice, *he got on the scale and weighed himself.* This cop wasn't fat or thin. He was just a regular, goyishe thirtysomething white dude with a crew cut and a badge, but that scale was calling out to him. He gave himself a little nod of approval, and stepped back down to continue our conversation. If I didn't understand before, that cop on the scale proved to me that we live in a society that is ridiculously obsessed with fat. In that moment, how could a cop be more curious about his weight than my safety?

I left thinking about the headline on the next day's *New York Post*: SCARED THIN. I was lucky to be alive. I stopped by the ATM to refill my wallet, and bought a box of Entenmanns's Chocolate Chip Cookies to celebrate my longevity. Fine, I bought two.

And determined not to let some petty crooks make me live my life in fear, I returned to my Weight Watchers meeting the following week. A security guard was posted by the door. The police had found the thieves. Turns out they were crackheads and had sold our jewelry for crack. Crack—also a very efficient way to lose weight.

Aside from the leader, I was the only person who returned. But that was the last time I went to Weight Watchers. The way I see it, being held up at Weight Watchers was pretty much a sign from God that I should be happy with myself the way I am. So every opportunity I get, I take my bagel with a schmear.

Mustorderitis

By Michael Showalter

I HAVE AN AFFLICTION called "mustorderitis." It's a common ailment, though largely undiagnosed. Mustorderitis is the obsessive-compulsive need to order certain foods when they appear on the menu, no matter what. This affliction affects both sexes of all ages.

I know what you're asking yourself: "Do I have mustorderitis?" Well, if you're like millions of other men and women then the answer is yes. Most assuredly, yes.

"What are the symptoms?" Dry mouth, excitability, telling stories about "the way my grandmother does it," unexplained weight gain, guilt, shame, embarrassment. These are the telltale signs.

"What causes mustorderitis?" Debates have raged for centuries. Is it a sin against God? Or a disease that attacks even the most pious of our kind? (e.g., Ralph Waldo Emerson was said to have had a desperate yen for jalapeño peppers). Some doctors say it's hereditary, but studies have shown that it can also be attributed to excessive exposure to fluorescent lighting commonly found in shitty restaurants. Other experts have put forth the Phantom Taste Bud Theory. They propose that mustorderitis is psychosomatic and that the craving is nothing more than the sensory recollection of a previously enjoyed meal.

Now, there are the lucky ones. Those select few with the sweettoothmustorderitis variation, which applies to tiramisu, milkshakes, pralines and cream and Skittles. These are low-risk items that lead to few or no major consequences. If you have this variation, then you have dodged a bullet. A bullet made of food!

But for us real unfortunates, the situation is hopeless. There is no known cure for this ailment. Oh sure, there's a whole slew of ineffective home remedies, like eating bat penises, and those ridiculous homeopathic elixirs like St. John's Wort. There's an array of 12-step programs out there: Mustorder-Anon, Children of Adult Mustorderitis Sufferers Anon. The doctor-prescribed medications cause a whole buffet of terrible side effects such as trench foot, malaria, wet brain and the sniffles. It's like this: If you've got mustorderitis, you're fucked.

A personal case study: I'm on a country highway. It's January. I'm hungry. There are no fast-food service areas in sight. I exit into a small town and come to a greasy spoon diner. A vintage Merle Haggard tune crackles softly from the jukebox. Elderly men and women are playing electronic bingo. They all wear trucker hats and Windbreakers. They seem . . . dead.

A waitress straight out of central casting hands me a menu. I peruse it but I don't need to because I know what I want. I want grilled cheese with fries. Why? It's safe. If I order anything else I'll have explosive diarrhea for the remainder of my journey. I'm getting the grilled cheese with fries! End of conversation. Only, see . . .

This particular diner serves gazpacho. It's hidden in the bottom corner, handwritten and misspelled "*gazpatcho*," but it's there. I definitely don't want to order gazpacho, but . . . I think I'm about to have a mustorderitis flare up. I can feel it. The soup is calling to me in a seductive voice, "Michaaael, oooorder meeee!" Shut up, gazpacho-voice! You don't own me! But I love you! I can't say no to you! I can't! I can't! I can't! Ahhhhhhhhh!

Then, the voice of reason comes in. "Order grilled cheese! You can do it!" This voice is intelligent and stern. It sounds like Laurence Fishburne. "You're at a burger joint in the middle of West Virginia. They've never even *heard* of Spain here! Just order the grilled cheese and fries, eat it and run like hell! Run like hell and don't look back! Don't never look back!"

"Can I take your order?" The waitress is looking at me like she knows I'm weak. Why is she looking at me like that? I hate her. I hate her because I hate myself.

"Yes, I'll have the . . ."

"The what?"

Grilled cheese, Michael! Say it! Goddamn, just say it!

"The . . ."

"Yes?"

Suddenly the walls inside the restaurant start to spin. I'm drowning. Red lights flashing inside my head. Spinning! Throbbing! Pulsing! Color! Texture! Taste!

"GAZPACHO!" I blurt out. And I say it with a Spanish accent so that it comes out like "gazpatho."

She's incredulous. I'm panting, out of breath, heaving, confused. What have I done? Before I can even get my wind back the waitress has disappeared into the kitchen. I instantly regret my decision.

You know how this story ends: me eating a bowl of warm, ketchup-y, pale orange salsa with a grapefruit spoon, crying like a baby into my food.

So, why did I do it? Because I have a disease.

That day I vow never to do it again, like so many times before. But two weeks later I'm at a Chinese restaurant in Hoboken. They serve Reuben sandwiches. And fuck, I love a Reuben sandwich!

Boiling Point

Allen Salkin

I WAS ON THE INDONESIAN ISLAND of Flores, famous for its multicolored volcanic lakes, and I came across a bunch of backpackers talking to a restaurant owner about the possibility of him roasting them a dog for dinner. The backpackers were acting like it would be a real adventure. Here they were at the end of the earth, they seemed to be thinking, far from all the social mores that keep their friends and parents chained to desks, far from such wondrous places as Kelimutu, the volcano at the top of Flores. Why not live dangerously, break a taboo?

The restaurant owner was ready to do pretty much anything to get some money out of these travelers. Even the five dollars a day that backpackers could live on in Indonesia was a lot of money to the people of Flores. His restaurant, located in a village at the base of Kelimutu, sat on the side of a dirt hill. There was a circle of rocks to sit on and an open fire with an iron grate over it and two iron pots on top—one for frying, the other for boiling. A few feet farther up the hill was a smoldering pile of garbage. In the village, a flame was put to whatever garbage was left after the dogs and pigs and chickens were done rooting through the peels and plastic bottles the humans left behind.

So the restaurant owner was willing, if the travelers wanted to pay $20, to slaughter one of those dogs and have it butchered, cooked and ready for the travelers to eat the next day when they returned from their long hike up to see the turquoise, lapis and ruby-red volcanic lakes on Kelimutu's crown.

I had no interest in eating a dog. I was in Indonesia for two weeks, trying to see some of the wonders I hadn't had time to see when I visited years before. I'd just traveled from California to Guangzhou in China with my father to help him at the trade fair where he buys rubber duckies and rattles by the container load to import for dollar stores in the U.S.

I hadn't eaten dog in China, where it is a traditional dish for some people. Those who eat it believe they are ingesting the dog's life force, which will help keep them warm during cold seasons. I had heard that dog was something Indonesians would eat. Looking around the mountainside town where there was no electricity except the kind from batteries, where the people lived in shacks of corrugated iron and wood and rocks, it wasn't hard to understand that sometimes they were hungry here. During the seasons when the travelers didn't come and nothing was being harvested, they would eat whatever they could to avoid starving: leaves, cans of United Nations food-aid tomatoes, dogs.

"So you can do?" a woman from Holland asked the restaurant owner.

"Yes, yes. You want sure?" he replied.

I watched the faces of these travelers, young men and women from places like England, Norway and Germany. A light was growing in their faces. They liked the idea of how crazy, how daring they were about to be.

I wanted to smother that light. I didn't know why I felt so strongly about it, but the words just erupted. "Don't eat a dog here," I blurted before they could say another word to the restaurant owner. They turned to look at me. I was the only American. I am often the only American. I continued, trying to back up my outburst. "If you want to eat a dog, do it in China where they know what they're doing. Don't let these savages kill a poor dog for you. It's not right and it won't even be worth it because they won't cook it well."

I could see they didn't like me calling the Flores natives savages. It was very insensitive. It was something some colonial overlord villain would say in an old movie, as he ordered his slaves to paddle faster. The other travelers looked at me with hatred. I wasn't one of them at all. I was an American asshole.

On the way to Flores a couple days before, I had stopped at Komodo Island, a national park where 25-foot-long monster lizards with forked yellow tongues and poisonous fangs live. Before the hike to where the dragons congregated, each backpacker had been asked to pitch in a few rupees to buy a goat. Local guides led us and the little goat, which walked quietly, bleating rarely, on an hourlong walk. Up at the viewing area, the guides hacked open the goat's throat with a machete. They didn't look happy about having to do it. As the blood pulsed out of its neck into the sandy dirt and the little creature kicked and spasmed out the last of its life, its eyes slowly unfocusing, they held it down gently with weathered hands and looked away. When the goat was finally still, the guides gathered it in their arms and, after counting "1-2-3" to make sure the travelers were ready with their cameras, hurled the goat over a rail to the pack of Komodo dragons waiting on a dry riverbed below. Fifteen or 20 of the Caucasian-skin-colored beasts swung open their mighty jaws to attack the warm carcass and the goat was ripped in half and eaten—bone, fur, hooves—and all within eight seconds. Completely gone.

Back at the restaurant on Flores after my outburst, the other travelers kept the subject of the dog alive for a little while, but it soon fizzled. By the next afternoon we'd all been up to the volcano and back. We'd seen what we'd come to that village to see and by the next day we were somewhere else. One dog lived one more day.

The Eyes of
the Beholder

By Najla Said

I'M ARAB. I thought I'd just lay that out there before you get confused.

I don't look or act like an Arab . . . well, what I mean to say is that people don't *think* I'm an Arab. I guess that's because I'm not dark and swarthy or whatever people think I'm supposed to be. I am *really* hairy though.

My name is Najla. And that's totally Arab. It's probably the number-one way you can tell that I am Arab. I hated my name when I was growing up. My parents always tried to tell me it made me special.

"It may not be Jennifer or Laura or Amy, but your name is *beautiful* because it has a *meaning*."

"It does? What does it mean?!!"

"It means 'big black eyes like a cow'!"

Apparently, that is a compliment. And it felt that way for a while. But then, when I was older, I met a girl named Maha, who is part Arabian. (Arabian is totally not politically correct to say, but I like it, so I use it.)

Maha said to me, "Wow . . . Najla—that's pretty . . . I don't know that name. What does it mean?"

"It means 'big black eyes like a cow,' " I told her with a huge beaming smile.

"Oh my God . . . that's what my name means!" she said. Not the reaction I was expecting.

"Wait, what? You must be wrong. That doesn't make sense."

"No, I swear, Maha means 'big black eyes like a cow' too!"

At this point, I realized that my parents were evil liars. I was not by any means special if there was another name that had the same unique and beautiful meaning as mine. So I went to my mom, all outraged, and was like, "Um, excuse me? Maha says her name means 'big black eyes like a cow' too!' "

You could tell she was caught off guard, because she looked at me like a deer in the headlights. "Wait a minute, Naji," she said "They are similar. But they are different."

"How are they different, Mommy? There is not a lot of room for variety in 'big black eyes like a cow'!"

"Wait. Please. Give me a minute. I have to think about it."

So while she was thinking about it I went to the computer and found this—wildly popular, I'm sure—website called Arabic Names for Your Baby or something. And I looked up "Najla" and I looked up "Maha," and sure enough, they mean the same thing. But what is *weirder* is that there are also about 20 other names that mean "big black eyes like a . . . something"—big black eyes like a cow, big black eyes like a donkey, big black eyes like a horse, big black eyes like a monkey . . .

So I called my brother, who was being scholarly and studying Arabic at the time, and I asked him what the deal was.

"Oh yeah, Naj, but they're not exactly the same. That website is wrong. Maha actually means 'big black eyes like an ibex' so it's not totally the same. Plus, Najla has a second meaning anyway."

"Really? What?" I was certain he was going to tell me that Najla's second meaning is something like "really hot funny girl who everyone wants to make out with." Or like another Indian name on that website which means "One with full, rounded breasts." Instead my brother said, "Najla also means 'gaping wound.' "

Arabs are so weird. No wonder no one gets us.

But I guess my name sort of fits because I do have enormous eyes—and they're bigger than they're meant to be because I have another totally Arab thing going on: huge dark circles. Whenever I go out without concealer, I look like I have pneumonia. Every single time I venture out of my house without makeup, I run into someone who gives me a "poor thing" sort of look and then asks, "What's wrong?? Are you sick? Have you been crying?" and so I say, "No . . . this is what I look like without makeup." And the person is then usually totally startled and they don't know what to say and they give me this weird look like they're thinking, "Oh that's some weird ethnic thing I don't understand." So most of the time I just pretend I have a disease.

Or I pretend to be Jewish, because with my big features and black hair, I kind of look like a lot of my Jewish friends. Plus, who didn't want a Bat Mitzvah? All my friends were getting thousands of dollars in cash and prizes and loads of attention. Of course I wanted to be one of them. Unfortunately though, being Palestinian and all, I couldn't totally fake it. When I was in first grade, I remember sitting in the back of the car with my brother—my dad was driving us somewhere, and I started happily singing my favorite Christmas carol: "Noel, noel, noel, noel, born is the king of *Isra*—"

My brother smacked me.

"Owwwwwwwwww . . . why'd you hit me?"

"Because, Naj," he said. "You're supposed to say 'born is the king of *Occupied Palestine.'* "

Oh Jesus.

Finding My Kegel Muscles

By Stephen Glass

IT HAS BEEN A LONG TIME since I have discovered a new part of my anatomy.

Just last month, I thought my body was a lot like Earth, all mapped out. Indeed, I remember the very last portion of my body to be designated, a sliver of flesh, a small unlikely parcel, so tucked away between this and that, I did not know it—like the Kingdom of Monaco—had been deemed an independent land of its own. But this is not a story about that dark, nether region.

This is a story of a different secret geography.

Having recently moved to Los Angeles from New York, I decided to try to get into this Southern California living and get in better touch with my body.

I called my mother and told her of my plan.

"For my birthday, I'm going to get back into shape," I said.

"What do you mean *back* into shape?" she laughed. "You've never been in shape in your life. There's nothing to get *back* to."

My mother had a point.

The only focused effort I ever made at a gym was in the early 1980s when my mom signed me up for break-dancing lessons at the aerobics center she attended in the Chicago suburb where we lived.

Each Saturday for several months, African-American men and women were bussed in from Chicago to teach a few dozen junior high students—including me and an overweight girl whom the jocks called The Purple Cow—how to moonwalk, headspin and windmill.

After class one day, one of the African-American guys took me aside.

"You're being dissed," he told me.

I thought I knew what the word *dis* meant, but was not completely certain. At that time, my understanding of African-American expressions was limited to the poorly dubbed Eddie Murphy cassettes I had been illicitly passed at Camp Menominee.

"She's better than you," the break-dancer explained, pointing to The Purple Cow.

I never returned.

So, as you can see, my need, 21 years later, to prove that I could do something physical, anything physical, was desperate.

I signed up for Pilates lessons at a studio near my Silverlake home.

Pilates, I found out, even more so than yoga, is still overwhelmingly practiced by women. In fact, I was the only male in the studio and so right away I asked my instructor, Liza*, whether this was an acceptable exercise for men.

"It's great for men," Liza reassured me. "Josef Pilates was a man and he was the greatest Pilates practitioner of them all."

Liza told me that she had been a dancer before she was a Pilates instructor. She named several dance companies she had been a member of and appeared hurt when I hadn't heard of any of them.

"I worked at Jumbo's too," she said, naming the strip club on Hollywood Boulevard. "You've definitely been there."

I hadn't, but I pretended to have been. If not knowing any of her dance companies had hurt, I figured not knowing her strip club would have been devastating—to have revealed so much of herself and to go so unrecognized. It's probably what a porn star feels like when she gets a bad review.

* Liza's name has been changed to protect the Pilates method.

Liza put me through the classic Pilates paces. She taught me the Hundreds and we worked on the Reformer. But it was during the Series of Five, a set of stretches, that things between us unraveled.

"Do you know what kegel muscles are?" she asked me while my hands and legs were waving wildly, as if I were drowning.

"Yes," I squeaked out, although I had no idea why she was raising the female sex muscle.

"Your kegel muscles are your problem," Liza said. "You need to squeeze your kegel muscles when you do these exercises."

"I don't have kegel muscles," I said.

I thought this was obvious. Women have told me that they perform kegel exercises in order to have better orgasms. So I've always assumed that the kegel muscle resides inside the vagina. I don't have a vagina. Ergo, I do not have kegel muscles.

That was the logic I had been living with for decades.

"Of course you have kegel muscles," Liza replied.

I should have pleaded ignorance here. No one has ever told me that I *don't* have kegel muscles. They've only told me that women do.

In school, boys and girls were often separated during health class. I assumed that this was so the teachers could talk to the girls about their embarrassing things, like tampons and kegel muscles, and talk to us boys about our embarrassing things, which I'm still too embarrassed to mention here. But maybe for the girls it was just about tampons. And maybe the presence of kegel muscles was so obvious to everyone but me, that they went unmentioned.

Or is it kegel muscle in the singular? I don't even know how many a person can have.

I also read men's magazines, from which I have learned all kinds of things. But never has there been a mention of a male kegel muscle. You would think that if men had a kegel muscle we'd be developing it, making it bigger, stronger. We have the technology; where's the *Six Million Dollar Man* kegel muscle?

Further damning evidence against the male kegel muscle: My parents never spoke of it over dinner. For my father and mother—a doctor and a nurse, both Jewish and without shonda—no anatomical feature was off limits at dinner. Indeed, this was the very purpose of dinner. My brother and I would talk about school. My parents would talk about body parts. We talked about penises, testicles, nipples and uteri. But never the kegel muscle.

But here's the best evidence against the male kegel muscle: I don't receive spam about it. If it were inside of me, I'm sure I would get 10 e-mails a day.

Thus I proclaimed with great confidence, to Liza, a former stripper and Pilates instructor, who had probably seen more of the human anatomy than my father, a gastroenterologist for 25 years: "Men do not have kegel muscles!"

"After more lessons, you'll understand your body more and then you'll feel your kegel muscle," Liza explained. "So do you want our eight-class introductory special?"

This Pilates thing was starting to sound like a cult to me: We'll show you the wonders of the male kegel muscle and other secrets of the universe, but only if you spend more money. Sign here.

Having previously been deceived about the human body (a Hebrew-school teacher convinced us boys that we had one more rib than our female classmates because that's how Eve was born from Adam), I was determined not to be fooled again.

I told Liza that I had to ascertain whether I even had a kegel muscle before I paid her to find it.

In my car, on the way home from the studio, I called Ask Me Now. You may have read about this service. You call a phone number and leave a message with any question. The message is transmitted to an office building (read: probable sweatshop) in the Philippines where it is researched, and minutes later, your cell phone is text messaged with the answer.

"Do I have kegel muscles?" I asked an anonymous Filipino. "And if so where are they? By the way I'm a man."

Ah, the joy of globalization.

A minute later my cell phone buzzed. The answer had come back: "Due to our editorial policy, we are unable to answer certain types of questions."

Julie, my girlfriend, was home when I returned from Pilates.

"Do I have kegel muscles?" I demanded of her when I walked in the door.

"I don't know," she said. "I'm not a doctor."

"Then how do you know *you* have them?"

"I'm flexing them right now," she said.

That wasn't helpful. I couldn't see Julie doing anything. For all I know, the kegel muscle is just a fiction invented by a vast female conspiracy and, of course, Dr. Arnold Kegel. (Was he as good at flexing his muscle as Pilates was at his stretches?)

"You can exercise it by stopping your pee suddenly," Julie said.

That sounded like torture.

I Googled "kegel muscles" and found the KegelMaster 2000.

It looked like a pair of hinged salad tongs you insert inside of yourself and open and close.

"Don't suffer needlessly. Try the KegelMaster. The World's First Progressive Resistance Vaginal Exerciser. You owe it to yourself."

I do?

I called the 1-800 number.

"Kegelmaster, how can I help you?" a woman answered. She had a slight Southern accent.

"Do men have kegel muscles?" I asked.

"I've heard that they do, but I wouldn't be an authority on that."

"Well, will your device help me?"

"I can't imagine it will."

"Is that because I don't have a vagina?" I demanded to know. (My worldview was already blown apart. I wanted at least this to be clear.)

"That's right," she said.

"Is there anything I can do for my kegel muscles?" I asked.

"I've heard stories," she said.

"Like what?" I asked.

"Like sometimes men hang a towel . . ."

She then went silent.

"They hang a towel?"

"Yeah," she said, but she would not elaborate.

In the end, and after I had calmed down, I called Liza and signed up for those eight introductory Pilates sessions. I decided the male kegel muscle is a lot like the female G-spot: It's better to search and to hope, even when it seems to be against all odds.

And it sure beats hanging a towel.

Body Hair

By Annette Ezekial Kogan

AFTER YEARS OF EXPERIMENTING with all sorts of contraptions and chemicals, suffering voluntarily at my own hands as well as those of others, I have arrived at the calculation that 30 percent of my life has been spent removing hair.

Wax, bleach, razors, electrolysis, depilatory creams. I have developed a process as efficient and streamlined as possible for someone of my—let's call it exotic—coloring. Family photo albums illustrate all too clearly the different stages of my search and struggle to find the ideal brow line—from their untamed wild days at my Bat Mitzvah, to their overplucked anemia at college graduation. I keep a magnifying mirror hidden in the drawer of my desk. When I return home from a trip, no matter how brief, I rush immediately to the mirror so I can examine how far my brows have strayed in the course of my absence. I can occasionally lose myself in a plucking binge. I could write a dissertation on the advantages of the round-edged tweezers.

At a recent dinner party, the conversation turned to dictatorship and the central role the mustache plays in any cult of personality. Hitler, Stalin, Tito, Enver Hoxha. My heart was suddenly racing as I stared down at my plate, avoided eye contact and furtively raised my hand to cover my upper lip—which was of course impeccably smooth. I've come a long way from the days on the school playground when someone (a boy, generally) would suddenly stop whatever he was doing and stare at my face. "Hey," he would blurt out, pointing at me as I talked faster and faster about Mr. Driscoll the gym teacher's droopy sweatpants. "Hey—you've got a mustache!"

Since then there's been a lifetime of waxing. I don't go to the fancy places, the so-called urban spas where they light candles, play mood music and lather you up in expensive lotions—a rather comical prelude to ripping out the hair from your most sensitive and delicate areas. Instead, I frequent the narrow storefront tucked between the newspaper stand and the fish store. It has a neon sign in the window blinking the word NAILS, with half the letter *A* missing.

The place conforms perfectly to my slightly shameful feelings about the whole procedure, and I enter furtively, as if ducking into a triple-X movie theater in the middle of the afternoon. When the "girls"—immigrants so recent they can barely say hello in English—ask what I want, I mutter as quietly as possible, "Bikini wax." The madam of the place points to one of the girls, and I follow her dutifully yet stealthily upstairs. In the tiny closet of a room, with only a doctor's bench covered in crinkly paper and a makeshift stove keeping the pot of wax warm, the girl doesn't even bother to step out while I undress. Instead, she stands behind me, arms folded, and watches as I remove my shoes, socks and pants and hoist myself up on the table. Tact not being these girls' strong point, they usually take one look at my inner thighs and let out a heavily accented "Oh my God!"

"Sorry," I answer in total sympathy, wishing I could pat the poor thing on the shoulder without seeming condescending. "I shouldn't have waited so long."

But she is already busy slapping powder on my legs and tucking protective cloth beneath the edges of my underpants. I continue staring off to the side, deep into the eyes of my own reflection in the mirror on the opposite wall. The girl is so quick and skillful that I almost forget the pain as she blows on the steaming wax, slathers it onto my skin with a Popsicle stick, pats it down with a rag, then tears it mercilessly from my body without a moment's hesitation, rhythmic as a machine.

The pain is intense but I never so much as wince: To make even the slightest jerking movement is totally out of the question. I remain perfectly still, gazing at my own face, deeply proud of my valiance. If—and it has happened, albeit seldomly—I receive a compliment, for example, "You tough lady," it is as though a gold medal for bravery has been placed over my modestly bowed head. My eyes closed and head still resolutely turned to the side, the girl continues yanking my legs up and down, shifting me over on my side, furiously ripping out the hair with quick snaps of the wrist. By this point she is sweating more than I am.

Before I can unclench my teeth, she is rubbing baby oil roughly into my inner thighs. I pull on my clothes, my skin still tingling, as she crumples the paper from the table into a ball and throws the wax, thick with my hair, into the trash can. In seconds, all traces of my visit have vanished. Downstairs, I slip her a tip almost as large as the bill itself.

But hair removal does have its limits. When I met my best friend, Lina Katz, we were standing in front of the Xerox machine of the university French department, clutching our lists of texts to prepare for our exams. I glanced searchingly down the row of titles on Lina's paper and spotted Garnier's Renaissance tragedy *Les Juifves, The Jewesses*.

Half an hour later we were sitting at a nearby café sipping double espressos, dividing a raspberry brownie down the middle and interrupting each other as we talked shop.

"Calves?" I asked.

"Shave," she answered.

"Thighs?"

"Wax." Then it was her turn. "Underarms?" she threw out.

"Wax," I countered.

"Eyebrows?"

"Pluck."

I pointed to my upper lip. "This?" I asked, pausing dramatically.

She took a sip of coffee, I held my breath.

"Pluck."

"Amazing!" I cried, lurching forward and knocking the remains of the brownie off the table. Our hair-removal technique was absolutely identical—I was in disbelief. Then Lina threw me for a real loop.

"What do you do about your arms?" she asked.

"My arms?" The idea had never even occurred to me. I thought it was a hirsuteness I would just have to live with, like a purple birthmark or a raised scar. We lay our forearms on the round café table, side by side, and studied them objectively. Lina's were just as well-adorned as mine.

A week later, the two of us were in Lina's apartment taking the last drags of a nice-sized joint. The lights were low, Rembetika purred on the stereo, and a large box of Jolen Creme Bleach was already opened. I waved the little white plastic spatula like a sword in the air. "Shall we?"

We stirred what seemed a huge amount of powder and cream together as directed, and carefully spread the mixture onto our own left arm, then each other's right. Covering the whole area, elbow to fingertips, took a good 20 minutes, and then we had to wait another 15 while the concoction stiffened and crystallized on our skin.

"Time!" Lina shouted.

We both gasped as we took turns scraping off the solution. The results stunned us into shock. I could not recognize my own hands with the invisible blondeness now coating them. "Whose arms are these?" I repeated over and over in a stoned drawl.

"This changes everything!" Lina breathed, standing before the mirror trying out endless variations of gestures and expressions: hands defiantly on hips, arms nonchalantly folded across chest, chin resting dreamily in the palm of her hand.

"I'll never wear long sleeves again," I declared, going through the five basic ballet arm positions and pas-de-chatting giddily around the room. At that very moment, one of my flailing limbs hit the Jolen tray. It wavered for a second and then overturned, landing on the seat of Lina's navy blue velvet armchair. We froze.

"I just had it reupholstered!" she yelled. I ran, trembling, for a towel.

We scrubbed and scrubbed, but there was nothing we could do to get rid of the white splotch in the center of the seat cushion. The Jolen's had only touched the material for a mere instant, but it was too late. We couldn't take our eyes off the stain.

I felt horribly guilty, but then something else hit me. The white patch on the dark blue seat cushion glared at me. "If that's what it did to a chair, just imagine . . ." Our arms began to sting unbearably all over again, if only in our imaginations, and we pledged, right then and there, never to bleach our arms again.

Masturbating Class:
A Hands-on Experience

By Alix Strauss

I'M GOING TO BE HONEST WITH YOU. I'm a terrible masturbater. I've tried. Late at night in bed or in the shower. Nothing.

I was frustrated (who wouldn't be) and tired of hearing from friends that I was missing out. So in 2001 when *Self* magazine said they'd pay for me to go to masturbating school to write an article about the experience, I threw a ready hand in the air and jumped at the offer.

I grew up in Manhattan on the Upper East Side. Born to overly traditional, we-don't-talk-about-that, neurotic Jews, I never received any sex information from my parents, who as far as I can tell, had sex only once, and even that's debatable.

I did my homework and found that sex therapist and masturbating guru Betty Dodson Ph.D., was the "it" person to see.

Over the phone, Betty, who has more than 30 years experience teaching women the how-tos of "self-pleasure," tells me that a private session runs about three hours and costs $900, though some people, she adds, need a little more time. We're talking about a four-inch area, how much extra time could I need?

When I arrive for my "lesson," a stocky woman with cropped gray hair who fashions matching black spandex T-shirt and shorts, greets me at the door.

Please tell me this isn't Betty—that it's some wayward student or dressed-down butler. Sadly, it's Betty. Great. I have enough trouble masturbating alone. Doing it in front of a woman older than my mother is jarring. Still, I compose myself and follow her into the living room—which is all gray—gray carpeting, furniture, walls. She points to a pair of gray chairs and gets right to the point.

"What do you hope to accomplish today?" she asks, as we both take a seat.

"I'd like to learn how to have an orgasm on my own, not just with a guy," I reply, feeling oddly calm.

For the next 20 minutes, we talk about my past relationships. All my life I've been the good girl. I pay my taxes on time, can hold down a job and have never needed an AIDS test. For me, self-pleasure is a white sale at Bloomingdale's.

"If you can't please yourself how can you expect someone else to do it for you?"

She has a point.

With that, she tells me to shed my clothing and asks if I want a T-shirt, which I gladly accept. The only other person I've stripped down naked in front of was a natural healer—another article, don't ask—who insisted that for $400 she could channel Jesus.

We move from the chairs to an area by her window. Set up on the floor is a purple towel, goose-neck lamp and round mirror.

Betty sits beside me, hands me the mirror and asks me to spread my legs. We stare at the reflection in silence until she announces that I should masturbate at least once a week to tap into my sexual energy. Once a week? I can barely make it to the gym that often. Then she hands me a mint.

"We'll be sitting close to each other," she says.

For a second I have no idea where she wants me to put the mint. Technically there are two places it could go. When she pops the candy into her mouth I do the same as relief fills me.

Next it's look-see time. "You should name your vagina and make her your friend," Betty informs me. "She wants you to visit on a regular basis. How about 'little Alix'?"

How about not? I counter with "Julia?" I have no idea where this name comes from. I don't know any Julias or even anyone who knows anyone named Julia, but Betty nods in approval, pulls on a pair of latex gloves, and like a session with my gyno, she explains all of my formerly private parts.

"Since you've only been with a handful of men, your vaginal muscles aren't stretched." Terrific. "Here's your vagina, your urethra and your clitoris," she says as I follow along in the mirror. "You've got a lovely clit," she adds, touching me. "See?"

Yes, I see. How can I not see. You're touching my woo-woo! This is more than I bargained for.

Next, Betty takes out a bottle of Charlie Sunshine massage oil, applies it to my hands and watches me touch Julia. As instructed, I start off with small round circles, then add in some stroking. When I feel nothing, she takes over. *$2.50 a word*, I remind myself. *I'm getting $2.50 a word. I can do this.* My neck muscles tighten, my jaw clenches. I want to go home.

Betty hardly seems to notice my discomfort, and moves on to the next exercise. It's time to try the "vaginal barbell," a metal bar about six inches long with a knob on either end. Once I learn this is going in me, I ask if it's been sterilized. Generally, I have trouble inserting a supertampon, but with the amount of oil I've got slathered on, I could probably fit a small Chihuahua inside. I'm amazed at how far in the contraption goes. I insert and remove it a few times. I have no idea how this is going to help me have an orgasm, but Betty seems impressed.

"For someone who hasn't masturbated often," she says with a wink, "you seem to know what you're doing."

What can I say, I've good motor skills.

Once I've mastered the barbell move, we move to another area—the middle of the floor, where a large gray towel has been placed over an even larger zebra throw rug. Several pillows are in a pile.

"Sex," Betty shares, "is dancing lying down."

Oh, let me put that on a T-shirt.

As I get comfortable, as if that's really possible, the battery-operated appliances make an appearance. I've not used them before and I'm hoping this will give me the orgasm I've been trying to have on my own.

I start small, choosing the Water Dancer, a vibrator about the size of a roll of quarters. Betty slips a condom over the device, turns it on and instructs me to run it over my clitoris. So far, this part feels the nicest, like a light tickling sensation. As if reading my mind, Betty tells me that the clitoris has more than 8,000 nerve endings, adding that I'll get better results if I throw in some pelvic movements and a few moans.

"I'm not big on talking," I say. Apparently, making any kind of sound during sexual activity reinforces the message to the body (and brain) that you're doing something pleasurable. Before I can really get going, she adds more direction.

"Now rub your nipple and breast."

I return to my money mantra, *$2.50 a word, $2.50 a word . . .* and force myself to mutter a few half hearted yeses, skip touching my breast and yet somehow still feel like I'm performing a porn movie. There are too many directions to follow and everything feels fake and too constructed. Whatever happened to just enjoying the moment?

"Any kind of sound you can make that lets your body know this is pleasurable is important feedback. Most women masturbate silently, when in reality they should be letting out sounds so their body can learn that this feels good." Betty calls this positive self-loving affirmation.

I try to breathe as a third component is added, the ball bearing. Betty oils it down again, stating that vaginal penetration on a regular basis promotes vaginal lubrication. "No man wants to put a dick into a dry pussy," she says.

We add more oil.

She instructs me to move the vibrator with my left hand while inserting the barbell with my right. As I start to get the hang of circling and the slow in-outs, I have a revelation: I'm having sex with myself. A numbing tingling starts in my fingers even though it feels as if it's happening somewhere else deep inside me. At 4:47 I have my first mini-orgasm.

"Congrats," she says excitedly. "Good job." Acclamations such as these are embarrassing. I'm also disappointed. I expected more, something earth-shattering. "You're orgasms will be," she insists, "but you have to practice. If you think you're going to dance *Swan Lake* after you've just tied on your first pair of ballet shoes, you're full of it."

The final part of the lesson happens when Betty hands me the magic wand, the Big Daddy of vibrators, which looks like a large microphone. It's really just a large massager, like the kind you'd use to relax tense neck or back muscles—I know this because it says so on the box, which makes me feel better when I see real people using it for something other than what I'm using it for.

As instructed, and with Betty sitting in front of me like some sort of birthing coach, I move the vibrator back and forth. At this point, all bets are off. I feel drugged and disoriented. What was in that mint? I can't believe I'm doing this, and in front of a total stranger. *$2.50 a word. $2.50 a word.* With no other choice, I decide to just pretend I'm home, by myself. Within minutes the tingling starts in my hands, my hips are moving and I'm sailing into the great unknown. As sexual tension mounts, Betty's voice fades and I go deeper into myself. My breathing quickens, my heart speeds up and a little shudder rushes through my body. The tingling increases and I notice that my right hand is gripping the blanket and my body is moving in tiny convulsions. I feel euphoric, like I've had several small, pleasurable seizures. Then it feels like one large one is happening—in my head, in my chest, in my insides, certainly in my vaginal area, and then something warm and wet comes out of me, caus-ing me to stop.

"The female ejaculation," Betty shouts, sounding as if I've won some-thing. "Men love it when you come on them."

"How come my feet are cold?" I ask.

Betty attributes this to poor circulation from anxiety or fear. Fear? What could I have to be fearful about? That I'm masturbating in front of a total stranger? And when did this become therapy 101? Perhaps I should be masturbating on her couch.

"And you have pleasure anxiety. Everyone does. When you start to get close to sexual pleasure or feelings it makes you anxious."

I look at the clock: 5:50 p.m. Betty stands and motions me back to the chairs.

"You went to war with your sexual repression," she says as I get dressed.

"Did I win?"

She nods yes. "Sex doesn't come naturally. It's an art form. You have to learn the technique, then you have to practice. You have the rest of your life to perfect what you've learned today."

On my way out the door, Betty hands me the magic wand, a party favor, then hugs me. "You did very well."

I leave Betty's a changed woman and a new member of a not-so-exclusive club. And as I wait for the elevator, I think: A visit with Betty, $900. Vibrator, $65. Batteries, $2.50. Orgasming on your own . . . priceless.

Contributors

REBECCA ADDELMAN is a Canadian writer and comedian living legally in the United States. She has written for magazines (*The Walrus, Maclean's, Bust, TORO*), television (CBC, Much Music, the Comedy Network) and the stage. Rebecca can be seen as the host of the monthly stand-up and variety show The Hour of Power in Hollywood. Check her out at *www.raddelman.com.*

MIKE ALBO is a writer and performer who lives and loves in Brooklyn. His first novel, *Hornito,* came out in 2000 from HarperCollins. He collaborated with his longtime friend Virginia Heffernan for his next novel, *The Underminer: The Best Friend Who Casually Destroys Your Life,* which was published in 2005 by Bloomsbury. He's performed numerous solo shows including Spray, Please Everything Burst, and My Price Point, also cowritten with Ms. Heffernan. Check out *www.mikealbo.com* for upcoming shows, his spaced-out blog, performance clips and recent writing.

STEVE ALMOND is a novelist whose book, *Candyfreak: A Journey Through the Chocolate Underbelly of America*—described as "half candy porn, half candy polemic"—was published by Algonquin. His quite filthy story collection, *My*

Life in Heavy Metal, is out in paperback. He lives in Somerville, Massachusetts, and teaches creative writing at Boston College. To find out more about his various perversions, check out *www.stevenalmond.com*.

JACOB AUSTEN is the editor of *Roctober* magazine, produces the cable-access kiddie dance show *Chic-a-Go-Go* and has written for magazines including *Time Out Chicago, Vice* and *International Tattoo Arts*. His books include *TV-A-Go-Go: Rock on TV from American Bandstand to American Idol* and *A Friendly Game of Poker*.

CARYN AVIV teaches Jewish Studies and directs the Certificate in Jewish Communal Service at the University of Denver. She is also a cofounder and the director of research for Jewish Mosaic: The National Center for Sexual and Gender Diversity. Aviv is the coauthor/editor of three books, *Queer Jews* (Routledge, 2002), *New Jews: The End of the Jewish Diaspora* (NYU Press, 2005) and *American Queer: Now and Then* (Paradigm, 2006). She also blogs for *haaretz.com*. Aviv is currently working on a book about American Jewish involvement in Israeli-Palestinian reconciliation movements. When not teaching and making the Jewish world safe for homos, Caryn can be found hiking in the foothills of the Rocky Mountains with a 3-year-old kid strapped to her back.

D.C. BENNY is a Brooklyn comedian who makes a living playing Puerto Ricans, Italians, Greeks and Arabs on both the small and big screens. For years he produced and hosted the comedic storytelling show Urban Myth, where Dave Chapelle, Colin Quinn and other comedian friends told their rawest, funniest stories. Check out clips of his stand-up at *www.dcbenny.com*.

ANDY BOROWITZ is a comedian, actor and writer whose work appears in *The New Yorker, The New York Times* and his award-winning website, *BorowitzReport.com*.

Contributors

RACHEL KRAMER BUSSEL (*www.rachelkramerbussel.com*) is a New York author, editor and blogger. She hosts and curates In the Flesh Erotic Reading Series and is a former sex columnist for *The Village Voice*. She's edited over 20 anthologies, including *Best Sex Writing 2008, Dirty Girls, Yes, Sir; Yes, Ma'am* and *Spanked: Red-Cheeked Erotica*, and written for *Cosmopolitan, Newsday*, the *New York Post, Time Out New York*, and other publications

American stand-up comedian JORDAN CARLOS has done a lot in his short life. He's been a Madison Avenue "Mad Man." He's hosted a live kids show on Nickelodeon (lotta pees and poops!). He's played Stephen Colbert's "black friend" on *The Colbert Report*. And recently when handpicked by the good people of Trojan condoms for their Trojan College Comedy Tour, he did his best to undo the evils of abstinence education . . . but ended up getting fractured with college kids. He did try though!

ROBBIE CHAVITZ, writer/director, has written for John Cleese, Sigourney Weaver, Michael J. Fox, Martin Short and others. Robbie spent his 20s abroad as a performer. His film *Time Out* debuted at the Sundance Festival and his most recent script is for National Lampoon. Robbie is the creative director of IKA Collective.

MATTHEW LOREN COHEN is a classically trained pianist. He is musical director of *The Next Big Broadway Musical!* and *The Nuclear Family*, two long-running improvised musicals. He has performed on cruise ships and cable TV, and is a published fiction writer and a columnist for *Metrosource* magazine.

OPHIRA EISENBERG is a MAC (Manhattan Association of Clubs and Cabarets) Award Finalist for Best Female Comic. She has appeared on Comedy Central's *Premium Blend* and *Fresh Faces of Comedy*, VH-1's *Best Week Ever* and *All Access*, E! Channel, the Oxygen Network and the Discovery Channel. She performs stand-up across the country and her writing has appeared in the anthology *I Killed: True Stories of the Road from America's Top Comics* alongside that of Jerry Seinfeld, Chris Rock and Joan Rivers. She is also a regular contributor for *US Weekly*'s Fashion Police and *The Comedians* magazine.

LIZ FELDMAN is a writer/comedian living in Los Angeles. Her parents brag about her writing for the 79th Annual Academy Awards show, writing/performing for Nickelodeon's *All That* and writing for the WB's *Blue Collar TV*. But they really kvell over her four Emmy awards for her work as a writer/producer for *The Ellen Degeneres Show*.

JOEY GARFIELD, a native of Evanston, Illinois, has worked in New York film production since 1991. He has directed music videos for Langhorn Slim, Kid Sister, Aesop Rock, EL-P and Airborn Audio. His music video for RJD2 entitled *Work It Out* was nominated for an MTV award and helped Joey obtain the Emerging Filmmaker award at Fuel TV's Swerve Festival. Garfield's award-winning feature documentary *Breath Control: The History of the Human Beat Box* charts the history of making music with nothing other than the human voice. Additional documentary film work can be seen on the upcoming film *Beautiful Losers* as well as the 20th anniversary reissue DVD of the seminal film *Style Wars* and the film *The Run Up*, which profiles several current urban artists including two from Chicago. He also directed *Heeb* magazine's first foray into viral media with the short film *Borscht Belt Horror* (check it out on YouTube). He has written and directed promos for MTV and Comedy Central with the Bert Fershners. Joey is a contributing writer to *Juxtapoz* and *Stop Smiling* magazines. He contributed several articles to *The Beastie Boys Grand Royal* magazine and, as compensation, was given the role of Octopus Monster in their music video *Intergalactic*. You can see some of his work on *www.ghostrobot.com*.

AVI GESSER is an attorney in New York City.

STEPHEN GLASS is the author of *The Fabulist: A Novel* (Simon & Schuster, 2003). He lives in Los Angeles.

LORI GOTTLIEB, a commentator for National Public Radio, is a journalist and the author of the national bestseller *Stick Figure: A Diary of My Former Self,* and coauthor of *Inside the Cult of Kibu* and *I Love You, Nice to Meet You.* She lives in Los Angeles with her son, Zachary.

MICHAEL GREEN's mother is surprisingly supportive of her son's career as a television writer/producer, though of course she would prefer something else. She likes that he is the creator of NBC's *Kings,* and enjoys telling people he used to write for *Heroes, Smallville* and *Sex and the City,* though she forgets some of the others. She doesn't really understand why he wastes his time writing that "Superman/Batman" comic every month, and his *Batman: Lovers and Madmen* she had trouble getting through. Of his occasional journalism she is largely unaware.

STEPHANIE GREEN is a writer whose privileged life was interrupted by stage II breast cancer at 32. She shopped, Botoxed, pill-popped and partied her way through a bilateral mastectomy, reconstruction and four months of chemo. "Benzos and Breast Cancer" will also appear in her upcoming memoir *Cancer Is the New Black.*

BEN GREENMAN is an editor at *The New Yorker* and the author of several books of fiction, including *Superbad, Superworse, A Circle Is a Balloon and Compass Both* and *Please Step Back.* He lives in Brooklyn.

LYNN HARRIS is author of the comic novel *Death by Chick Lit* and its prequel, *Miss Media.* She is cocreator of the venerable website *BreakupGirl.net.* An award-winning journalist, she writes for *Glamour, Salon.com, The New York*

Times, and many others. She writes the Rabbi's Wife column for *Nextbook.org*, about her own experience. *www.lynnharris.net*

ELLIOTT KALAN is a segment producer for *The Daily Show with Jon Stewart*, weekly columnist for the newspaper *Metro* and occasional stand-up comedian. In previous lives he hosted the talk show *The Midnight Kalan*, cohosted the Internet radio show *Fist City* and formed half of the sketch comedy group the Hypocrites.

MARK KATZ is an ex–political operative, recovering copywriter and failed sitcom writer, who went on to become the founder of the Soundbite Institute, a creative think tank for strategic communications. His essays have been published in *The New Yorker, The New York Times* and *Time*. He is the author of *Clinton & Me: A Real Life Political Comedy* (Miramax Books), an account of eight years as the in-house humor speechwriter of the Clinton White House.

BYRON KERMAN is a journalist and comedy writer living in St. Louis. They laughed at him at the academy, but someday he will show them all.

JONATHAN BARUCH KESSELMAN (yes, he is Jewish), the godfather of the Jewxploitation film, was born and raised in the San Fernando Valley. *The Hebrew Hammer*, his first feature film, premiered at the 2003 Sundance Festival, and was released by Strand Releasing in conjunction with Comedy Central and Paramount Home Video. Jon wrote and will direct *The Orbit of Bob* for Nickelodeon, and the live-action feature film *Odd Todd*, based on the web cartoons of the same name, for Paramount. *The Hebrew Hammer 2: Hammer vs. Hitler* as well as the stage musical version are also in production. Jon recently wrote (with *Da Ali G Show*'s writer/producer, Jamie Glassman) the film *Pure Air* and directed an episode of David Wain's *Wainy Days*. He writes a humor column for *Suicide Girls* and teaches comedy writing for the screen at Yale University.

ANNETTE EZEKIEL KOGAN is the founder, singer and accordionist of the New York klezmer-rock band Golem. She's been writing songs and short stories all along her wild ride through the contemporary Yiddish world. She lives in New York City.

LISA KRON is known for her plays *Well*, which premiered on Broadway in 2006 and garnered her a Tony nomination following an acclaimed run at the Public Theater, and the Obie Award–winning *2.5 Minute Ride*. Lisa is also a proud founding member of the Obie and Bessie Award–winning theater company the Five Lesbian Brothers.

TODD LEVIN is a writer and comedian living in Brooklyn. His words can be read in *Salon, Glamour, Esquire, McSweeney's* and *RADAR*. His face can be seen on Comedy Central and stand-up comedy stages all over NYC. And his voice can be heard on Public Radio International's *Fair Game*. And also: *www.tremble.com*.

ADAM LOWITT is a senior producer at *The Daily Show with Jon Stewart* and has been a contributing writer for *Saturday Night Live*'s Weekend Update. He currently hosts and produces IT IS IT, a bimonthly comedy show on the Lower East Side of Manhattan.

JOSHUA NEUMAN is the Publisher of *Heeb* magazine. A graduate of Brown University and the Harvard Divinity School, he has taught undergraduate courses in the Philosophy of Religion at New York University, written for Slate, eMusic and ESPN and appeared on VH1, Food Network, Court TV and National Public Radio. His first book, *The Big Book of Jewish Conspiracies*, was published by St. Martin's Press in 2005.

SIMON RICH is the author of two humor collections, *Ant Farm* and *Free-Range Chickens*. He currently writes for *Saturday Night Live*.

DAVID J. ROSEN lives in NYC, where he attempts to write books and TV shows between walking his dog and eating cheese. He is the author of the novel *I Just Want My Pants Back* and the nonfiction book *What's That Job and How the Hell Do I Get It?*

TODD ROSENBERG is a freelance animator who runs the website *www .oddtodd.com*, featuring cartoons about an unemployed guy who sits around in his apartment doing nothing. Todd's animated segments have been featured on *ABC News*, *America's Test Kitchen*, the National Geographic channel, Comedy Central and *the IFC Media Project*. He is the author of *The Odd Todd Handbook: Hard Times, Soft Couch*. He lives in Brooklyn.

NAJLA SAID is an award-winning actress, comedian and writer. She has appeared Off-Broadway, regionally and internationally, as well as in film and television. She is a founding member of Nibras Theater Collective, and is currently working on her one-woman show, *Palestine*. Najla is a graduate of Princeton University.

ALLEN SALKIN cast industrial films in Hong Kong, wholesaled rubber duckies in Las Vegas, picked oranges in Crete, peddled oil paintings door-to-door in Western Australia and spent much of his 20s standing in the corner at parties scrawling notes in his journal. He is now a reporter at *The New York Times*, where he has written about robot dogs, doom tourism and unicorns. He also wrote the book *Festivus: The Holiday for the Rest of Us*.

WENDY SHANKER has written for *Glamour, Self, Shape, Us Weekly* (Fashion Police), *Cosmopolitan, Marie Claire, Seventeen, Bust* and *Bitch*, as well as MTV. She published the humorous, hopeful memoir about women and body image, *The Fat Girl's Guide to Life* (Bloomsbury USA), for which she appeared on *The View, Good Morning America, CBS Sunday Morning*, and on a national tour sponsored by Macy's. *The Fat Girl's Guide* has been published in Italian, German, Spanish, Chinese and Polish (but not French—because French women don't get fat). Her latest book, *Does This Book Make Me Look Fat?: 14 Writers Weigh In*, was published by Clarion Books/Houghton Mifflin in 2008. *www.wendyshanker.com*

ABBY SHER has been published in *The New York Times*, the *Los Angeles Times*, *SELF, Heeb, Jane, Redbook* and *Lost*. Her first young-adult novel, *Kissing Snowflakes*, was published by Scholastic in the fall of 2007. Abby also has pieces in *Modern Love: 50 True and Extraordinary Tales of Desire, Deceit, and Devotion* and the upcoming *Behind the Bedroom Door*, published by Bantam and due out in January 2009. Before returning to her native New York, Abby wrote and performed for *The Second City* in Chicago, where she was a company member for five years. Abby currently performs improvisation weekly at the Magnet Theater in New York, and is working on her memoir, which she recently sold to Scribner.

MICHAEL SHOWALTER wrote and directed the romantic comedy *The Baxter* (IFC Films). He is also one-third of the comedy trio Stella. He cowrote, coproduced and starred in the cult comedy *Wet Hot American Summer* and was a founding member of the MTV sketch troupe the State. Currently, Michael is performing stand-up and working on a new TV project. His favorite food is gazpacho.

LAURA SILVERMAN first caught the attention of television viewers with her memorable vocal performance as the bitingly droll receptionist also named Laura on the popular animated sitcom *Dr. Katz: Professional Therapist*. She followed that with turns in the movies *Half Baked* and *State and Main* as well as numerous television shows including *King of Queens, Curb Your Enthusiasm* and *Home Movies*, and was a series regular on the cult HBO comedy series

The Comeback. In 2005, Laura joined her sister briefly onscreen in the stand-up feature *Sarah Silverman: Jesus Is Magic.* More animation work was soon to follow as Silverman voiced characters in *Freak Show* and *Metalocalypse,* and in 2007 she reunited with her sister on the critically acclaimed Comedy Central series *The Sarah Silverman Program.* In 2008, Silverman guest-starred opposite Hugh Laurie on an episode of Fox's hit series *House.* She was recently named one of the "Top 100 People of 2008" by *USA Today.*

HAL SIROWITZ is the former Poet Laureate of Queens, New York. His first book, *Mother Said,* was translated into nine languages, including Hebrew. He shared the National Jewish Foundation Rosenberg Award for Contemporary Music with composer Alla Borzova, who set some of his poems to music.

RAVEN SNOOK, a writer, performer, diva and proud Jewish mama, has penned articles for *Time Out, The Village Voice,* the *New York Post, TV Guide, New York* magazine's website and *Heeb,* told stories at the Moth and *Heeb* Storytelling, and hosted myriad burlesque shows, including the all-Jewish Kosher ChiXXX. For more info, visit *www.ravensnook.com.*

JOEL STEIN grew up in Edison, New Jersey, went to Stanford and then worked for Martha Stewart for a year. He was a sports editor at *Time Out New York,* then lucked into a job as a staff writer for *Time* magazine, where over seven and a half years he wrote a dozen cover stories on subjects such as Michael Jordan, Las Vegas, the Internet bubble and—it being *Time* and he being a warm body in the office—low-carb diets. He has appeared on any TV show that asks him: VH1's *I Love the Decade You Tell Me I Love,* HBO's *Phoning It In,* Comedy Central's *Reel Comedy* and E! Entertainment's *101 Hottest Hot Hotties' Hotness.* After teaching a class in humor writing at Princeton, he moved to L.A. at the beginning of 2005 to write a column for the *Los Angeles Times.* He still contributes to *Time* and whatever magazines allow him to.

ALIX STRAUSS is a media-savvy social satirist and lifestyle trend writer. She has appeared on national morning and talk shows including those on ABC, CBS, CNN and VH1. She has written for *The New York Times*, the *New York Post, Time, Departures, Marie Claire, Entertainment Weekly, Self* and *Esquire*. Her novel *The Joy of Funerals* (St. Martin's Press) was optioned by Stockard Channing, who is attached to direct. Recently she edited the anthology *Have I Got a Guy For You*. *www.alixstrauss.com*

DARIN STRAUSS is the international bestselling author of the *New York Times* Notable Books *Chang and Eng* and *The Real McCoy*. Also a screenwriter, he is adapting *Chang and Eng* with Gary Oldman. The recipient of a 2006 Guggenheim Fellowship in fiction writing, he is a Clinical Associate Professor at NYU's graduate school. His latest book, *More Than It Hurts You*, was published in June 2008.

JOSH SWILLER has been deaf since the age of 4, and now hears through a cochlear implant. His first book, *The Unheard: A Memoir of Deafness and Africa*, was published in 2007 to rave reviews, and Josh is hard at work thinking about being hard at work on his next one.

NOAH TARNOW is quizmaster, producer and writer of the Big Quiz Thing, NYC's live trivia spectacular. He's hosted quiz events throughout the city and around the country, and was a contestant on both the VH1 game show *Name That Video* (champion—won a car) and *Jeopardy!* (second place—curse you, Trebek!). Elsewhere and elsewhen, he's the chief copy editor for *Time Out New York*, a writer whose work has appeared in *Rolling Stone* and *Jane*, a stand-up comedian and a karaoke singer of stunning ferocity.

ERIC D. WIENGRAD, a native Philadelphian, resides in West Hollywood, California, with his wife. He's an established reality television producer and director, published writer and photographer. His Transformers sleeping bag, mentioned in the story, can be viewed on display at the Smithsonian museum in Washington, D.C. Just kidding . . . they said no.

RENA ZAGER is a comedian who has appeared on Comedy Central's *Premium Blend* and on NBC's *Late Friday*. She is a featured performer for the variety show *Nice Jewish Girls Gone Bad*, which, most recently, has been wowing them at the Zipper Theater. She's also a writer for the VH-1 show *Best Week Ever*.